A LIFE HALF LIVED

DARRYL RODGERS

A LIFE HALF LIVED

A True Story of Love, Addiction,
Tragedy, and Hope

CMR PUBLISHING  Cary, North Carolina

Helpful Links

Visit the link immediately below to get my next book, "Taking the Fight to the Enemy" FREE on Amazon Kindle! How will you hold up when faced with personal tragedy? What will you do when faced with adversity and pain? It was the great football coach, Vince Lombardi, who said, "The best defense is a good offense." Learn the strategies and attitude you need to be able to come out on top and get through your darkest hours. Become an instrument of change and empowerment for others. Sign up now to get "Taking the Fight to the Enemy"!

http://speedy34.com/get-my-next-book-free-on-kindle/

Visit My Youtube Channel

https://www.youtube.com/channel/UCD2UuvY2-OyujPBga3SzVig

Follow Me on Twitter

https://twitter.com/JDRodgers61

Go to My Facebook Fan Page

https://www.facebook.com/ALifeHalfLived

This book is dedicated to my father and mother, the late Mr. and Mrs. Morgan W. Rodgers of Lyman, South Carolina. I learned many valuable life lessons from both of them. My father, an ordained Southern Baptist minister for many years, showed me through the way he lived his life what it means to be a real man. He dedicated his life to serving God and loving people. My sweet mother believed in me and in my abilities as a writer and encouraged me to publish some of my works. I'm sure she is beaming with pride right now, knowing that I finally followed through.

CONTENTS

FOREWORD

WHAT FOLLOWS IS A TRUE STORY. I have changed the names of most of the people in this book in an effort to protect their privacy. It is not my intention to hurt, embarrass, offend, or otherwise inflict pain on anyone. I ask for forgiveness in advance from those whose lives are depicted in the pages ahead as part of the story. I have written this book from my perspective, and as you well know, we all see life through our own lens. At times I have been brutally honest about some of my own shortcomings as well as those of others whose lives were intertwined with mine over the years.

A LIFE HALF LIVED

Photograph courtesy of Mike Legeros.

BLUE COROLLA—MAY 29TH, 2014

IT WAS A SUNNY MAY AFTERNOON in Cary, North Carolina. The skies were bright blue at 4:45 pm on a Thursday. People were getting off work and in a hurry to get home. Chase Morgan Rodgers was one of three young adults in a 2004 blue Toyota Corolla which took the on ramp from Harrison Avenue onto I-40 Eastbound. The speed limit was 65 miles per hour, but the traffic was thick and it was necessary to drive at about 70 miles per hour to stay with the flow of traffic.

There were three eastbound lanes and three westbound lanes separated by a grass median. Behind the wheel of the Corolla was a young blonde woman, 18 years old, who had some driving experience but had never had a driver's license. In the passenger seat beside her was Chase, 20 years old. The Corolla belonged to him, but he had decided to let the young lady drive. In the back seat was another young man, about 18 years old.

After passing the very first exit they came to, the young lady decided to change lanes. She gave a signal and started to come over to her left when a horn blared from a vehicle that was in her blind spot. Suddenly she lost control of the blue Corolla. White smoke came from the tires as the car spun 90 degrees out from the direction of travel and careened off the road. In that moment, lives were changed forever.

One

THE EARLY YEARS

EVEN BEFORE HE WAS BORN, Chase was a very active child. His mother's belly was constantly moving. He squirmed, flipped, and kicked. One time my wife, Kim was in a meeting at work when Chase got very active. She was wearing a dress with a bow in the front. The bow kept jumping and moving around with each of Chase's movements. No one was paying attention in the meeting because everyone was watching the bouncing bow.

Chase Morgan Rodgers was born to Jon Darryl and Kimberly Wood Rodgers on Monday, November 22nd, 1993 at 5:12 pm at Rex Hospital in Raleigh, North Carolina. He weighed 5 pounds 10 ounces. The name Chase means Hunter. My father's name was Morgan. It means, "by the sea." Rodgers means, " prowess with a spear." We didn't plan it this way. The name Chase was a popular baby name at the time and my wife liked it. We wanted to name him after my father, Morgan, and we were blessed with the last name, Rodgers. It wasn't until years later that I searched out the meanings of all the names. Combined they form an idea. Chase Morgan Rodgers—A hunter/warrior who is good with a spear and lives by the sea. When I first discovered the meanings of the names, I wondered, where the sea would fit into this equation.

Chase's birth changed my life forever. Before he was born, I was a nice guy, but sometimes selfish and inconsiderate. I would go on hunting and fishing excursions and not tell my wife when I would be back. I never asked her opinion. I made my own plans for my free time. She never complained. When Chase was born, I thought everything would continue the way it always had. One night I got a rude awakening. Kim was elbowing me. "It's YOUR turn," she said. Huh? What was she talking about? Chase was crying. She meant that it was my turn to get up in the middle of the night and go feed him with the bottle. Until then she had been taking care of the feeding duties. At first it wasn't much fun waking up in the middle of the night, but after a while I got used to it, and I enjoyed holding and feeding Chase. I even got good at changing diapers.

When Chase was about fourteen months old, Kim went to pick him up from day care one day, and the day care workers told her that Chase had learned to walk. She couldn't wait to get home to see Chase walk. Kim got Chase all set up to walk down the hallway with me coaxing him toward the other end. He would take a couple of steps and fall. He would get up, take a couple more steps and fall. Chase was determined to walk. Over and over he went, time and time again until he finally lay down in the floor, completely exhausted. Chase always had so much energy. Kim says this was one of the few times she'd ever seen him out of energy. I would have to agree.

I was driving on Maynard Road in Cary one afternoon with Chase in his car seat in the back. I don't recall where we were going or why it was only the two of us. I had heard Chase make a lot of sounds, but I had never heard a word come out his mouth. I couldn't believe my ears.

Chase in his car seat

"BALL! BALL! BALL!" I heard his little voice ring out. I quickly glanced over my right shoulder to see Chase's tiny outstretched arm, his little index finger pointing. I followed the direction of his point to see two young men kicking a soccer ball around in a field across the street. I have a ball player on my hands, I thought. This is gonna be fun!

Chase made people laugh without even trying. Once he stood at Kim's feet with his arms stretched towards her. "Pick my up, mommy. Pick my up," Chase said.

Kim tried to correct him. "No, honey. Pick ME up."

"Uh Uh," Chase replied. "You too heby." Once when Chase was in day care, the kids were learning about birds. They had colored a picture of a toucan. Kim held up the picture Chase had colored and asked him, "What is this?" He shrugged his shoulders.

"Come on, you know what this is. What is it?" Kim persisted. Again Chase shrugged his shoulders.

Finally, Kim gave him the answer. "This is a toucan", she said.

"Uh Uh! That's One Can," Chase responded. Kim cracked up laughing, and then Chase started laughing. "One Can. One Can." He said it over and over just to hear his mom laugh.

One time when Chase was little, he asked his mom to buy him something that she didn't think he needed. She told him that she didn't have any money. Chase told her that she should just go to the ATM machine and get more money out. This attitude about money continued over the years.

Not many years after we bought our home, I went to a local nursery and bought several wax myrtle shrubs. They were small plants that were knee high or less when I bought them. They grew fast however, and after about ten years they had grown into small trees. They were six to eight feet tall. Each one had multiple thick trunks and bright green foliage. One day I went out back and noticed that a couple of my wax myrtles had been broken down to the ground. All of the wax myrtle trunks had been broken off just above ground level. The limbs were still lying on the ground. I questioned Chase about the wax myrtles. He told me that he and one of the neighbor's kids were climbing in the bushes when one of the limbs broke. Then the neighbor's kid said, "Hey! Let's break all the limbs down and use them to build a fort!" I didn't yell at Chase or punish him in any way. I did explain to him what I didn't like about it and said, "Never do that again." I also let the neighbors know what their child had done. They offered to reimburse me for the plants. I told them that would not be necessary since Chase participated in the destruction of my bushes. This little boy turned out to be a bad influence on Chase and I eventually told him he was not welcome at our house. His family finally moved away, making things easier for us. One thing I learned early about Chase was that he always told the truth even if it got him in trouble. He wasn't a liar. I also discovered that Chase was more often a follower rather than a leader and was often influenced by other kids to join in on activities he otherwise wouldn't have participated in.

Early on we discovered that Chase didn't have a filter. He was quiet, but when he did talk, he told you exactly what was on his mind. When Kim and I bought a new television at Circuit City, Chase was three years old, and TVs were a lot bigger and heavier then. We went to the shipping and receiving area where someone was supposed to help us load the TV into our truck. We were standing there with Chase in line and there were two people who were together in front of us. One of the gentlemen was very large. We're talking close to five hundred pounds. Kim was saying a little prayer that Chase wouldn't say anything. Then it came out. "Mom. That guy's got a biiiiiiig behind!" The two men were too busy talking to each other to notice, but Kim was still embarrassed.

Another time Chase was riding with me. It was a hot summer day, and I stopped at a convenience store to buy something to drink. Outside the convenience store, there was a group of Hispanic men standing around a car talking. They had clearly been hard at work. None of them were wearing shirts. "Dad", asked Chase. "How come Mexicans don't wear shirts?"

From the time Chase started kindergarten, his teachers urged us to take him to a doctor for a possible ADD/ADHD diagnosis. Kim and I resisted this for a while, because we felt that our society is too quick to diagnose kids with ADD/ADHD and then medicate them. Chase had always had an excess of energy, but he was kind-hearted and not a troublemaker at all. He was quite shy in most situations.

We did come to realize that Chase's trouble focusing in class was going to be a problem for him in school. Finally we did take Chase to a psychiatrist to have him examined. Chase was diagnosed with Attention Deficit Disorder and only mild Attention Deficit Hyperactivity Disorder. He could, however, be quite hyperactive at times. Chase's doctor recommended Concerta as a medication for the ADD. We kept Chase on the absolute lowest dose that the doctor advised. Even so I could tell a difference in Chase when he was on his meds. He wasn't the zombie the way that some people describe their kids on meds for ADHD, but he wasn't completely himself either. I was never entirely happy about this, but I came to accept it.

It was apparent early on that Chase was going to be a small but gifted athlete. While the ADD/ADHD had its drawbacks, agility, quickness, endurance, and great hand to eye coordination seemed to be some of the pluses that came with it. So when Chase was five we enrolled him in T-ball. While Chase excelled at hitting and running, he could often be seen in left field tossing his glove into the air and catching it. When a ball finally did come his way, the coach would have to refocus him, then Chase would have to get his glove on, get to the ball, and throw it. He got better as the season progressed, but focusing remained an issue.

We also enrolled Chase in a recreational soccer league that year. He loved the game and played hard every time he was out there. Chase's coach taught his team how to juggle a soccer ball; that is, he taught them how to keep the ball suspended in mid-air by using the tops of the thighs, the feet, the head, etc. The coach suggested that his players practice at home a little every day. I never forced Chase to play any sport, but I did tell him that, if he wanted to play, he should practice. Chase began practicing his juggling and other soccer skills at home. Within a few months he could get up to one hundred touches before allowing the ball to reach the ground. He began to exhibit some of his ball-handling skills in the games. It was both amusing and impressive to watch.

I remember well one of Chase's soccer games when our team was down, 4–0 at half and it appeared we were in for a blowout. In the second half, Chase relentlessly attacked the other team's goal. From the looks on their faces it was clear that our opponents wished Chase would go away. They were tired, but Chase was only getting started. We won that game, 5–4. Chase scored four of our five goals in the second half. Chase didn't like losing, though he was a good sport about it when he did. He worked harder than anyone on the field because he liked winning a whole lot more than losing.

I learned that I had to be careful what I taught Chase. I was playing around with him one day when we were eating in a fast food restaurant. I tore off the end of my straw paper cover, slid it to the end of the straw and blew a puff of air into the straw, sending the paper cover flying into Chase's face. Chase learned how to do this quickly and he continued to do it, over, and over, again and again. The more annoyed I became, the more he would grin and do it until I finally had to let him know how serious I was by raising my voice. He stopped, but every so often Chase would whip out the old straw trick again. It was part of his weird sense of humor to annoy others until they would become exasperated.

When Chase was around seven or eight years old, we were visiting my parents in South Carolina. They lived about a four and a half hour drive away, and we visited them two or three times a year. My parents were in their late seventies at the time and Chase became bored easily. They lived on a large lot with woods in the back. I would throw the football around with Chase out in the yard or he would play with some toys my mother had for him inside. Sometimes he and I explored the woods in the back. Over time Chase explored these woods by himself. One day while we were visiting Chase brought in a small flat stick. He used a black marker he found in the house to write the words, "I Love You" on the stick. He presented the stick to my parents. That stick sat on my parents' fireplace mantel until they passed away. Today it is on the bookshelf in Chase's room at our house.

Little kids loved Chase. He knew how to make them laugh. At church Kim and I sometimes worked in the nursery. Chase would stay in the nursery with us and entertain the toddlers the entire time. The other parents noticed how much their kids loved Chase. When they dropped them off at the nursery, their children didn't complain as much as usual, and when they came to get them they were having so much fun playing with Chase, they didn't want to leave.

When Chase was seven we enrolled him in flag football with a local recreational league called Carolina Copperheads. Chase had played baseball and a lot of soccer, but this was his first experience with football. Once, while playing on defense, Chase grabbed another player's flag. He threw the flag to the ground, stomped on it, and ground it into the turf with his foot. Fortunately the referees had their backs turned. This was typical Chase behavior. He was quiet, kind, loving, and gentle, most of the time, but when he was engaged in sports, he was aggressive. The soccer fields, baseball fields, and football fields were his stage, and if you were on the opposing team, you were his enemy until the game was over. Not once in his career was he ever flagged or penalized for unsportsmanlike conduct, but the tenacity that an athlete needs to be able to win was always there.

Kim had told me she would not have any more children after the age of forty. As she approached forty, we learned she was expecting. We struggled to find a name for the child. At some point, I blurted out just in Chase, "meaning just in case." Justin. We laughed it off and continued to search for names, but nothing stuck and we came back to the name Justin, which was spawned from the joke. We also joked that he was "just in time," because of my wife's deadline of forty. No one was more excited than Chase when Justin was born. In fact, Chase had made

Chase is excited about his baby brother.

it very clear that he was not going to be happy if this child turned out to be a girl. He wanted a baby brother, and he was thrilled when he got one. They were seven years apart.

There was no doubt from the very beginning that Justin was going to be quite different from Chase. He was much calmer in the womb. The kicking and wiggling were present, but much less than with Chase. When Justin was born, Kim and I decided that I would be a stay-at-home Dad temporarily. I fed Justin, changed his diapers, and Justin went everywhere I went. I had read that listening to classical music improves toddler brain development. I had classical music on when Justin was eating and at other times throughout the day. I read to Justin. When I drove around town, I pointed out and named various things for him. I read traffic and street signs to him. Very early Justin surprised me when he began to talk and read.

I'll never forget once when I pulled into our auto mechanic's lot to drop off my car. There was a warning sign in the lot to let criminals know the lot was under camera surveillance. Justin pointed at the sign and asked me why there was a warning sign there. I had no idea he could read the word *warning*. Another time I had Chase and Justin in the car with me. We went through a fast food drive through lane. The company was looking for management people and had a sign on the drive through window stating this. They were looking for people with an entrepreneurial background or aptitude. Justin, still not in kindergarten, looked at the sign and asked me, "Dad, what does *entrepreneurial* mean?" He pronounced it perfectly. I asked him how he knew that word.

"I don't know," he answered.

Chase laughed uncontrollably. I was as tickled at Chase's reaction as I was that Justin knew the word. Justin was an inquisitive child. He has always asked questions. Some parents might become aggravated with this, but I was excited that Justin had such an appetite for knowledge. I'm also honored that he thinks I know so much. Once in awhile, when I'm feeling overwhelmed by his questions, I sometimes say, "Justin, where Dad's knowledge ends, Google's knowledge begins. Google it."

Chase and Justin occasionally fought, as all brothers do, but at the end of the day they loved each other as only brothers can. They shared a room until Chase became a teenager and I gave up my office space so that he could have his own bedroom. When Chase and Justin were in the same room for all those years, we had problems getting them to go to sleep. They would talk with each other after they were in their beds and often times we would hear Justin cackle as Chase said or did something funny. After I had made several visits to their room to get them to quiet down and go to sleep, Kim and I would hear them continuing to whisper.

When Chase was 4 years old, a new family moved in next door. The previous owners had grown children. Our new neighbors had a boy younger than Chase and a little girl older than Chase. It wasn't long before Chase was playing with the neighbors' children, Alex and Katherine. He would go ring the neighbors' doorbell and when the dad would come to answer the door, Chase would just stand there and look at him.

The neighbor would ask, "Do you want something, Chase? Chase, do you want to play with Alex?"

Chase would nod, but say nothing. Then our neighbors would invite him in.

Like many little boys Chase and Alex loved playing Army. They spent hours together with their toy guns and camouflage. Later when Alex's family moved down the street into a cul de sac, they would play in the woods directly behind Alex's home. Alex's parents told me how Chase had frightened them when they discovered that he had climbed to the very top of a tree. In the trees Chase was like a monkey. He saw a tree as another challenge to be conquered. Much like Chase, I used to climb to the very tip top of the pecan trees in our yard when I was a boy. My mother would warn me to be careful as she looked on from our kitchen window.

Alex and Chase played pick up games of football together with other kids in the neighborhood. Alex's father, David, says that Alex told him Chase was so athletic that Alex would seek out other kids to form a team to play against so that he could play on Chase's team. He got tired of playing against Chase and his endless supply of energy.

In 2001 when Chase was 7 years old, I founded Tree of Life Outdoor Ministries. This was a non-profit Christian organization that initially offered a summer day camp for boys ages eight to fifteen. We started out on church property but in our second year we moved to a 150-acre farm which the owner was generous enough to let us use. Later I added an outdoor program I called Elite Force primarily for "at-risk" boys in the same age range. Our Elite Force program offered a weekly 90-minute meeting always held outdoors, weather permitting, and frequent camping trips.

Chase was with me every day for summer camp, which lasted most of the summer, and he was also a member of Elite Force. He never missed a meeting. At camp, he helped me prepare in the mornings by carrying items and by filling water and Gatorade jugs for me. He helped me set up our large military surplus tent and our obstacle course. He never complained.

We had a lot of different activities lined up for the kids, but the most popular one was "capture-the-flag." We had access to a big chunk of woods and fields where we could play capture-the-flag. Chase would come home covered in mud, with scratches all over his legs from running through the briers. His mother fussed, but that was Chase's way. He always went all out at sporting events.

Most of the time, I organized, and sometimes officiated the capture-the-flag games, but I also participated in a game once in awhile. On this particular day, Chase was on the opposing team and I wound up in his team's territory trying to get their flag. Chase spotted me and came after me. I was running in the woods, through the briers, and doing whatever I could to lose him. My breathing was getting labored, and Chase was right on my heels. I couldn't let him catch me. I looked ahead and spotted a small tree with no low-hanging limbs. I jumped as high as I could up the tree trunk and began to pull myself up, but before I could get out of his reach, Chase tagged me on the heel. I looked down to see him grinning from ear to ear. Then I knew I could no longer outrun Chase. We both had a good laugh about it, but Chase definitely enjoyed the moment more than I did.

In Elite Force we practiced survival skills. We made and tested slings to sling rocks, snares, and all kinds of traps. We hiked and explored, shot bows, and fished. We camped regularly. E.L.I.T.E. stood for Experience Life In The Extreme. The ELITE Force group was small. We had about ten members at our peak.

We built various kinds of survival shelters, including a lean-to and a root shelter. One night, Chase and T.J., one of our other Elite Force regulars, decided they wanted to spend the night in a root shelter they had constructed. The other campers and I stayed in the large tent while T.J. and Chase were in the nearby root shelter. It rained that night, but the boys never complained. They made it through the night. The next day I asked how it went. They reported that they had shared their shelter with some crawling insects, but that otherwise, it wasn't bad. They stayed relatively dry and warm throughout the night.

Part of the rank advancement requirements for ELITE Force involved memorizing scripture verses. Chase memorized quite a few verses, but his favorite was, "I can do all things through Christ who strengthens me." I had to give up Camp High Adventure and Elite Force. I didn't have the financial support or the help that I needed to keep it going. As much as I loved working with the boys, I had to close it down after our 2006 season.

Chase was disappointed when I closed down these programs. I suggested that he join the Boy Scouts of America to help fill in the void. Chase agreed reluctantly. I told him to try it to see how he liked it. Obviously Boy Scouts wasn't going to be the same, but I explained to him

Chase scales the wall on the obstacle course at Camp High Adventure.

that Boys Scouts go camping, go to summer camp, and do a lot of the other things that we did with Camp High Adventure and Elite Force. Chase joined Boy Scouts a year after he was eligible at age twelve. That put him behind a little, but he jumped right in and started advancing through the ranks.

When Chase was in the fifth grade, one day near the beginning of the school year, he came to me and told me about a little boy named Kordell who whacked him on the back of the head at the bus stop. I told Chase to ignore him, that he would probably stop. I completely forgot about it and Chase never mentioned it again.

Late in that school year, Chase got kicked off the bus for standing up while it was moving. When I asked him why he had stood up, he told me that he was defending himself from Kordell. He was sitting in his seat when Kordell came over and began to hit him. The principal was expecting a baby and was on leave, so there was an acting principal. I called her and tried to reason with her about the situation. Chase had never been in any kind of trouble at school, and Kordell had a history of being a troublemaker. She admitted this to me. To her, it was a black and white issue: there was zero tolerance for standing up on the bus, period. It didn't matter to her why Chase had stood up or that he had never been in trouble before. I asked Chase about any other run-ins with Kordell, and he told me that Kordell had whacked him on the back of the head again.

"Chase, how long has this been going on?"

"All year," he said.

"He's been whacking you on the back of the head every day all year long?"

"Yes", he answered. "Not only that, but he sometimes does it several times a day."

I asked him to tell me more. He went on to say that Kordell intimidated younger students on the bus and took their snacks every day. I tried to reason with the acting principal. I told her that she and the bus driver had a responsibility to make sure that Chase and the other children could ride the bus in safety without being harassed. "Something needs to be done about Kordell. He doesn't belong in school."

"Mr. Rodgers," she said, this *is* a public school." Exactly! I thought. My tax dollars pay your salary and the salary of that bus driver. You work for me, and my child has the right to ride that bus without being harassed every single day. Do your job! I wish I had said those thoughts, but I didn't.

Against the principal's edict, I put Chase on the bus the next day. Then she called me in and we had a long discussion. I felt sorry for Kordell and I expressed this to her. There must have been something terribly wrong with this boy for him to be acting out the way he was. Finally, I gave in to the principal. We kept Chase off the bus for a week, even though I thought it was unfair.

After his week of punishment was up, it was time for Chase to ride the bus again. It was also time for Kordell to ride the bus again. So that morning, I walked with Chase to the bus stop and confronted Kordell. "Kordell, I've told Chase that he is to keep his hands to himself and not touch you under any circumstances. I recommend you do the same and we'll keep you both out of trouble. The school year is almost over. Can you do that for me? Can you promise to keep your hands to yourself and not touch Chase for any reason?"

"Yes sir," Kordell replied.

When Chase got off the bus in the afternoon I watched him walking home from the bus stop to our house. Kordell walked a few feet behind him and I could see him taunting Chase. Chase ignored him and kept walking. I never saw it at the bus stop, because Kordell was too smart for that, but not long after that Chase told me that Kordell was whacking him on the back of the head again every day. Kordell was also continuing to intimidate the little kids and take their snacks. When Kordell wasn't looking Chase would sneak and give the snacks back to their rightful owners. I wanted to give Kordell what he deserved. I went to the store and bought a laxative that looks like chocolate candy. I also bought some chocolate cupcakes. My plan was to put a generous supply of the laxative into the cupcakes and have Chase put them where Kordell would be tempted to take them. I came to my senses however when my wife, pointed out this would not be the adult thing to do. So I said to Chase, "This is what I want you to do. I want you to keep your hands to yourself, but I've already warned Kordell. The next time he puts a finger on you for any reason, you have my permission to beat him up." Kordell was a much larger kid than Chase and he had failed a grade, so he was older, too.

The time had slipped up on me, and I wasn't watching for Chase this particular afternoon. I heard a frantic knock at the front door and when I opened it, Chase was standing there in tears and out of breath.

"What is it, Chase? What happened?"

"I think I hurt Kordell, he said."

"Is he bleeding?" I asked.

"No. I don't think so," he said. "We started fighting and the fight went to the ground. I ended up on top of him and I punched him several times in the face. He started crying."

"If he's not bleeding, then you probably should have hit him harder." I heard a knock at the door. There stood Kordell.

"I was getting off the bus and I tapped Chase on the shoulder to tell him something and he started kicking me and punching me."

I looked at him. "Kordell," I said, didn't I tell you to keep your hands to yourself? You promised me you wouldn't touch Chase for the rest of the school year for any reason." He stared back at me for a moment, and then he walked away. I didn't believe his story about tapping Chase on the shoulder for a moment.

About fifteen minutes later, someone knocked on the door. Kordell was standing there with his father this time. His father said, "Kordell said that he just tapped Chase on the shoulder when he was getting off the bus to tell him something and Chase turned around and started kicking and punching him."

So I told Kordell's father the story of how Kordell had been whacking Chase on the back of the head every day for the entire school year, and how Kordell was taking snacks from the little kids on the bus. "I don't understand why Chase and Kordell are having so much trouble getting along, but maybe we should take the two of them to get ice cream one day and let them get to know each other a little better." He stared back at me and without saying a word, he turned and walked away with Kordell in tow.

Kordell still had not learned his lesson, and though the harassment was not as bad as before, he kept at it. He would get up to sharpen his pencil, walk by Chase's desk, and whack Chase on the back of the head when the teacher wasn't looking. On the next to the last day of school, Chase was sitting at his desk working on a project. Kordell reached over and grabbed Chase's artwork and crumpled it. Chase had had enough.

He got up and body slammed Kordell to the classroom floor and began to punch him until the teacher and other students stopped Chase and dragged him off of Kordell.

Kordell and Chase were both suspended for the rest of the school year, which was only one more day. This upset Chase because he liked his teacher a lot and wasn't going to get to say goodbye to her. Since he would be moving up to middle school the next year, he thought he might never see her again. We called Chase's teacher and explained how Chase felt. She invited us to bring Chase over after school. The two of them went to the basketball court and shot some hoops for a while. Now that's a good teacher, in my book.

I learned later from one of my neighbors that Kordell had been terrorizing his daughters the entire school year. Kordell now has quite a criminal record. His mugshots can be found online. Below is a letter Chase wrote to his teacher. I saved it on my hard drive all these years. He did this completely on his own.

DEAR MS. Johnson
I will miss you. You are the best teacher in the world.
My phone number is 467-xxxx.
I hope you have a good summer.
I will. Maybe sometime you can eat dinner at my house.
I will visit you a lot.
My address is xxx Kingsland drive.
I will miss you.
I will miss you.
I will miss you.
See you later.
See you later.
See you later.
Bye Ms. J

Kordell lived right down the street from us, and despite his bad behavior in school, he showed up at our house once in awhile and wanted to play with Chase. I invited him in, and we tried to befriend him. I did keep a close eye on how he interacted with Chase. I suggested to Chase that we buy a Christmas present for Kordell as a peace offering.

Chase and I went to the mall together and found a man selling nice sports cards from a kiosk. At the time, Julius Peppers was with the Carolina Panthers and was a very popular and upcoming football star. We purchased a rather expensive Julius Peppers football card, had it gift wrapped, and gave it to Kordell for Christmas. Kordell never thanked us.

Chase got a new bicycle for Christmas. It was a Schwinn Stingray; chopper style, black with orange and yellow flames. When he learned about it, Kordell looked Chase right in the eye and said to him, "I like that bicycle. I'm going to steal it."

Chase told Kordell that he had a chain and a lock to protect his new bicycle from people who might steal it.

Kordell's answer was, "That's okay. I have bolt cutters to cut the lock with." Fortunately, Kordell never acted out on his threats to steal Chase's bike.

When he was about nine, I asked Chase if he would be interested in playing Pop Warner tackle football. He was interested right away. So we enrolled him, and he got picked for a team. That first season he didn't get a lot of playing time, mostly because he didn't have any previous tackle football experience. Understanding and remembering plays on offense, and using good form on tackles are things that take time for kids to learn.

The next season, however, things were different. By this time, Justin wanted to play sports and I knew it would be difficult getting both of them where they needed to go, especially with Chase playing three sports. During his first season of tackle football, Chase also played soccer. He was good enough at soccer that he was ready to move up to a more challenging level of play, but the tryouts for that level were only held in the fall, and now Chase was playing football in the fall. I talked to Chase and asked him if he had to pick one sport, which one would it be.

Without hesitation, he said, "*football!*"

"Chase, are you sure?"

"Yes! *Football.*"

"Chase, you're small for a football player, and last year you got yelled at a lot by the coaches because you couldn't remember formations and plays. Are you sure you want to play football?" He was sure, so we dropped all of the other sports and let Chase concentrate on foot-

Chase during his second year of Pop Warner football.

ball. His second season with Pop Warner Chase was on a different team with a coach who was excited about his speed and agility. Chase now had one season of tackle football under his belt. His coach would run a simple pitch sweep to get Chase the ball out in space. If Chase picked up one block on the edge and he could turn the corner, he was gone. No one was going to catch him. Chase became the go-to guy. Just pitch the ball to Chase and he'll get the first down or score.

Chase and I spent a lot of time together practicing different sports, mostly in our front yard. I would throw him the football, most of the time slightly out of reach. Chase would make attempt after attempt at diving catches. He loved every minute of it. We played one on one football in the front yard. I taught him how to spin and how to juke. He picked up on it quickly and during his first season of Pop Warner football, Chase embarrassed a few of his teammates at practice during drills. They would attempt to tackle him and he would spin or juke, leaving them grabbing at air and colliding into one another.

Chase had been asking me for a basketball goal. Christmas wasn't far away, so I put it on the Christmas list. In the meantime I took him to a nearby park where he and I spent some father and son time shooting hoops. One Sunday afternoon we were playing basketball when a gang of ten teenagers showed up. These boys were in their late teens to early twenties. Chase and I had been there a little while, but we weren't quite ready to leave yet. One of the boys said that Chase and I were in their way. He said they play basketball on that court every Sunday at the same time. I told him we weren't ready to leave and that he would have to wait a little longer. He asked me why I didn't put a basketball goal up at our house. I said, "Okay. Why don't you go down to the store and buy it for me, big man?" He shrugged his shoulders as if I was the one who didn't get it. The court behind us was open, but they wanted to play full court. There was another full court next to us, but apparently they didn't think they could bully the people who were playing there.

They kept the pressure on. They started playing half court behind us. They kept complaining. Then they started playing full court right around us, bumping into us in the process. When Chase's ball got in the way, one of them kicked it so hard that it went right over the fence. I crossed my arms and glared at him. He quickly ran out to go get the ball. I told them that I could call the police if they would like. "No! Don't do that," one of them said. Chase and I played a little while longer until I felt I had made my point. I didn't want to endanger Chase, but I wanted him to see that you have to stand up to bullies.

Christmas came, and I bought that basketball goal for Chase. Our house is not the ideal location for a goal, but I was determined to make it work. I filled the base with water and antifreeze. This was a mistake. I should have filled it with sand. The base was made of plastic and after dragging the goal around to reposition it a few times a hole was worn in the bottom. We weren't aware of the hole. I woke up one morning to find the basketball goal lying across our driveway. The rim was irreparably bent. I had good intentions to go get another goal for Chase, but he wasn't so patient. He used some chalk to draw a goal on the chimney under our carport. He used his imagination. I liked that. The remnants of that chalk basketball goal can be still be seen on the chimney.

Chapter Two

MIDDLE SCHOOL

T HE LAST YEAR CHASE played Pop Warner football, we sometimes didn't have enough people at practice to have players on offense and defense. One afternoon we were short on players. I had played baseball in high school, but never played football. I agreed to play corner back and Chase was at running back on the offense. The head coach did a sneaky thing and ran a reverse to my side. For those not familiar with football, a reverse is when one of the running backs takes a hand-off and runs to one side of the formation in an attempt to draw the defense in that direction, then quickly and smoothly hands the ball off to another running back who is headed in the opposite direction.

Of course, I got fooled and moved inside, following the original ball carrier. Here came Chase to the outside. So I took a good angle and sprinted for all I was worth. I had on no pads or helmet, just shorts, a T-shirt, and cross trainers. I caught Chase by his left shoulder pad and he dipped his shoulder. When he did, my feet left the ground and I became airborne, but I held on to Chase's pads and spun him around and out of bounds. We both tumbled out of bounds, and I rolled, my elbows and knees taking the impact. There was a gravel trail around that side of the practice field, so when I got up, my elbows and knees were bleeding. Do you think I cared? I was grinning from ear to ear and so were Chase and the head coach.

The last Pop Warner football game Chase ever played was a close game. We needed a first down if we wanted to win. Chase was lined up at wide out and he ran a deep fade route down the left sideline. Our quarterback reached back and let it go. I watched the arc of the ball and my mind quickly calculated how this would work out. It was a pretty pass, but a little too long. I didn't think Chase had a chance. At the last moment, Chase dove for it, the defensive back right on his heels. Chase was completely outstretched, parallel to the ground as the ball came in over his right shoulder. He caught it with his fingertips and pulled it in to his body. We won that game by a touchdown. After the game, one of the fathers on the opposing team approached me in the stands. "Is that your son who made that catch near the end of the game?"

"Yes,"

"Man! That was an NFL catch," he said, excitedly.

I have always loved animals and so had Chase. I've rescued several baby squirrels that fell from trees. As a child I had pet dogs and cats, and at one point a couple of turtles. Yet I grew up in an area and a time where hunting was a tradition. I've always opposed any type of animal abuse and I believe in treating animals, wild or domesticated, with the utmost respect. I'm telling you this story, because it was father and son bonding time that Chase and I spent together.

When I was leading Elite Force, I partnered with a local chapter of a hunting organization to provide an opportunity to youth who wouldn't ordinarily have the opportunity to go hunting. Chase had been hunting with me a few times, but this was a great opportunity, not only for the other boys of Elite Force, but also for Chase and me to have a father/son outing. All of the boys with Elite Force, and the other young folks in attendance had an adult mentor with them for the hunt. North Carolina Wildlife officers were in attendance, and youth model rifles were provided for the hunters. Time was allotted for each participant to take target practice so they could become acquainted with their rifle.

When we were ready, Chase and I were escorted by one of the property managers to a field where we would hunt for the evening. He pointed out an elevated box stand across the field and told us which direction to expect the deer to come from.

It was a very cool day in December with temperatures in the teens. I was pleasantly surprised that our stand had a small propane heater inside to keep us nice and toasty. We were seated in swivel chairs and I decided to keep watch out the front of the stand while Chase kept watch out the back. I made sure to keep Chase's expectations for the hunt realistic. I told him that if we even saw a deer at all, to consider it a success. He understood. Sometimes that's the way hunting goes. You brave the forces of nature and sit there for hours without seeing a thing. I was surprised about twenty minutes into the hunt when Chase whispered excitedly, "Dad! Dad! I see a deer!" I carefully turned my swivel chair in his direction and peered through the slit in the stand to see three deer about 150 yards away approaching our position. We had been instructed by the landowners to shoot only does. This was a policy designed to manage the deer herd, as the does outnumber the bucks about ten to one in our area. I asked Chase if he saw antlers on any of these deer.

"No."

The deer continued to meander in our direction, grazing a little as they walked. I asked to hold Chase's rifle so I could look at the deer through the scope. I looked carefully, but I couldn't see any antlers either. I handed the rifle back to Chase. By now the deer were about 100 yards away, and Chase and I couldn't stand it any longer.

"Okay," I said. "The one in the middle looks to be the biggest. Why don't you shoot that one?"

"Okay."

I coached him as he took a deep breath and pushed off the safety. He put the crosshairs on the deer in the middle. He slowly let out his breath as he squeezed the trigger. BOOM! The .45 caliber lever action rifle belched. I watched carefully as the three deer scattered into the woods to our right. Chase looked at me with a huge grin on his face and impulsively gave me a high five. Chase was so quiet most of the time that it was out of character for him to show this much emotion. We both knew he had made a good shot.

I told Chase that we should wait twenty minutes before coming down from our stand. Otherwise, if the deer were still alive, she would run from us, prolonging her death and making her more difficult to find. When we came down and went to the spot where the deer had been standing we tracked the deer into the bushes. We didn't have to go far. Chase had made a good shot. It has been important to me to make careful, clean shots so as to minimize any suffering the animal might experience.

As we were climbing back into our stand, we saw a group of deer about 300 yards out on the other side. That would have been a long shot for Chase, especially with this rifle, and we didn't want to be greedy. The deer caught our scent in the wind and snorted and huffed at us, hoping we would leave so they could come into the field to eat. We sat there until it was close to dark and the ranch hand drove back to get us. We put our deer in the back of the truck and met with the other hunters back at a metal building where all of the deer were prepared for human consumption. We hunted again the next morning, and Chase had another shot which missed, but we were happy with the results of our hunt. All but one of the Elite Force boys had taken their first deer.

One summer we took a quick weekend camping trip to the beach. We looked for activities to enjoy while we were there. I found a brochure advertising a serpentarium, a facility that housed snakes. There were a wide variety of snakes there, including several highly-venomous species and constrictors. There were also several other reptile exhibits, including small alligators. We took our time and enjoyed each exhibit. I noticed that all of the animals were becoming more active and guessed that feeding time was around the corner. A good-sized crowd was gathered in the serpentarium now. Sure enough, a man came in and educated us on the different snakes. He fed a dead chicken to one of the large constrictors and mice to the Gaboon vipers.

After the feeding, we made our way upstairs to see other exhibits. Chase and Justin moved ahead of Kim and me. I caught up with them at a large aquarium that housed a three-foot alligator. The alligator sat there like a statue, not moving a muscle, with his mouth hanging wide open. "Dad, put your face down next to the glass right by the alligator," Chase insisted.

"Why?"

"Just do it, Dad!"

"Okay." So I put my face next to the glass right by the small alligator. Suddenly he snapped at me, bumping his snout against the glass with a loud thump. I jumped back, startled. Then we all laughed. Kim was still walking around behind us looking at other exhibits and was completely unaware of what was going on with the alligator. Chase and Justin got her attention, and she made her way over to us.

"Mom, put your face next to the glass near the alligator," Chase urged. He could hardly contain himself.

"I'm not putting my face next to the glass!"

"What are you guys up to?" Kim asked suspiciously.

"Just do it Mom," Chase and Justin urged. Reluctantly, my wife moved her face next to the glass and peered at the alligator. Suddenly the alligator snapped at her, bumping his snout against the glass. She jumped back and let out a blood-curdling scream. Prior to this, there had been a steady buzz of conversation. As soon as Kim screamed, you could have heard a pin drop. People looked around, but no one spoke. I could almost read their minds. "What happened?"

"Did a deadly snake escape somehow?" "Was someone bitten?" After a few seconds, people returned to their walking around the exhibits. Fortunately, because of the echo it would have been hard to pinpoint precisely where the scream came from. Chase and Justin fell to the floor laughing, holding their bellies. I laughed, too. Kim didn't think it was so funny at first, but after awhile she laughed too.

I wanted to teach Chase and Justin a lesson about hard work, the free market, and how to earn money, so I encouraged them to set up a lemonade stand in our front yard during the summer. We live on a good street for it. It's busy enough to provide plenty of customers for the budding entrepreneurs but not so busy that it's dangerous. We set up a shade structure in the front yard, and I helped them make some bright signs to capture the attention of drivers.

Business was good. Most of our neighbors were impressed that the boys were willing to work to earn money, and they were very supportive. Some people just driving through stopped to buy lemonade. At the end of the first day, the boys had made $80. Soon Justin had friends who wanted to get in on the action, so they came to help out some days.

One neighbor didn't seem to be so impressed. He asked me if I was trying to turn my boys into little capitalists. I looked him straight in the eye, smiled, and said, "Yes. That's *exactly* what I'm trying to do." He looked stunned. Speechless, he turned and walked away. I can't tell you how many times I've bought Girl Scout cookies from his daughter. Never pooh-pooh someone else's success. Go out and create some success of your own.

One day Chase brought home a small snake. Its body was slightly thinner than a pencil and it was eight inches long. The snake was brown with grey markings. I knew right away that it was non-venomous by the shape of its head. I thought I knew what kind of snake it was, and an internet search revealed that I was correct. It was a brown snake.

We went to the local pet store and purchased a Critter Keeper to keep the snake in. The Critter Keeper is a plastic aquarium with a vented lid and folding handle. You can also buy a light for it that snaps into the lid. We put dirt, sticks, and rocks in the Critter Keeper to create a habitat for the snake. Also, there was a small dish that held water for the snake to drink. Another internet search revealed that brown snakes like to eat earthworms. The large night crawlers that people buy for fish bait were too big for him to eat. They were almost as big as he was. The small red worms that are indigenous to North Carolina worked better.

It wasn't long before we had the snake trained to lift his body up like a human being standing on his tiptoes, to take the earthworms in. We would watch in amazement as he swallowed the worm whole. Chase kept a logbook chronicling his daily feeding, and watering, as well as any observations about the snake's behavior. He did this because it was part of the Boy Scouts reptile and amphibian merit badge requirements. Then Kim fed the snake one day and did not put the lid all the way back on properly. I later discovered that the lid wasn't all the way on and I looked for the snake in the Critter Keeper. It wasn't there. We never saw the brown snake again. We don't know if he found his way out of our house or not.

Another day Chase and I went for a hike in the woods and he found and caught a small banded water snake in a creek. We brought him home and put him in the Critter Keeper we had used for the brown snake. The banded water snake needed a different type of habitat. We put it in water with some sand, branches, and a small hollow log for a hiding place. After a little research, we learned that the best way to feed the banded water snake was to buy feeder guppies at the local pet store. So we purchased ten feeder guppies for a dollar and dropped them into the water with the snake. He would chase them around in the water and eat them one by one. At the time I was a leader in Chase's Boy Scout troop. He and I both went off to Boy Scout summer camp one summer and when we returned, the banded water snake was dead. We had left it in my wife's care. We're not sure what happened, but he didn't survive.

I received a phone call from one of Chase's eighth grade teachers one day. He said that he had left the classroom for a few minutes, and when he returned, Chase was standing on top of the teacher's desk. I can't recall now the exact story, or even if we ever got the whole story. Chase never admitted to it. I didn't think his teacher would make up something like that, but Chase had never lied to me before.

I scheduled a parent/teacher conference a few days later. Another of Chase's teachers said that Chase had decided to take a nap on the floor by his desk in the middle of class. Again, he denied this. Finally, it dawned on me that Chase had been going through a growth spurt and that we had not made any adjustments to his medication. I scheduled an appointment for him with his doctor right away, and she bumped his ADD meds to the next dosage level. I didn't have any other reports of unusual behavior from any of his teachers for the remainder of the year. I was very disappointed, however, that he had lied to his mother and me about his behavior.

One time when we went to Greenville, South Carolina to visit family and friends, we forgot Chase's meds. At first I blew it off, but after awhile some of our family and friends were asking about those meds. Chase couldn't sit still. He was wired up and exhausting us all. Finally I called our neighbors and had them get Chase's meds from our house and overnight them to us.

Chase wasn't a stellar student, but he made mostly As and Bs with an occasional C. What hurt his grades more than anything was that he sometimes completed his assignments but forgot to turn them in. This is apparently a common issue with middle school boys. Chase was disorganized and forgetful. I stayed on him about keeping his grades up. I told him that in the eighth grade, his grades would begin to matter more if he decided he wanted to go to college later.

We had introduced Chase to video games when he was little. That decision I later regretted. Chase became addicted to video games and would play for hours if I let him. When I made him stop, he sometimes became very angry and even threw a temper tantrum.

In middle school Chase ran the 800 meter and the mile and competed in the long jump. He was competitive but never won any of those events. He did, however, earn the nickname "Bunny Rabbit" for his ability to jump so far for such a little guy.

One day I was watching an interview with NFL wide receiver Terrell Owens. I watched him workout and heard him say that for practice he catches three hundred passes per day from all different angles. Chase had great hand to eye coordination and was blessed with a natural ability to catch. I believe that the way to go from good to great at anything is to practice, practice, practice. After that I threw the football out in the front yard to Chase every day; over the shoulder catches, low passes, high passes, passes that he had to dive to catch.

I used to tuck in Chase and Justin every night at bedtime. Sometimes I told them a story or we read a book. Chase was never ready to go to bed and he would do anything to stall. One night, as I went to tuck Chase in, I grabbed a football. I went to the far corner of his room. Chase was lying in bed on his back. I said, "Here, Chase." I tossed the football to him underhanded, putting spin on it. He reached up from his position lying flat on his back and snagged it. I kept throwing them, each time making them more difficult to catch. I threw them hard, threw them high. We counted them. 100, 200, sometimes 300 passes at bedtime. He got even better at catching. At bedtime Chase would call out to me, "Dad! Dad! Come throw me some passes!" Every night for the longest time, this was our father and son ritual.

Chapter Three

HIGH SCHOOL

W HEN CHASE STARTED THE NINTH GRADE, we went with him to freshman orientation. Katherine, the girl next door to us, Alex's sister, saw us as we were going from room to room helping Chase get familiar with the layout. Katherine was a rising junior. She was warm and friendly and seemed genuinely excited that Chase was there. She welcomed him to high school. Chase was so shy, he hardly said a word to her even though they had grown up next door to each other and played together over the years.

Katherine had friends who were twin girls and lived right down the street from us. She rode to school with them, and they offered Chase the opportunity to ride along as well. According to Katherine, Chase rode with them all the way to school every day without saying a word, unless they asked him questions. Even then he wouldn't talk much. This was typical of Chase who was very quiet in groups most of the time, but friendly, funny, and playful, one on one. Chase felt a little intimidated by girls.

When Chase had been preparing for high school in the eighth grade, he decided to join the NJROTC (Naval Junior Reserve Officers Training Corps). Participants develop leadership skills and learn the basics of military bearing and naval operations. The NJROTC holds an annual ball that cadets and family members can attend. Cadets may bring their dates. The cadets wear their uniforms, and their dates dress formally.

We encouraged Chase to invite a girl to go with him to the NJROTC ball in his freshman year. He apparently felt too awkward to invite any-

Kim and Chase prepare to attend the Cary High NJROTC Ball.

one. Chase's mom told him that if he didn't invite a girl to go with him that she would go as his date. We thought this would prompt him to invite a girl. What teenage boy wants to be seen with his mom at the dance? It didn't work. Chase refused to invite a girl to the ball, so his mom went with him. It turns out that Chase wasn't the only cadet who brought his mother. All of the kids danced together, and Chase got in on the action. The next year his mother went with him to the NJROTC ball again.

One of the things that Chase especially enjoyed about NJROTC was the field events. He competed in NJROTC athletic field events as part of a team. Chase excelled at this and he was proud of a medal that he earned as a part of that team.

I came across the book *"Raising a Modern Day Knight."* I liked the concept. The book was about fathers banding together to raise their sons with strong Christian values. Knights were known for their virtue. Like the knights, the RMDK program used ceremonies to celebrate each stage of the progression from boyhood to manhood. Later when my friend Bob approached me about participating in a RMDK study, I was excited. Part of the program involved the father asking his son to tell him how he was doing at being a father, and if there was anything he could improve on. It was a great way to get feedback. Chase was so quiet and respectful that he didn't normally give me much criticism, even when I specifically asked for it.

One of the exercises in the book was to create a manhood crest to represent what the men in the family were about. Chase, Justin, and I talked it over, and with their input, I began to sketch out what I thought should represent the Rodgers men. Once the sketch was complete I hired a graphic artist to use our sketch as a guide to create a digital image. My plan was to have high-quality prints made of the artwork that I could then frame and give to Chase and Justin. I still have the digital artwork, but I haven't yet had it printed and framed.

There were four stages in RMDK, each celebrated by ceremonies, outlined in the book: Page, Squire, Knight, and the Promise/Oath stage. The Page ceremony is informal. Chase and I drove about an hour and a half to a place where we rode zip lines through the treetops. The ride there and back gave us ample time to talk about what it means to be a man. We discussed some of the challenges he would face along the path to Christian manhood. Chase listened while I talked. We listened together to a CD that discussed some of the issues he would face during the early stages of becoming a man.

Manhood Crest created by Chase, Justin, and me

My friend Bob also introduced me to a program called "Letters from Dad." This program encourages dads to write frequent letters to their children, encouraging them and giving them guidance as they grow. It also teaches the art of writing good letters. Thanks to "Letters from Dad," I wrote several letters to Chase and Justin, and I still practice this today.

One of our neighbors approached me and asked if I thought Chase would be interested in mowing lawns to make extra money. Her step-son had been mowing the lawn of one of her friends and another lawn or two in the same neighborhood. I had owned a lawn care business for five years so I knew I could help Chase get started with this. I thought it would be a good way for him to begin earning money and learning the work ethic. Chase didn't yet have his driver's license and the neighborhood where the opportunity existed was too far to walk with a mower and other yard equipment.

I asked Chase if he was interested in the job and he said he was, so I agreed to drive him there and to do the trimming and some of the blowing if he would mow the lawns. He agreed, so we started with a couple of customers and soon grew to having five or six regular customers whose lawns we mowed every two weeks during the spring and summer. I opened a custodial bank account for Chase and began to deposit some of his paychecks for him. I allowed him to have some spending money, too. The rest of it went to pay for expenses. Chase and I made a pretty good team. It was tough sometimes, especially in the summer heat when he also had football workouts. Chase had an abundance of energy, but I know there were times when he would have rather been doing something besides mowing lawns.

Chase played football on the JV team his freshman year, but he didn't get much playing time. I felt like he was being overlooked because of his small size and the fact that he was so quiet. By this point in Chase's sports career, I had learned that coaches have a tough job. Maybe the toughest coaching job of all is that of a football coach. So I tried to be patient and not complain about Chase's lack of playing time. I did email the coach and ask him what Chase needed to improve on. The reply I got was vague. It's frustrating as a parent to watch your child sit on the bench, especially when you know in your heart he's a good athlete. I decided that it's not uncommon for a freshman to ride the bench. Besides that, Chase was small. I never said anything else about it and hoped he would get more playing time his sophomore year.

In Chase's freshman year we took a family vacation to Washington DC for his spring break. I thought it would be both educational and fun. Kim had a co-worker who had a relative who was with the Secret Service. He was able to get us on the list to visit the White House on short notice. The first stop we made was at Arlington National Cemetery. We also visited the WWII Memorial, the Lincoln Monument, the Vietnam Memorial, and the Washington Monument. Justin complained about how his feet were hurting. I gave him piggyback rides. I wasn't sure when we would get back to Washington, so I wasn't going to let him slow us down.

We saw a lot of the sights, but one of my most fond memories was at the Smithsonian Air and Space Museum. There was a full-motion airplane simulator ride there that two people could get in together. They were seated in tandem and one would pilot the aircraft while the other was the gunner. It was an expensive ride, but I took great pleasure in listening to Chase and Justin's belly laughs as the simulator rolled upside down and made sharp movements over and over. I'm not sure what Chase was doing in there, but he had Justin cracking up.

When I was Chase's age, I was painfully shy too. As I matured I learned some things that helped me overcome my shyness. One was how to start a conversation and be a good conversationalist. Being an active listener is one of the keys. I wanted to pass on some of this knowledge to Chase, but he wasn't ready for it.

One thing he did learn was how to break the ice with people. One of my favorite ways was to pay a sincere compliment. Chase used these ideas along with social media and his cell phone, to get his romances started. He found girls whom he found attractive on social media sites and paid them a compliment. He got the conversation going with them and then he got their number and moved to texting, phone calls, and finally meeting them in person. This was how he overcame his shyness. He got good at it; too good.

When Chase entered the tenth grade we finally got him a cell phone. With his busy schedule of football practice, NJROTC, track and field, and Boy Scouts, we had to have a way of staying in touch so we could get him where he needed to go. About that time he also started a Facebook account.

I discovered that Chase had gotten into a dispute on Facebook with a boy who was a high school student at a high school across town called Panther Creek. The other young man dared Chase to meet him at a middle school football field after school so that the two of them could duke it out. Apparently this kid had made some disparaging remarks about the Cary High School football team on Facebook. Chase didn't take kindly to that, so he returned the favor with remarks about the Panther Creek football team. It had gone back and forth until it got out of hand.

One of the conditions I had put on Chase at the time for having a cell phone and a Facebook account was that I should have access to his accounts at any time to see what kind of messaging was taking place. I discovered the conversation between the two of them in Chase's Facebook private messages. I confronted Chase with this information, and he assured me he had no intention of meeting with this young man named Ronald. Chase said that the time Ronald wanted to meet him was during football practice which he had no intention of missing, and besides that, he had no transportation other than me. Satisfied with Chase's answer, I let the issue go and cautioned him about what he posts on Facebook in the future.

It was less than a week later that I got a call from one of the assistant principals at Cary High School. Ronald had shown up at Cary High School after school with a carload of kids who were looking for Chase. Chase was still at football practice working on his position drills, when Ronald and his crew came upon some other football players and asked them if they knew where Chase Rodgers was. The football players asked him what he wanted with Chase. When he told them that he was looking to fight him, they quickly let him and his gang know that they would have to fight the other football players before they could lay a hand on Chase. Ronald and company decided it was time to leave.

The assistant principal at Cary High School contacted Panther Creek to alert them to the incident involving Ronald. He and some of the other kids got called into the office to be questioned. Chase also got called into the principal's office at Cary High School to be questioned about the incident. At some point, Chase was asked how he knew these boys at Panther Creek or how they knew him. Chase didn't realize Ronald was one of the boys who had showed up. He didn't know who these boys were who had come looking for him. He was then asked if he knew anyone who was a student at Panther Creek. He mentioned Carla, a girl he had met who went to school there. He had met her at a track meet, and they had been texting. I was totally unaware of this. Carla got called into the office and questioned at Panther Creek. She knew nothing about the incident, but when Chase's name was mentioned, that caused a big problem.

One evening not too long after the school incident, the Cary Police called me. The officer said, "Mr. Rodgers, I need to talk to you about your son Chase." He explained that Carla's father was very upset because Chase had been texting Carla and calling her at home. She was no longer interested in Chase and did not like the attention he was giving her. This was the first girl to my knowledge that Chase had ever shown any interest in and this was how I learned about it. Apparently Carla had shown interest in Chase in the beginning but had decided at some point that she was no longer interested. This baffled Chase and he wanted an explanation. Carla didn't feel like she owed Chase an explanation but he kept pestering her. When she got called into the principal's office she told her father, and he called the police to report everything that had happened.

So the first thing I did was to tell Chase about the phone call I had from the police. I kept my cool and he and I went down to the Cary Police Department to talk with the officer who had called me. I had talked to the officer in advance to let him know I would like to take this course of action. He had a good talk with Chase about the dangers of texting and Facebook. I got Carla's father's number and called him to apologize. When I explained the situation to him, he was very understanding and the entire matter was resolved.

When I looked at their Facebook photos, Ronald and his friends looked like a bunch of street punks to me. They lived in nice neighborhoods, but they were obviously smoking weed. They did not look like the friends I would want Chase to have. Some of the staff at Panther

Creek confirmed for me that Ronald was a troublemaker. I then contacted the assistant principal at Cary High School who had initially alerted me to the incident. I expressed my concern that this might not be the end of the problem. He promised me that he would submit the paperwork necessary to protect Chase. If Ronald ever set foot on the Cary High campus again, he would be arrested for trespassing.

In Chase's sophomore year he was in the starting lineup at cornerback on the J.V. Team. He had some competition for the starting spot, however. He made the first interception of his career in the game against Fuquay-Varina. I can still see it in my mind. I can't remember the second interception he made that season, but the third interception is still as crystal clear in my memory as his first.

By now it was early October and Our J.V. Team was having a good season with five wins and only two losses. We were playing at home versus our main rival, Apex High School. Chase was good with his coverage all night long and the quarterback never tested him. It was a close game, and we were ahead by less than a touchdown. With time running out in the game, Apex was driving down the field. If we couldn't stop them, we would lose the game.

Their quarterback took the snap in the shotgun formation. He couldn't find anyone open. Chase had tight coverage on his receiver. The quarterback looked around but didn't see anyone open and decided to try Chase's receiver. The receiver was considerably taller than Chase, so it was worth a try. Chase had good position and went up with the receiver. He made the interception and was immediately tackled as time ran out. Our entire team rushed onto the field and surrounded Chase. I have a photo of Chase and me that was taken immediately after the game. He has the biggest smile on his face.

Then the night came when our JV team played Panther Creek at Cary High School. I sat in the stands enjoying the game as usual. Chase was starting at cornerback. He had been having a good season with a lot of good tackles and some interceptions.

After the game I was walking around the field in the direction of the field house. Kim and I liked to wait for Chase to come out of the locker room. As I was walking along outside the chain link fence that surrounds the field, I saw Ronald. People were leaving the game and the

Chase and me after his game-ending interception.

crowd was thinning quickly, but Ronald was standing there talking to another young man and a young lady. I had no way of knowing what his intentions were, but he had already brought a carload of boys from another school all the way across town after school to beat up Chase. Apparently he had been too chicken to take Chase on alone. Still, I didn't trust him. The assistant principal had said that if Ronald was caught on the Cary High School campus again, he would be arrested for trespassing. I walked straight up to him. "Ronald?"

He looked back at me. "Yeah." He nodded his head.

"You're not supposed to be here. You're trespassing."

"I'm just here for the game."

"The game is over now, so you can leave."

"I'm not doing anything wrong," he whined. "I'm just here hanging out with my friends."

"You and your friends need to leave now and hang out someplace else," I insisted. A group of about three or four police officers were standing probably fifty to sixty feet away. "I have every right to be here," Ronald said.

"Then, let's go talk to the police about it."

"No! I don't want to talk to the police."

"Yeah, let's go." I grabbed his jacket and started to pull him towards the police. I called out to them, but they didn't hear me. A gentleman who works concessions approached me and asked me what was wrong. I asked him to go get the police and tell them that this boy was trespassing. He laughed at me and hesitated. He didn't know the story and thought I was joking around. I told him again, this time more emphatically, to go get the police. He started walking towards them. Ronald's eyes were like saucers. He was scared to death.

Suddenly he jerked away from me hard. He let his arms come out of the jacket and I was left standing there with a souvenir—his jacket. He took off running through the parking lot. I didn't bother to run after him. Ronald's friend, Andy, and the girl were still standing next to me. While I was watching Ronald, Andy snatched Ronald's jacket from my hand. Kim and I talked to the police and the assistant principal we had been dealing with all along. He never did get the paperwork completed that he had promised me. I must have scared Ronald though. He left Chase alone after that.

When Chase was playing football at Cary High, I frequently gave his teammates a ride home. Being a stay-at-home Dad, I was available and more than happy to help out. I enjoyed getting to know the guys and talking football with them. There is no telling how many different Cary High School football players rode in my truck at one time or another. One day, Chase asked me if I would take him and a bunch of his football buddies to a movie called "The Expendables." I was more than happy. We packed my little Isuzu Trooper. We had to put one guy, William, in the cargo compartment. I sat there and watched the movie with them. I loved it, but thirty minutes into the movie I looked around and noticed a lot of them were texting. The movie didn't have much of a plot. It was just a shoot 'em up tough guy movie. We still had a good time. I drove them all home afterwards.

One of Chase's teammates from the Cary High football team, Xavier, sometimes came over and had dinner with us. When Xavier came over I often grilled T-bone steaks and served the best ice cream I could find for dessert. Xavier often spent the night and sometimes went to church with us on Sunday mornings. He was a short but muscular linebacker with a big smile. He had a warm, friendly personality and you couldn't help but like him. Xavier lived with his mother. His father lived out of state. He was excited one evening when he came to our house to view some video I had shot of one of the J.V. games he and Chase had played in. Chase had laid an especially big hit on a wide receiver in that game just as the receiver caught the ball. Chase's hit had caused the ball to pop out, resulting in an incomplete pass. We all watched that play several times. Xavier got a big kick out of that hit. Outside of football, Chase and Xavier didn't have a lot in common. I soon became closer friends with Xavier than Chase was.

Chase had another friend named Ethan who was a punter on the Cary High School football team. Chase and Ethan had attended middle school together at Reedy Creek Middle in Cary. According to Ethan, he and Chase got in a little trouble in middle school for goofing off at PE one day and had to do up-downs in the long jump sand pit. Up-downs have been used for conditioning and discipline by football coaches for a long time. It's a drill in which the athlete or person being disciplined chops their feet quickly, running in place. When the coach commands him to go down either with his voice or a whistle, the person must go down to the ground as quickly as possible. Usually this is immediately followed by the "UP" command and more chopping of the feet. This can go on for some time with the ups and downs and can be very tiring. That's the point. Doing the up-downs in the sand pit makes them even more miserable, because the person doing the up-downs gets sand all in their clothing and shoes.

At some point during his sophomore year, Ethan introduced Chase to a girl he was dating named Kylie. Kylie's best friend was Shannon. Kylie introduced Chase to Shannon, and they hit it off right away. Chase still wasn't driving, so I chauffeured them around quite a bit. I would drop them off at the mall and the movies. Sometimes Shannon came to our house for dinner and the two of them would hang out and watch TV. Other times, Chase went over to Shannon's house. At least once that I know of, the four of them, Ethan and Kylie, Chase and Shannon went out on a double date to a nice restaurant. Shannon was a sweet girl with long brown hair and pretty brown eyes. Every time I've been around her she has been upbeat, cheerful, and polite. She really loved

Chase and often came with Kylie to the Cary High School games to cheer him on.

A friend of mine, Monte, offered me a temporary landscaping gig spreading pine straw. As a stay-at-home dad I was always looking for day jobs to make a little extra cash. We had a large area to cover, and it was going to take all day Saturday to complete. Chase had gone with my friend Bob and his son Robert to help with an Eagle Scout project at their farm. Robert had completed all the requirements to become an Eagle Scout except for his Eagle project and final review. It is customary for other scouts from the unit to serve as helpers on the Eagle Scout project under the direction of the Eagle Scout to-be.

We were almost finished with the pine straw that afternoon when my cell phone rang. It was Bob. He told me they had finished the Eagle project and that he had let Chase and Robert take their two go-karts out for a spin. Chase had flipped his go-kart and hurt his arm. Bob said that he didn't think Chase's arm was broken, but he was going to take him to the emergency room just in case.

I got a big lump in my throat. "Oh, No," I was thinking. Please don't let it be broken. I called Kim to let her know, and then I kept working so as to try and finish the job. I got a call back a little later from Kim. She was with Bob and Chase at the emergency room. "It's broken," she said. "You need to come to the hospital." I informed my friend, Monte of the situation and took off for the hospital.

These go-karts are not the ones you see at the track. They're made for off-road use with larger, off-road tires. They have a higher center of gravity than track carts and thus are much more susceptible to rolling over. They are equipped with a roll cage and five point restraint to protect the driver. Robert and Chase both were strapped in to their respective carts and wearing helmets.

Chase apparently got a little too comfortable with his gokart handling skills and pushed it to the limit. He was doing power slides in the dirt when he must have hit a hard piece of ground. The two tires on the side in the direction of the slide suddenly grabbed, flipping the kart. Chase's hands were on the steering wheel, but the centrifugal force must have caused his elbow to swing outside of the roll cage and it struck the ground as the kart rolled over.

When I arrived at the emergency room, I went back to see Chase. I pulled back the curtain to find him reclined in the hospital bed. Bob, Kim, and Justin were with him. His left forearm was laid across his chest bent at the elbow almost 90 degrees. The arm was swollen to an amazing degree and crooked. It looked horrendous. Chase never complained, cried, or whimpered. Bob told me that Chase had not complained of any pain on the drive to the emergency room either.

The doctor came in and the news wasn't promising. The X-Rays showed that Chase's elbow had been shattered into many little pieces. His upper arm and forearm were broken. It would take a lot of screws to put Chase's arm back together, and with his elbow joint being shattered so badly, he didn't think he would be able to have full use of that arm again. Fortunately Chase was right handed. Chase had to have a temporary cast put on and we made an appointment as soon as possible to see an orthopedic surgeon.

Chase had an excellent surgeon. He had his private pilot's license, so he and I were able to talk flying. He was also an Eagle Scout. By this time, Chase was a Star or a Life Scout, and the doctor encouraged him to finish up and get his Eagle rank. Chase's doctor had been the valedictorian of his college graduating class. He was a very intelligent man. He assured us that this type of surgery was his specialty and something that he was very good at.

About a week after Chase flipped the go-kart, this doctor performed the surgery on his arm. It took two hours, and it seemed forever to Kim and me. The surgeon told us that he had put twenty-one pins and a plate in Chase's arm in order to put it back together. He said that once he got his cast off Chase would have to go to physical therapy and that he wasn't sure how much of his range of motion he would be able to get back.

Soon we were able to see Chase in recovery. The nurse gave him a small device he could hold in his hand that had a button on top and a wire coming out of the bottom. She told him that if he felt a lot of pain, he could press the button and it would give him some morphine that would help with his pain. She said that he could press it as often as he liked but that he would only get the morphine every fifteen minutes. Chase pressed the button. We sat and talked to him. He pressed the button again. After Chase was moved into a hospital room, he continued to push his button, again, and again. The nurses asked him what his pain was on a scale of one to ten. He would always say "a ten", but he never complained. Kim stayed in the hospital room the first night with Chase, and I came home.

I went to the hospital the next day to see how Chase was doing. He was complaining that the little thingy in the back of his throat was stretched out and getting in the way when he swallowed.

"Your uvula," I asked.

"My what?"

"It's called a uvula," I said. I looked into his throat. His uvula did look longer than normal. There was a white board and marker on the wall in his hospital room. It had the name of the nurse on duty and also a place for any questions the patient or family might have. I wrote a note on the board asking the nurse about Chase's stretched uvula. I even drew a picture of the uvula just to be funny.

Chase's nurse came in and read the note while I was still there. She looked puzzled. "What's a uvula," she asked. I was thinking, Didn't they teach you that in an anatomy class? I explained it to her. She didn't know why it was stretched, but she came back later with an answer. Sometimes when a person is put under for surgery, the breathing tube that is inserted into the windpipe will stretch the uvula. It would return to normal after a few days. That was all we needed to know. Chase wouldn't have to go through the rest of his life with a stretched uvula.

It wasn't long before Chase was back in school with his arm in a cast. After six weeks we were back in the doctor's office getting the cast removed. Then off to therapy we went. I took Chase to most of his therapy visits. Once in awhile I went back to watch. Usually I waited in the lobby and read a magazine. The progress was slow and painful. The therapist had to try to make Chase's arm go places it didn't want to go anymore. The therapy took several months, but eventually, it was over. The physical therapist had done all she could do. Chase had regained about 95% of his range of motion in his left arm. Gradually, Chase returned to exercise, and even lifting weights. Whenever we did bench presses I asked him how his elbow felt. He admitted that it hurt, but he was getting stronger. He eventually regained 98% of his range of motion in his left arm. His doctor was surprised.

During the summer between his sophomore and junior years, Chase went back to football practice. He never missed a beat. As scrawny as he was at 135 pounds, he still tackled the big guys at practice. It was amazing to me that Chase had literally crushed his left elbow and arm but was back playing tackle football after only a few months. He had moved up to the varsity team. He wasn't a starting player. Another cornerback outweighed him by forty pounds and was a good player. Chase rode the bench most of his Junior season. Every time he did get an opportunity to get on the field, he performed well. During one game Chase was put in on the kickoff team. We kicked an onside kick and Chase dove over the top of the opposing team's player to recover the ball. Xavier laughed as he recounted to me that the kid Chase dove over to make the recovery left the field in tears.

During his junior year Chase's grades began to drop. I talked to him about this, but I couldn't get a handle on what the root of the problem was. His Spanish teacher approached Kim and me at one of the football games and expressed her concern about Chase's performance in her class. She was worried that he might fail Spanish I. Chase had never failed any class before.

I got Chase enrolled at Sylvan Learning Center to give him some after-school help with Spanish and the other classes where he was struggling. His grades showed signs of improvement at first but then began to trail off again. It was about this time that video gaming became an issue. I had to restrict his video games until his grades improved. Sometimes I had to take the Xbox away and hide it in the attic. This made Chase very angry. Once he punched a hole in the door to his room. He was challenging our authority in our home. Things became very tense between us at times. Meantime, Chase's grades and his attitude were on a downward trend. Chase and Justin were also arguing more than usual.

Chase began to let his pants sag a little, allowing his boxers to show. This bothered me as a dad, but the more I said about it, the worse it got. Chase had a new habit of not making eye contact during conversations between us. He mumbled, especially in reply to questions he didn't like. Sometimes when we clashed and he was disrespectful, I reminded Chase of the scripture verse, "Honor thy father and thy mother that thy days may be long upon the earth." I asked Chase, "So what happens when people don't honor their father and mother, Chase?"

"They don't live to be very old," he would mumble.

Kim began to have issues with involuntary leg jerks. It was worse when she was trying to fall asleep at night, but it happened other times too. It wasn't restless leg syndrome, which was my initial thought. Sometimes while she was sitting, one of her legs would suddenly jerk and her foot would come way up off the floor and slam back down. She went to our family doctor and then to neurologists. They ran every test on her they could think of, but they couldn't find the cause of the problem. Later the neurologists told her that it was due to stress. They had eliminated everything else. She was stressed about her job but I think she was more stressed over the shouting matches Chase and I sometimes had. Her worry over Chase's declining grades and rebellious behavior were taking a toll on her physically.

Chapter 4

MILITARY SCHOOL

C HASE SEEMED TO BE HEADED in a bad direction and nothing I was doing was working. It wasn't one particular thing that bothered me, but rather a combination of things. The situation with Ronald, the call from the police about Carla, the fact that I caught him in an inappropriate text with a young lady, his slipping grades, his increasing obsession with video games, his sagging pants, and his defiant attitude were things that combined, raised a red flag for me. I shared my concerns with my friend Les.

"Have you thought about a military school?" Les asked.

"No. I haven't considered that."

My impression of military schools was that they were for bad kids, and I didn't think Chase was that bad. When I thought about military schools, the name Hargrave popped into my head. I Googled Hargrave Military Academy and researched it online. It was in Chatham, Virginia, a two-hour drive from us. Then I remembered Elliot and Parker. Elliot had played soccer with Chase when they were younger. I had bumped into his younger brother, Parker, a couple of years earlier at Boy Scout summer camp and he had told me that Elliot was at Hargrave Military Academy. Remembering this and an ad I had seen recently in Boys Life magazine, a Boy Scout periodical, had planted a seed in my mind, and now I remembered where I'd heard of it. When I first approached Chase with the idea of attending Hargrave that was definitely not on his list of things he wanted to do. He was comfortable where he was. He had never been away from us before. He also didn't want to part ways with his high school friends or give up the football team.

"Chase," I said, "one thing about Hargrave is that it's a smaller school. There will be less competition for starting spots on the football team. You're a good athlete, but the competition is pretty stiff for your position here at Cary High. If you go to Hargrave, I'm pretty sure you will be a starter on the football team."

I set up a time for Chase and me to go to Hargrave and take a tour of the school. It didn't hurt that we saw Elliot when we had lunch in the cafeteria. There was someone he knew even though it had been awhile since they had seen each other. Eventually Chase succumbed. I never told him that he had to go to Hargrave. I didn't think I was forcing him to go, but Chase may have seen it that way.

Chase could easily make good grades. Some of his problems were letting himself be distracted and not having good discipline. I thought the structure of a military school would be good for him and help him with these issues. When I went with Chase to take a tour of the school, my main questions were about girls and social media. I was fine with Chase's interest in girls, but if he dated, I wanted to be sure he could get his schoolwork done. Facebook, Skype, cell phones, and video games seemed to be the obstacles that prevented Chase from getting his homework done.

I was assured by the lady I talked to in Admissions that Chase would have no access to Facebook or Skype. He could have a cell phone, but only on the weekends. It would have to be turned in every Sunday evening. This reassured me that Chase would not have the main distractions he had at home. Hopefully this would keep him out of trouble and focused on his studies. It took a few weeks for Chase to be accepted into Hargrave and for us to get everything ready for him to move in. The day I took Chase to Hargrave to check in, the same nice lady told me that Chase would have access to Skype at certain times. Maybe I misunderstood her the first time, or maybe things changed; I don't know. I was disappointed that Chase would have access to Skype.

"Some of the parents like to use Skype to stay in touch with their sons," she explained.

I was thinking Chase won't use Skype to call us unless he wants something, but he'd use Skype to talk to girls when he should be doing his homework. I sent Chase the following letter once he was settled in at Hargrave:

Chase, I am proud of you for choosing to attend Hargrave Military Academy. I know you are thinking to yourself, "I didn't CHOOSE to go to Hargrave; you MADE me go! That's not true. At first you didn't want to go, but you soon realized that Hargrave would bring out the best in you and help you become the man God has created you to be. You decided not to fight our decision to send you. You made a wise decision.

As with anything new, it is going to be a little painful and uncomfortable at first, but as you get into the routine you will embrace their methods. Learning is a lot like exercise. It is exercise of the brain, and exercise is always uncomfortable to some degree, but you always feel better after your exercise session, and the long-term benefits of exercise are many. After awhile just as with physical exercise, you learn to enjoy the mental stimulation of learning new things.

Hang in there and things will get easier in a few weeks. One day you will look back on your days at Hargrave with pride. You will be proud of what you have accomplished.

I Love you,
Dad

P.S. I heard about the "Grizzly" prank. Were the missing light bulbs part of the prank? If so, it was a pretty good prank.

Chase had a roommate named Andrew. He seemed like a nice kid. He was polite and friendly to me when we went up for visits. He was a year younger than Chase and seemed to look up to him. Andrew's parents seemed nice too. According to Chase, there was only one issue with Andrew. He sometimes made up stories out of the blue. In other words, he would tell lies about past accomplishments. Chase liked Andrew otherwise, but he couldn't understand why he felt the need to make up stories. Chase and Andrew seemed to get along okay. As far as I could tell, Chase had no enemies. He got along with everyone and if he did make an enemy, they didn't stay enemies for long. Chase was a fun guy to be around once people got to know him.

Another young man named Brice had befriended Chase on his very first day at Hargrave. He had helped Chase get fitted for his uniform. He lived in a room by himself which was adjacent to the room Chase and

Andrew were in. I later discovered that he and Chase poked a hole in the wall so that they could pass notes back and forth. This is something I would have been completely against, had I known about it at the time. For one thing, it was destruction of school property. For another, Chase needed to be concentrating on his homework, not passing notes back and forth with Brice.

In the spring of Chase's junior year at Hargrave, there was a military ball. Chase had stayed in touch with Shannon after he left for Hargrave, and he invited her to the ball as his date. Shannon was excited about the ball and went to a lot of trouble to find just the right dress to wear. She looked very pretty. Kim and I attended the ball and had the opportunity to talk with Shannon's parents and some of the other parents. The cadets posed for photos with their dates and danced the night away. Chase had never had any dance lessons, but he was never at a loss for moves and he kept Shannon laughing most of the night.

Chase had reached the rank of Life Scout in his troop back home. He was well on his way to becoming an Eagle Scout by the time he started at Hargrave. There was a Boy Scout troop at Hargrave, so I encouraged Chase to get involved with it as soon as he could and to continue working towards his Eagle rank. Chase began working with the younger Boy Scouts at Hargrave, teaching them some of the basics. He was always good with knots, and other basic scouting skills.

Chase had usually gone to Boy Scout camp with his troop back home in the summer. He earned several merit badges every year at camp. By the summer before his senior year, Chase was seventeen and eighteen is the cutoff to make Eagle. If he didn't get it done within the next nine months he would never be an Eagle Scout. The Hargrave troop was not going to summer camp that year so they helped Chase hook up with another troop out of Roanoke, Virginia.

After summer camp was over and Chase was back at Hargrave we paid a visit to him. When we got home, I sent him the following letter.

Chase, I love you, and I'm sorry I left without saying goodbye. I get frustrated with you sometimes because I know what you are capable of. I know you have a lot of potential but sometimes I feel you aren't using all the potential God gave you. You're selling yourself short. You are capable of much more than even you realize. God didn't make any junk, and he made you a special person and designed you to succeed. Have confidence in yourself and your maker. Reach down inside and find all the talent, intelligence, and determination God has blessed you with. Use it to succeed so that you may be a blessing to yourself and others. I hope OCS (Officer's Candidate School) is going well for you and I look forward to hearing about it. I can't wait for football season and I am going to be getting my camera equipment ready. I'll see you soon.

I love you,
Daddy

The candidate for Eagle Scout must complete a Project. He has to come up with the idea for his project. He may get suggestions from his parents or scout leaders. The candidate then must organize the project by determining the staff and supplies needed. He must write up the proposal for his project and have it approved by scout officials before he can proceed. Once the project is complete, it will be reviewed and the candidate will sit for an Eagle Scout board of review. If everything goes well, the Eagle Scout candidate will become an Eagle Scout and later have the opportunity to participate in a ceremony to recognize his accomplishment.

I stayed on Chase about planning his Eagle project. He went to the Hargrave staff and asked them for suggestions. They proposed that he rebuild a partially sunken floating dock in the pond on the Hargrave grounds behind the dorms. There is also a trail that can be used for hiking or jogging around the pond. They also wanted Chase to pick up any trash along the trail around the pond as well as weed-eat it to make hiking and jogging easier.

It was near the end of the summer before Chase could get his project approved and get everything organized to move forward. It was now or never. Once school started back he would be way too busy with school and football to finish the project. The only problem was that many who could be of help to him were gone for the summer. We were able, however, to get my friend Bob and his son Robert to help us. Chase had helped Robert on his Eagle project a couple of years earlier. That was when he flipped the go-kart.

We helped Chase gather all of the necessary supplies and tools and Bob and Robert drove up to Hargrave and met us by the pond. Before they arrived Chase and I began picking up trash around the pond. I was surprised when I found what looked to be a homemade bong in the grass. A bong is a pipe used for smoking marijuana that sends the smoke through water to make it colder. It was made from a Gatorade bottle. The label and lid were faded. It had obviously been there a while. I thought about reporting it to the staff, but I didn't. Nothing much they could have done with that information. I'm sure they were aware that some of the boys sneaked around to smoke marijuana.

We spent all day on the project. Chase was in charge. Learning to be a leader is part of becoming an Eagle Scout. Being in charge of such a project wasn't something Chase was good at. He hadn't had much experience at organizing and leading projects. He needed a little nudging, but he got the job done. We rebuilt the dock, we cleaned and cleared, and it was a hot day. We also replaced boards on a couple of old bridges along the jogging path that allowed joggers to cross the creek or marshy areas. When Bob and Robert left, Chase and I did still more weed eating.

Chase and Justin after Chase's Eagle Scout Ceremony.

We were exhausted at the end of that day. Mission accomplished! A couple of months later Chase became an Eagle Scout.

We had enrolled Chase in summer school at Hargrave so he could catch up on his English requirements. While he was there for the summer Chase participated in a leadership training course offered to tenth, eleventh, and twelfth grade students called Officer Candidate School. Once he completed the leadership course, Chase earned some rank and was given more responsibility. He worked in the cafeteria supervising other cadets in the clean up after meals. He was able to wear a saber with his dress uniform when appropriate and the tabs that marked the entry-level officer's rank.

Near the end of the summer we went up to Hargrave for a parent/teachers conference and to visit Chase. This was the most memorable one for me of the early visits. Chase was always genuinely happy to see us all. He missed his family. Kim and I made our rounds, visiting each classroom and meeting with Chase's teachers to get the scoop on how and what he was doing. Overall, I was happy, though there were a couple of classes in which he needed to work a little harder.

Finally we visited the football coach. His face lit up "He's been working with my quarterback all summer, catching passes. He's fast! And he can catch! He will be a starter and he will play both ways! I'm looking forward to the season, and I know Chase is going to do really well. I asked him if he had any interest in playing college football, and he said he did. I told him that I believe that he could play at the college level if he wants to. I see no reason why he couldn't."

I was grinning from ear to ear. Finally! Chase was going to get his chance on the football field to show what he could do again. I was amazed to hear Coach Tanner say that Chase could play college football. I hadn't completely written that idea off, but with Chase's small stature, I had thought it was a long shot.

As the season approached an article came out in the Chatham paper about the Hargrave football team. Coach Tanner mentioned several key players to watch and he referred to Chase as, "the speedy Chase Rodgers." It stuck. All of Chase's friends at school started calling him "Speedy." Chase wore number 34 when he was on the varsity team at Cary High, so he picked that number at Hargrave, too.

I was excited about Chase's opportunities and decided I would attend every football game, home and away and take along my video camera and tripod to see if I could capture some good footage in order to make a highlight video. It was a two-hour drive to Hargrave, and away games were often another couple of hours drive.

Chase played football with what could be called reckless abandon. Chase always gave it everything he had. He wasn't satisfied simply to provide good pass coverage or make tackles. He was the second leading tackler on the team, right behind the middle line backer. That was not because of Chase's speed, agility, or talent. Chase made so many tackles because of his desire and his hustle. It was not unusual to see Chase come all the way across the field so he could be in a position to make a tackle when his teammates failed to bring down a running back. He played like this for four quarters of every single game. I'm not stretching this. Others will back me up. In the first game of the season Chase played so hard that he had to come out of the game and go throw up on the sideline. He stayed out for a couple of plays, got some water, and went right back in.

Shannon, Kylie, Justin, and one of Justin's best friends, all piled into my Yukon XL along with Kim and me to travel to Hargrave to watch Chase play a home football game. They all had watched Chase play at Cary High School, but this was the first time they had been to a game at Hargrave. Chase played well and made a lot of tackles as usual. By this time, Chase had become good friends with Ross, a junior and a good player on both the offensive and defensive lines. Ross later became known as "Pancake Man" because of the blocks he made in which he "pancaked" or flattened the defenders. Ross and Chase had weekend passes and rode back home with us after the game. Ross was originally from Raleigh, not too far from where we live in Cary. Ross was quiet, polite, and a very bright kid. I plugged my video camera straight into the video player in my truck and the boys watched the game they had just played as we drove back to Cary.

At some point I discovered that Chase had a new girlfriend whom he met while at Hargrave. I sent Chase to a military school partly to limit his exposure to girls. I was fine with Shannon. It wasn't Shannon I was worried about. Imagine my surprise when I found out that Chase had a new girlfriend at Hargrave. I didn't know anything about her, but I was skeptical.

"What about Shannon," I asked him during a telephone conversation. "Have you told her yet?"

"No. I can't have a girlfriend who lives that far away." I guess that made sense. It probably goes with the whole ADD thing.

I was hurting, however, for Shannon. I knew this news would be devastating for her. It hadn't been that long since her parents had driven her to Hargrave to attend the military ball with Chase. She had gone to such great pains to pick out just the right dress. Chase let Shannon know via text. I explained to him that I knew it was a difficult thing to do, but that was not the correct way to handle it. That was the easy way out, but it required no moral courage whatsoever. The distance made it difficult for him to let Shannon know, but he could have picked up the phone when he was allowed to make phone calls and told her that way.

Chase told me very little about his new girlfriend except that her name was Wendy and she attended an all girls school nearby. I thought Chase now had a girlfriend with behavior issues! I wondered how Chase had managed to find a girlfriend at an all boys military school. Social media? That was how. Facebook, to be specific. The more I talked to other parents, the more I found out about the social media habits and cell phone habits of the Hargrave cadets. Some of the cadets had two cell phones. They would turn in one Monday morning and keep the other. Other cadets were good hackers. They found all sorts of ways to get around the school firewalls so that they could use the internet when they weren't supposed to. Chase had used Facebook to find Wendy and strike up an online relationship.

Not long after this, Kim and I attended another Hargrave home football game. After the game there was a table set up where the players could grab snacks. We met Chase over by the snack area after the game, and he couldn't wait to introduce us to Wendy. He was grinning from ear to ear. Standing there was this cute little blue-eyed blonde, quiet and shy, but with a friendly smile. She was polite, said "yes sir" and "no sir," "yes ma'am" and "no ma'am." She had a slight Southern drawl and Southern charm. I remained skeptical. I was determined not to like her and to figure out what was wrong with her.

"Tell me about your school," I ordered. "What grade are you in? What do you plan to do after high school?" I was trying to be polite and start a conversation, but I was also in my military intelligence gathering mode. Much to my dismay, I couldn't find a thing wrong with her other than the fact that she had failed a grade, which she admitted right up front. I found it difficult to not like her. She had a smile that would melt the most hardened of souls.

Chase literally counted the days until he got to see Wendy again. He put that on Facebook and on his Skype account. "Four days until I get to see Wendy." "Three Days." Finally when the day came, Chase would write, "It's going to be a Wendy day!"

At Hargrave everyone had off some weekends. These were known as open weekends. Cadets had to earn other weekends if they wanted to leave the campus by making good grades and having good behavior. Chase rarely earned a weekend off. The weekend after Chase met Wendy, he knew she was going to be in downtown Chatham. Chase left school without checking out. He walked off campus and followed the train tracks into town and met Wendy, her roommate Beth, and Ross. Ross had earned the weekend off. The four of them hung out together in downtown Chatham.

It wasn't long after Chase and Wendy started dating that I got a phone call from a staff member at Hargrave. "We have an issue concerning Chase which we need to discuss," the gentleman said. "Can you come up and talk with us?" I made an appointment and drove up the next day. Apparently a couple of young men from Hargrave had decided it would be a good idea to make a night time visit to the nearby all-girls boarding school, Chatham Hall where Wendy was a student. I was relieved to find out that Chase was not one of the two young men who had started this plan but still disturbed that Chase was involved.

I met with the leadership staff, and then we called Chase in to discuss the situation. Apparently, Chase had masterminded the entire operation. At the very last minute Chase had decided that the idea was no good. He tried to talk his friends out of going to Chatham Hall, but it was too late. Their minds were made up. Two young men had somehow climbed onto the roof of Chatham Hall, and one of them actually got inside. There was a security guard on duty, however, and he called the police. One young man ran all the way back to Hargrave. The other caught a ride back with a police officer.

I later found out from Wendy why Chase had changed his mind and not participated. Chase had told Wendy of his plan, and she let him know in no uncertain terms that their brand new relationship would be over before it got started if he followed through with his hair-brained idea.

When questioned about the trip to Chatham Hall that night, Chase had lied to the Hargrave staff. One or maybe both of the other two young men had told the staff of Chase's involvement. When he lied to the staff Chase broke the school's honor code. "I will not lie, cheat, or steal, nor tolerate those who do." Chase lost his rank and the privileges and responsibilities that went with it, including the right to wear the saber.

Later in this season of Chase's senior year, the Hargrave Tigers football team had an away game scheduled at Randolph-Macon Military Academy. It was Randolph-Macon's homecoming game. I shot video of Chase's games. I had agreed, however, to keep the stats for this game for Coach Tanner. I needed a good vantage point, so I went to the press box and asked if I could count stats from there. The good people with Randolph-Macon invited me right in. They asked me if I had a son in the game, and what jersey number he wore. As the game progressed they congratulated me every time Chase made a good tackle. Their big bruiser star running back who already had committed to the Citadel came Chase's way, and Chase went down low and took his legs right out from under him. The gentlemen in the press box were amazed at how aggressive Chase played for his size.

With time winding down to under a minute, Randolph- Macon was ahead by a touchdown and we had the ball somewhere around our own twenty-yard line. Chase had been on defense all day, but I saw him go in at wide receiver. I knew what was about to happen. I didn't want to do anything to tip off Randolph-Macon's staff in the booth, but I could barely control myself. As the Tigers broke their huddle and moved into their formation, I moved to the edge of my seat when I saw Chase line up at wide receiver. Chase later told me when he came to the huddle, our quarterback, Cole, said to him, "Just run as fast as you can straight down the field, Chase! I'm going to throw it to you! Run as fast as you can!"

I watched anxiously as Cole took the snap and Chase sprinted past the opposing cornerback. Cole lobbed a 60-yard bomb to Chase. He caught it over his right shoulder in stride, but there were two defensive backs right on his heels. They tackled Chase inside their own ten-yard line. Inside my own mind I was screaming and shouting to the top of my lungs, but I sat there emotionless as I listened to the groans and moans from the press box staff. We went on to score a couple of plays later to tie the game, and we eventually won in triple overtime.

You could have cut the tension in that press box with a knife. I knew it was time for me to get my stuff and get out of there. Then I found out that Chase had broken his foot in the first quarter in a pile-up and had played the entire game that way. He never told anyone because he didn't want to come out of the game. This is testament to Chase's toughness and determination on the football field.

After the Randolph-Macon game, Chase had to wear a rubber boot on his foot and hobble around on crutches for several weeks. The boot was easy to remove and Chase didn't like using the crutches. He was hardheaded about it. I had several talks with the school nurse and she and the teachers kept an eye on Chase and used disciplinary actions against him when necessary to get him to keep the boot on. Chase's doctor finally cleared him to stop wearing the boot on his injured foot and to return to football.

The football season was coming to an end with only one game left when Chase sneaked off campus again. This time he walked off with a bunch of his buddies without signing out. He met Wendy at a little cafe downtown Chatham called ChathaMooCa. Of course, he got caught. Between the Chatham Hall Affair and his sneaking off campus to see Wendy, it seemed like Chase was always in trouble. Chase thought the rules were stupid and if they were stupid, they didn't apply to him as far as he was concerned.

There was a white rectangle painted on a paved area behind the dormitories, known as the bullring. Cadets who had broken rules were often required to march around inside the bullring in full parade uniform carrying a weighted dummy rifle on their shoulder. Examples of infractions that would likely result in time in the bullring were fighting, cursing, dirty rooms, not turning in homework, or arriving late for formation. Cadets who had to walk the bullring missed out on any sports practices or games and were the last to eat dinner. It was not uncommon during a visit to Hargrave to see a number of cadets marching inside the bullring. Chase made a number of visits to it.

There was a bulletin board in the hallway close to the visitors' lounge where cadets could sign up for different trips and activities. There weren't a lot of activities Chase was interested in, and often he was not able to sign up because of his disciplinary actions. He signed up to play paintball every chance he got. It was one of the activities he thoroughly enjoyed. I know he was good at it, because of his athleticism and experience playing capture-the-flag. One trip he had signed up for he was especially looking forward to. It was a trip to see the University of Virginia play Virginia Tech in football. Chase had never been to a college football game, and he badly wanted to go. He was not allowed to go on this trip because of disciplinary violations.

Less than two weeks after his last escapade of sneaking off campus to see Wendy, I got a phone call from one of the TAC (Training, Advisory, and Counseling) officers. Chase was missing. He thought that he might have run away. Had I heard from him? I assured him that I had not. They were doing everything they could to find him, and he asked me if I heard from him to please call the school right away.

Kim and I talked the situation over and decided I should try to call Chase's cell phone in case he had it with him. My call went straight to voice mail. I tried it several times, leaving messages asking him to call me right away so we would know that he was okay. I then texted him. Finally Chase responded to one of my texts. He was on the bus headed to the University of Virginia for the game. He had hidden on the bus. The TAC officer had looked for him before the bus left, but Chase had hidden too well. I called the TAC officer right away to let him know that Chase was on the bus. By this time the bus was well on its way, and they were not going to turn it around for Chase. He went to the game, and I later saw pictures of him sitting there. He looked miserable. He couldn't enjoy himself because he knew he was in the wrong, and he knew there would be consequences for his actions.

Chase had played six football games, but had to miss the next two because of his broken foot. However, because of his previous misbehavior, Coach Tanner thought it would be best for Chase to sit out the final game of the season, even though the doctor had cleared him to play. This was not something Coach Tanner wanted to do. Hargrave is a small school with about three hundred cadets there when Chase was enrolled. The staff is very strict about not letting cadets participate in sporting events when they have misbehaved. Cadets who are good athletes but who have behavior problems sometimes drop out or get booted from the school. So winning consistently is not easy for the coaches.

Hargrave was close to having the first winning season in many years. Coach Tanner and the team needed Chase there, and in spite of Chase's recent lapses in judgment, the staff was not preventing Chase from participating in the final game. They left it to Coach Tanner to make the call, and I respected him for it. He was a man of great character. Nobody wanted that final win more than he did. I had been to all of the football games that season and videotaped them; even the final two that Chase did not participate in. This one was no different. It was an away game and I was determined to be there to support the team and shoot some video just like I had done all season long. We got off to a good lead early on, but our team made a lot of mistakes and gave up one big play too many near the end. We lost. It was heartbreaking to watch. As I discussed the game later with Coach Tanner, he confided in me that he knew if Chase had been in the game we would have won. We had needed him to provide the pass coverage that only he could provide.

The Hargrave Fall Sports Banquet was scheduled for a couple of weeks after the final game. Chase had been in a lot of trouble, but he had played his heart out on the football field. I hoped he would receive an award. On my two-hour journey to Hargrave, there was a wreck that backed up traffic and put me behind schedule. The drive to Hargrave from Cary has a lot of two-lane hilly country roads. There are some lonely stretches of road that are very dark at night. In some spots you lose cell service. It never fails that if you're in a hurry you get behind some old-timer who refuses to drive faster than 50 miles per hour. I got stuck behind such a driver. Finally I got a break, and I put my foot into it. When you got a chance to pass on this drive you had to act quickly because there is always a curve or a hill coming up to make passing impossible. I shot around the car in front of me, and I hit about 70 mph before decelerating back to the speed limit. As soon as I completed my pass, I saw blue lights flashing in my mirror. I don't know where he came from, but I got a nice speeding ticket that night. Nevertheless I made my way to the Fall Sports Banquet.

I sat with Elliot's dad at the dinner. Once the banquet started I pulled out my video camera. As they announced the football team award winners, I waited for Chase's name to be called. Then it finally sunk in that Chase's name wasn't going to be called. His behavior had prevented him from receiving any awards for football. I was disappointed, but I understood. I hoped that Chase got the message.

Then Christmas was upon us. Wendy invited Chase to a Christmas party at Chatham Hall. I was at Hargrave that day for a parent/teacher's conference. Chase told me that Wendy was going to stop by Hargrave and pick him up to take him to the Christmas Party. I was invited to attend also. Wendy and her mother showed up in a red Cadillac rental car. We rode over to Chatham Hall and we chatted, trying to get to know each other. When we arrived at Chatham Hall, Wendy and Chase went off to join in activities with the other young people. The school was serving a meal in the cafeteria and Wendy's mother, Laura, and I sat down and talked as we ate. Laura was a Southern belle. She was elegantly dressed, a classy lady; very intelligent and articulate and carried herself with an air of confidence and dignity. She was friendly and polite and possessed that certain charm that is only present in Southern ladies.

Laura asked about my occupation. I told her I had been a pilot and found out that she was a private pilot herself. She told me that her father had owned a construction business and that he used to own a King Air that she had piloted on some trips. The King Air is a twin turbine engine Beechcraft that seats eight to ten passengers. It's used by corporations to transport executives and customers. I was familiar with the King Air because the first flying job I had, I served as a co-pilot on one. I was impressed that Laura had piloted one of these and even more that her father's business had owned one.

Laura told me a little about Wendy. She thought Wendy was absolutely crazy about Chase. She did warn me that the relationship might not last long based on Wendy's past relationships. I told her that it was okay and that Chase seemed to be crazy about Wendy, too.

We left the dining hall and joined some of the other parents and teachers out in the courtyard. I got Laura a glass of wine. Laura was an Ole Miss Alumn. Wendy had filled Laura in on Chase's exploits on the football field, and Laura suggested I consider Ole Miss as a possibility for Chase.

"He's good, but he weighs 145 pounds. I don't think a school like Ole Miss is going to give him the time of day."

"What about the Citadel?" A gentleman who knew Laura chimed in.

"Yeah. I'm from South Carolina. The Citadel would be awesome, but again, with his grades and his size, the Citadel is also well out of the realm of possibilities. He's going to need to look at smaller schools if he wants to play college football, but I think he's good enough to play somewhere," I said. After the party, Laura and Wendy drove Chase and me back to Hargrave and dropped us off. We said our goodbyes and I left for the drive back to Cary after delivering a pep talk to Chase about keeping his grades up.

Chase had pulled up his grades during his junior year but was off to a bad start with his grades as a senior, so I had continued to follow his Facebook posts to get some idea of why his grades were dropping. You remember Brice who had passed notes to Chase through a hole in the wall during Chase's junior year. Chase had moved into a room with him at the beginning of his senior year. I realized from Chase's Facebook posts that he and Brice were having a party in their room every night when they should have been studying. I wanted to put a stop to this so that Chase could pull up his grades and stay out of trouble.

Chase and Brice were popular. Chase admitted to me that sometimes his room was packed with people at night. Everybody wanted to hang out with the cool guys, Chase and Brice. Ross would sometimes spend the night in Chase's room sleeping on the floor. I told Chase that I wanted him to run people out of his room in the evenings and study. I reminded him that if he didn't bring up his grades he would not qualify to play college football or perhaps even attend college.

I decided to take a look at Brice's Facebook posts as well, because I wondered what kind of influence he was having on Chase. Brice's poor attitude showed in his posts. Every generation of Teenagers rebels and with each new generation the rebellion seems to get worse. It seems to me, Teens these days emulate "gangstas" and rappers. Brice wore his "gangsta" attitude like a badge of honor. He had a chip on his shoulder, and I didn't want Chase to be influenced by him. Chase, was quiet and shy and in many respects seemed to thrive on the attention he got from his peers when he acted out in defiance of authority.

Brice was a leader among the cadets. He was a Company Executive Officer, so I expected more of him. Brice had said some bad things about the Commandant of the school on his Facebook timeline. I copied all of Brice's posts and downloaded the videos and photos he posted. Next I sent Brice a private message on Facebook telling him that he needed to set a better example for Chase. I complained about his Facebook posts and all of the people in their room at night. Brice was polite in his first response to me, and took down the bad posts about the Commandant, but things heated up when he made more obscene posts on Facebook. I messaged him on Facebook and we had a chat about it.

"Wow! You're setting a great example. If you are the company XO what does that say about Hargrave? Can you explain to me the humor in that? Maybe I'm just an old fart who doesn't understand."

"That is the name of a rap song and I don't know why you are so offended. I also don't know why you are trying to take your anger out on your sons' seventeen year-old roommate. What I post on my Facebook is posted because I wanted to post it. If it involves you or Chase I can understand your concern but that has nothing to do with either of you. We all post silly things on our Facebook even though we are not serious about them. After all you are a "natural born killer" right?" He was referring to a photo of me on my Facebook page holding an M-60 machine gun when I was in the military. I had made fun of myself with the caption, "Natural Born Killer." The argument went back and forth. I explained to Brice that it was my business what he put on his Facebook timeline, because he was a representative of the school and as Chase's roommate and Executive Officer, he had an influence on Chase.

I sent an email to one of the staff members at Hargrave about Brice and Chase. I didn't say anything in the email concerning Brice's vulgar Facebook posts about the Commandant, but I did write about some of his other Facebook content and the late-night parties in their room. The staff member that I had contacted talked to Brice and got his attention. Brice took down the obscene posts. He also promised me he would be a better influence on Chase and would make sure there was sufficient quiet time in their room for Chase to get his homework done.

I kept track of Chase's grades over the next few weeks and they didn't improve. I could still see evidence of he and Brice playing when they should have been studying. I contacted Brice again and asked him to help Chase by having a quiet place to study in the evenings. Then I threatened him. I told him that I had downloaded the things he had said about the school Commandant from his Facebook wall and that I could get him kicked out of Hargrave for good. He didn't want that because he was only a few months away from graduation.

"That's blackmail," Brice exclaimed in his message to me.

"You're doggone right it is," I wrote in return, "and I intend to use it if necessary to make sure my son graduates from Hargrave with the best possible grades." What Brice and Chase didn't know at the time was that I had also managed to hack into Chase's Facebook account. In this way I was able to see Chase's private messages, giving me a tactical advantage. I had complained to the Hargrave staff for a long time about Chase's ability to be online all night talking with Wendy and who knew what else. They ignored me. There was a firewall that was supposed to be in place after 10 p.m. and they assured me that Chase was not online after ten. I told them that I could see when he was online via Facebook and Skype and that I knew he was online way after ten. I had even had conversations with him online after 10 p.m. telling him to go to bed. Their excuse to me was that Chase would have unlimited access to the internet when he attended college and that he needed to learn now how to use it responsibly. They still didn't believe Chase was online after ten, however.

Cadets were issued a laptop. This was the only computer they were supposed to use for their studies and homework while at Hargrave. While waiting for Chase in the visitors' lounge one day, I spoke to one parent who admitted helping her son smuggle in his laptop from home. She even bragged to me and Kim about how smart he was and how he had managed to hack the system at Hargrave to get internet access at night after hours.

After Chase got in trouble for the Chatham Hall Affair, sneaking on the bus, and a couple of other infractions, Brice was questioned about Chase by the Hargrave staff. Brice and Chase had become close friends, and Brice spoke highly of Chase to the staff in an attempt to lessen any punishment Chase might be given. During some of these talks with the staff Brice told them about the unauthorized internet access late at night being enjoyed by the entire school, with the result that the staff beefed up the firewall.

I stayed on the Hargrave staff about Brice. I asked several times if they could move Chase to a different room. Finally they did move him out of the room with Brice. Chase was in a room by himself for a week or two before his new roommate arrived from Saudi Arabia. People from all over the world send their sons to Hargrave. There were students from Germany, China, Saudi Arabia, and I'm sure quite a few other foreign countries. I thought it was good for Chase to have the opportunity to interact with boys from different cultures. Chase often laughed about his new roommate. "He brought all of this sand with him from Saudi Arabia! It's in everything. It's in my rug and I can't get it out! It's so fine it's almost like powder," he would say with a chuckle. I didn't have the opportunity to interact much with Chase's new roommate, but what little I was around him, he seemed like a nice kid. He was quiet and polite.

Chase's primary position was cornerback, often the lightest, most agile players on the field but Chase was thin for even a cornerback. I did everything I could to help him gain weight over the years through nutrition and weight training. He was a tough case. I used to buy him all kinds of snacks to eat while he was at Hargrave. Protein powder, protein bars, Ramen noodles, and Snickers bars were all part of the weight-gaining arsenal I supplied.

I would buy a 48-count box of Snickers bars and take it to Chase on our trips up to Hargrave. Then I found out that he was selling them for a profit. I wasn't angry with him. I thought it was rather funny and proved he was resourceful. He didn't sell them all. He ate a good portion of them, but he made some money on the rest. One day during a telephone conversation, Chase told me that one of the security guards was stealing his Snickers. He said he watched the guy go in his room and actually take a Snickers bar from his stash and eat it. I told Chase he should report it to the staff. I tried repeatedly to get Chase to report it; to go through the chain of command, but he refused. He didn't think the staff would believe him.

Chase had an annoying phone app that he liked to use. There were times when I was having a conversation with him, and instead of answering my questions he would hit the app button on his phone. It gave short, funny, pat answers to everything. He was good at using it. It was completely inappropriate most of the time, but I had to admit that it was sometimes funny. One time when we were riding in my truck I said something to him about studying for a test, and he responded by hitting the phone app button—"Ain't Nobody Got Time Fo Dat." I did my best to keep a straight face.

It was time for the military ball at Hargrave again. Chase was excited about inviting Wendy. I had decided that I wouldn't let him go because of his misbehavior and poor grades. He begged me, but my mind was made up. It was very difficult for me to stand my ground. I didn't want to deny him this opportunity, but I had to take a stand. I had to show him that there were consequences for his actions. Then his attention turned to the Chatham Hall formal party. Wendy had invited him. I said no. He begged and he pleaded. I discussed it with Kim. I was feeling bad about this one, because I was also punishing Wendy for Chase's behavior. I didn't want to do that, so I finally told him he could attend.

Spring break was right around the corner and Chase and Wendy had hatched a plan. Wendy had invited him to visit her home in Louisiana over spring break. I wasn't too crazy about the idea. I talked with Laura about it and then Wendy's father and I also talked. Chase and Wendy were intent on his spending the entire spring break there. Wendy's parents and I thought a week was way too long, but we didn't make a decision right away. I was still on the fence about Chase going. In the meantime, during a parent/teacher's conference, I spoke with Chase's math teacher, Colonel Smith about his grades. Colonel Smith assured me that Chase had a good mind for math, but that he wasn't focused on his studies. He asked me how Chase and Wendy were doing.

"How did you know about Chase and Wendy?" I asked.

"Oh, everybody around here knows about Chase and Wendy" He chuckled.

I told Colonel Smith that Wendy had invited Chase to her home in Louisiana for Spring Break, but that I had reservations about him going.

"Why don't you let him go?" He asked.

"Chase has made a lot of bad decisions lately, and he's a teenage boy with raging hormones. The last thing any of us need right now is a little Chase running around."

"He's going to be eighteen soon anyhow, and he'll be able to do whatever he wants to do then. Let him go and have a good time. Her parents will look out for her. Use it to your advantage. Tell him he can only go if he gets his grades up. I'll tell you something. A lot of Hargrave boys over the years have dated girls from Chatham Hall. Not many of those romances last. Did you know most of the girls who attend that school are from very wealthy families?"

"No. I wasn't aware of that."

"Yes! It's a very expensive private boarding school. Wealthy families, I tell you! Again, my advice is that you let Chase go and have a good time. Just tell him he has to get his grades up if he wants to go."

"Okay. That sounds like good advice, Colonel Smith." "Thanks!"

I still needed to think it over more and talk with Wendy's parents more before I could make a final decision.

For all the big events at Hargrave or Chatham Hall, there was only one place for out-of-towners to stay. The Hampton Inn in Alta Vista, Virginia; about fifteen minutes north of Hargrave on Highway 29. Wendy's dad and brother were coming into town for the formal. When Chase was released from Hargrave for the weekend, he wanted to stay at the Hampton Inn, too. There were a lot of parents, young ladies, and some Hargrave cadets there.

The Hampton Inn serves a Continental breakfast near the lobby. I had breakfast with Wendy's dad there a couple of times over the weekend. We had a lot in common. We were both sons of Baptist preachers, and both of us loved to hunt. He told me about how he had hunted zebras from a helicopter in Africa. The meat and most of the hides were donated to local villagers who must have been grateful. He described to me their old plantation in Louisiana with it's thousands of acres. We discussed Chase's upcoming visit to Louisiana over spring break. I expressed my concern about Chase's intentions.

Mr. Walters assured me that was taken care of. "Chase will be staying in our guesthouse. Besides that, Wendy's brother, Ralph, is very protective of Wendy." Ralph was a couple of years younger than Chase, but was a defensive lineman on his high school team. He was considerably larger. "Okay. I trust you," I said.

We agreed that a long weekend would be ample enough time for the visit. With that our discussion turned to college.

"Chase wants to attend Averett, right down the road from Hargrave in Danville. They had a scout at one of our football games earlier this year."

Wendy was a year behind Chase in school, meaning that if he attended Averett, he would be able to visit with her frequently. "I'm not sure that's a good idea," I said.

"Neither am I," replied Mr. Walters.

"There are other schools that are interested in him. We'll see how it works out."

Chase and Wendy got all dressed up for the formal. They looked good, Wendy in her evening gown and Chase in his tuxedo.

Finally spring break arrived. This was the first time Chase had ever been on an airliner. He had flown in a small plane before but never before in an airliner. I went with him to the airport and walked him through everything. I knew he would be fine. We stayed in touch via text, and he arrived in Louisiana on schedule. Chase and Wendy went swimming, went downtown Baton Rouge, went bowling, and saw the levee. Chase decided to jump up on a bale of hay while they were out on the plantation. There was a colony of fire ants that had made the hay bale their home. Chase got a lot of fire ant bites that had him scratching for days to come. He did, however, have a good visit. I picked him and Wendy up at the Greensboro airport and took them back to Chatham.

One day when I was waiting on Chase and in the visitors lounge, the Hargrave football defensive coordinator approached me, grinning ear to ear. He was literally glowing! I could tell he had something that he could hardly wait to tell me. "Did you hear?" he asked.

"Hear what?"

"Chase made First Team Defense All Conference!"

"Really?"

"Yeah! He also made Honorable Mention All State! I think if he hadn't broken his foot and been out the last three games, he might have made the All State team."

"Wow! That's great! Thanks for letting me know."

"Sure thing!" That made my day, and I forgot all about that fall sports banquet. I was beaming all day long. I couldn't wait to talk to Chase.

Chase submitted a lot of applications to colleges he was interested in. I took the game film that I had shot to a friend who edits video for a living. He made a really nice highlight video for Chase and burned it to DVD. The opening music on the highlight video is the old theme song from the original Amazing Spiderman cartoon. Chase had always liked the modern Spiderman movies, and when he was playing football, he reminded me of Spiderman. His slender build combined with his uncanny reflexes and agility—all he needed was a Spiderman costume and everyone would have been convinced that he was the real deal.

I sent letters and copies of the DVDs to coaches around the country. I also made phone calls and sent out emails. Chase and I narrowed it down to five colleges he was interested in. We arranged times to visit these schools. We did visit Averett University in Danville, Virginia. We also visited Ferrum College in the Virginia mountains and Methodist College near Fayetteville, North Carolina. All of these schools' athletic programs were NCAA Division III. They were small, private colleges. Under NCAA Division III rules, these schools were not allowed to offer any athletic scholarship money to students. Chase's grades weren't good enough for him to qualify for academic scholarships. He had a 2.7 GPA at the time. It was going to be expensive to send him to college.

I was impressed with the way the Averett staff handled the visit. A lot of athletes and parents were there that day. They took us all into a room where they showed us how they analyzed game film and prepared for upcoming games with their opponents. The athletes left the room while the staff talked further with the parents. Later the athletes returned wearing Averett football jerseys with their high school number on them. It was a great visualization exercise. I took a picture of Chase in the Averett weight room wearing that jersey.

I was trying to look for every opportunity that might be out there for Chase. I reached out to the head coach at Hargrave, Coach Tanner, and asked if he had any other ideas. He told me he would make a few telephone calls. The next day I received a call from an excited young defensive back coach in Illinois. "We're interested in Chase. We'd like him to come play cornerback for us here in Belleville," he said. It was a small school that competed in the NAIA conference. They were a spinoff from Lindenwood University in St. Charles, Missouri. They were just starting up a football program. The NAIA is a little different from NCAA Division III, in that they can offer athletic scholarship money. We set up a time for a visit with Lindenwood-Belleville, and another Division III school in Minnesota called Northwestern University. It's a small Christian school with a strong football program.

We bought our plane tickets and off we went. We landed in St. Louis, got our rental car and headed for the hotel. The next morning bright and early we headed over to Lindenwood-Belleville. We met with the coaches and they showed us around campus. It was an old high school campus that had been converted into a college campus. They had done a good job with the renovation. They were building a multi-million-dollar state crime lab right there on campus. The school has a criminal justice program and having the crime lab right there is a big plus for students pursuing a degree in criminal justice. At that point the crime lab was not much more than a hole in the ground. Construction on the football field was only beginning. There were plans for alternating maroon and grey Astroturf; not something you see every day. The mascot was a lynx and the uniforms were black and maroon with flat black helmets. All of the coaches seemed friendly and enthusiastic. We took it all in and then headed back to the hotel to relax.

Later that day, Chase and I headed over to the St. Louis Arch. We went inside and took the tour. We went up to the top in the pod. The pod is a ball that is suspended from a mechanism that sounds a lot like a roller coaster when it's ascending. There are a lot of metal clunking sounds as you go up. The pods are fairly small; enough room for four people, but a very tall or large person wouldn't fit comfortably in it. There is a small porthole that allows passengers to view the metal structure on the inside of the arch as you ascend.

Once at the top, the view was amazing. It was a beautiful day! The sky was clear and blue. There was a good-sized crowd milling about, moving from window to window. Chase and I shot some video and took pictures from the thick Plexiglass windows at the top of the Arch. We could look down inside the St. Louis Cardinals baseball stadium and see people walking around. We could watch people walking around and playing Frisbee on the lawn below the arch, and people enjoying helicopter rides from a landing pad that floated on the western bank of the Mississippi river. The St. Louis Arch is 680 feet tall and quite a feat of engineering.

The next day Chase and I visited an outdoor art museum on the outskirts of St. Louis. It was a large park with a wide variety of unusual large sculptures. Wendy had given Chase a special teddy bear that came with a camouflage military uniform. Chase, in turn, had given Wendy a bear. They both named their bears Willis after Willis on the old sitcom, "Different Strokes." Each bear came with a "birth certificate." Chase brought the bear that Wendy gave him along with him in his backpack. That bear went almost everywhere we went, his head poking out of the backpack as Chase walked from place to place. Chase took the time to take pictures of the bear in different locations and send them to Wendy. Chase took a photo of the bear in the airplane seat, as though *he* were the passenger and not Chase. He took photos of the bear at the Gateway Arch and on most of the sculptures at the outdoor art museum.

Later that afternoon, we boarded the plane for Minneapolis, Minnesota. We arrived late at night, got our rental car, and made our way to the hotel. The next morning we headed over to the campus of Northwestern University. It was another gorgeous spring day, sunny with a bright blue sky. The Northwestern campus is very pretty with a large lake out back. We enjoyed an unseasonably warm spring day there. The staff was very friendly, and I was impressed with the football coach. Northwestern was the farthest from home of the five schools we had looked at and the weather there would be the coldest by far. It was also the most expensive of the five, with very little scholarship money available. They really wanted Chase at the cornerback position.

Chase and I ate in the cafeteria, and before we left we stopped by the gift shop and bought matching purple ball caps with the school logo, an eagle, embroidered on them. We boarded the plane and headed home. We talked about all the schools we had visited and the pros and cons of each one. People on the plane noticed our matching ball caps and it turned out to be a great conversation starter. Everyone we talked to was excited for Chase that he had these opportunities in front of him.

After a lot of consideration Chase and I narrowed our search to two schools; Lindenwood-Belleville in Illinois, and Northwestern in Minnesota. I wanted Chase closer to home, but I felt Northwestern was the best school by far.

"Dad," Chase said, "That school is way too far from home and it's way too cold there."

Tunnels connected the buildings so that the students could go from class to class in the wintertime without having to go outside. Still, Chase was right. It did get very cold there, and they got a lot of snow. On top of that, I wasn't sure how we were going to afford Northwestern, and Lindenwood-Belleville was offering scholarship money. Financially Lindenwood-Belleville was the best deal by far. We're talking less than half the money. By this time Chase wasn't even asking about Averett any more. If he had wanted to go there, I probably would have allowed him to. I wasn't ruling it out. I thought it wasn't the best choice for him. Wendy being so close by would be a huge distraction for them both, once he had more freedom.

After more discussion with Chase and Kim, we finally decided on Lindenwood-Belleville. I picked up the telephone and gave the coach a call. I asked him if he could send me a Lynx ball cap for Chase to wear on signing day at Hargrave. He was happy to oblige. Signing day is when a student-athlete signs a letter of intent to attend and play ball for a particular college or university. The moment is often celebrated with ceremony. I was busy on signing day and couldn't attend, but Justin, Wendy, and Kim were there. Coach Tanner had some nice things to say about Chase. The shutters clicked, flashes went off, and Chase signed the forms. In a few months he would be on his way to play college football at Lindenwood-Belleville University in Belleville, Illinois.

Finally! He's going to make it out of high school, I thought. We arrived at Hargrave in our suits and ties, the ladies in their dresses. My wife's family was there. Her brother Eric, his wife Clare, and their daughter Erica drove up from Greenville, South Carolina. My wife's mother, Jean rode with them.

We gathered in the chapel for the graduation ceremony, and afterwards we stood outside and talked. Chase posed for photos with several of his friends, including one kid from the post-graduate basketball team who must have been close to seven feet tall. It was a funny photo with Chase's head not even reaching his friend's shoulder. Chase and Brice posed together for photos. In spite of my interference, they had remained close friends.

The boys kept an old tradition of smoking cigars to celebrate their graduation. From the look on his face, I don't think the new school president was all that happy about the cigars, but he didn't say anything. This class knew of the tradition and had been planning it for a while.

Wendy wore a bright green dress and a lovely smile as she posed with Chase for photos. Later Chase and some of his classmates could be seen throwing their clothing and other items from the second story window. I was concerned that someone walking by was going to get hit on the head. Chase didn't think it was smart to make a bunch of trips up and down the stairs or elevator when he could throw it all out the window. I decided it was harmless and stood guard to make sure no one got in the way of the falling items.

I was happy for Chase. He had graduated from Hargrave. He was going to college, and he would have the opportunity to play college football. Something inside of me, however, was sad, too. The Hargrave

Chase and me at Hargrave Military Academy.

era was over. Chase was going to be very far from home. I was going to miss him.

A long time later I came across a letter from Wendy to Chase. At first I didn't read it, but there came a point in time when I knew it would be okay. I asked for Wendy's permission to publish her letter. Here it is:

Chase Morgan Rodgers, No one is going to understand this message. No one else is going to know. I want you to know, life...it's hard. Every day can be a challenge. It can be a challenge to get up in the morning, to get yourself out of bed, to put on that smile, but I want you to know, that smile is what keeps me going some days. You need to remember, even through the tough times, you are amazing. You really are. I know that the weather may not be perfect. You might have to turn your back to the wind or feel the cold nipping at your nose, but you know what? At least you are there to feel it. At least you can enjoy the suns warm rays on your face or that cold February wind biting at your cheeks. You know what that means? You are alive. Everything will be okay.

I love you so much Chase. I love that you know me like no one else does. I love your facial expressions. I love the way you say my name. I love the way you want to tell me things. I love your smile. I love your laugh. I love that we have the same sense of humor. I love that we are both on the same wavelength. I love the friendly flirting. I love our conversations. I love that you care. I love how awkward you are. I love how you smell and how it lingers on my clothes. I love your hugs and how they're warm and safe. I love the way your eyes light up when you smile or laugh. I love how you're such a nerd sometimes. I love that our hands fit together perfectly. I love that you're concerned about me. I love that you make me do that cliché sigh. I love how you make me burst into fits of laughter after everything you say. I love how you trust me. I love how we're best friends. I love that I can trust you. I love that you're close by. I love that I was able to know you. I love you Chase. I really do.

Look, I don't care which car you drive, where you live, if you know someone who knows someone, if your clothes are cutting edge, if your trust fund is unlimited, if you are on A list, B list, or no list at all. I only care about the words that filter from your mind. They are the only things you truly own; the only things I will forever remember you by. I will not fall in love with your bones and skin. I won't fall in love with the places you have been. I won't fall in love with anything other than the extraordinary words that flutter from your mouth and mind. I want to wake up next to you, eat breakfast with you, get changed with you, play computer games with you, watch movies with you, hold your hand, send you cute texts, buy you gifts, nap together, wear your comfy hoody look into your eyes, be with you at sunrise and sunset, cook for you, walk in the rain with you, fall asleep while on the phone with you, snuggle with you, mess up your hair, kiss you goodnight. I would give up everything for you. I love you more than you will ever possibly realize.

I wanna do so much for, and with you baby. I wanna do crazy little kid stuff like build a fort out of blankets, take naps together, wear matching shoes, take photos of each other on our phones, draw on each other with paint, pass notes, judge people, write silly songs, tickle fights, wear each other's clothes, laugh, love each other infinitely. I just wanna hold your hand and lay in bed with you for hours. I never knew what love was before this. Sure I have said it before...but I never knew the real meaning. It's just when I look in your eyes I can hear you saying I love you, I miss you...etc. I know that means something. You're all I dream about. You're all I think about. You're cute, funny, sweet, loving, and I never want to let you go baby. I am such a lucky girl when I'm in your arms I don't have to look any longer for the one priceless thing everyone dreams of and too few find. The deep connection of "one and only", "soul mates." I love you

You're AMAZING.

Chapter Five

SUMMER TIME

C HASE HAD TAKEN DRIVER'S ED and gotten his permit while he was at Cary High early during his sophomore year. Once he moved to Hargrave in his junior year, however, there just wasn't time for him to go get his driver's license. A few days after he graduated from Hargrave, we got him scheduled for his test drive with DMV. He passed with flying colors. He wanted a personalized tag for the car his grandparents had left him. I had second thoughts about the tag, and Kim scolded me later when she found out I had gotten it for him. The tag read, "SPEEDY34." It had nothing to do with the car or with his intent to speed. He was proud of his nickname Speedy and his jersey number 34. Kim and I were concerned, however, that it was going to be a police magnet.

Since it would only be a couple of months before Chase would be hundreds of miles away at college, I thought he and I should do something fun together. I've always enjoyed all types of fishing. I grew up fishing in small ponds with my dad. Once I fished in the ocean, though, after that, fresh water fishing wasn't as interesting. It's a real adventure when you fish off shore. You never know what you will see or what you will catch. Chase enjoyed any kind of outdoor activity, and he was always up for an adventure. I booked us on a boat out of Atlantic Beach, North Carolina, for a shark-fishing trip. It's a nighttime gig. The boat leaves the dock a little after sunset and stays in fairly close to shore. There's no need to go out in deep water for sharks.

It was a rough ride out. There was a large cabin on the boat, but Chase and I sat outside and enjoyed the ride, that is, until we started getting wet. The bow of the boat rose up and then it came down hard on a swell, sending spray from the bow to the stern. The spray came right over the rails where we were standing. Chase looked like he had just gotten out of the shower. We decided to go inside and dry off. A few minutes later the boat arrived at the first fishing spot and we went back out, got our gear, and dropped our sinkers. Little fish kept stealing our bait. Not many people were catching sharks, and the sharks that were caught weren't very impressive.

A couple who looked to be in their forty's were standing right next to us on the boat. We started talking. This was their first time on a fishing trip like this. The lady made some comments about Chase and I standing there on the outside of the boat on the ride out.

"You guys were crazy to stand out there like that! It was a rough ride."

I smiled at her. "I've been on a lot rougher rides than that."

"Really," She asked in disbelief.

I had a bad feeling about her. She was a rookie and if she thought that was a rough ride, then she was likely to get seasick. It wasn't long before she was feeding the sharks with whatever she had to eat a few hours earlier. Then her husband started throwing up. This wasn't my first time out, and I was hoping Chase wasn't going to be bent over the railing next. A lot of times when people get seasick, other people around them get seasick, too.

Finally, Chase caught a small sand shark. They're good to eat. Then I caught a couple. I noticed Chase's fishing rod was bent over hard. He was hanging on, but it was obvious he had his hands full. This was the first time Chase had ever had a fish of some size on the line. His eyes got big. I think he was surprised at how hard it was pulling. He kept working it and soon one of the boat mates showed up to coach him. He finally landed a nice Atlantic Black Tip shark. It wasn't huge but it was the biggest fish caught on the boat that night; probably a good 20–25 pounds; the largest fish Chase had ever caught by far. It didn't meet the length requirements and we had to release it, but not before getting a picture of Chase holding it. This was another thing that the deck hand coached him on; the proper way to hold his shark for the photo so that he didn't get bitten. We took our photos and sent the shark on his way.

On the ride back in, Chase finally got seasick, too. It's one of those things that happens to most people sooner or later when fishing in the ocean. It wasn't a big deal for him. He had thrown up during a football game in high school and gone back in a couple of plays later. We didn't catch a lot of fish that night, but it was a fun trip and a good father/son outing. We brought home our sand sharks and cooked them up the next day. They were quite tasty. Chase shared his shark photo on Facebook. He was proud of the shark he caught.

When Chase graduated from high school he was 5'10" 145 pounds. I knew he needed to put on some muscle. Being ADD, this was a challenge. Chase was still on a light dose of medication for his ADD, which curbed his appetite a little. Over the summer he came off of his meds since he didn't need them to help him focus on his schoolwork. I fed him well and he joined a gym close to our house called Athletic Lab that I had learned about from Ross's mother. Athletic Lab is a special gym that concentrates on improving athletic performance. Over the summer Chase gained ten pounds of muscle and got a lot stronger, thanks to Athletic Lab and the hearty meals I was feeding him. While he was at Athletic Lab he set a gym record for pull-ups, thirty-three. To this day Chase retains the pull up record.

Wendy worked as a camp counselor over the summer on the coast of North Carolina. She was a couple of hours away from where we live, but she was busy at camp. Chase was hanging around the house and going to his daily workouts at Athletic Lab. Wendy met a young man who was also working as a camp counselor and posted photos on Facebook of the two of them together. It took a little while for it to sink in with Chase, but then he was bummed out about it. I told him that if he cared about her, he shouldn't give up so easily. Then it hit me like a ton of bricks. I've caused this. They were inseparable and now I'm sending Chase to school way up in Illinois.

Chase texted Wendy and managed to get her to meet him at the beach. It was his last ditch effort to save the relationship before heading off to college. They met and had dinner with one of Wendy's friends, but nothing really changed. It was over; or so it seemed.

A couple of weeks later Chase was feeling a little better but still licking his wounds over Wendy. I was out running some errands. I made it back home earlier than expected. Chase wasn't in the living room or dining room. I made my way down the hall towards his room.

"Hey, Chase! What are you up to?" I called out. His door was slightly ajar, so I tapped on it a couple of times and started to push it open. Chase jumped up from the foot of his bed with just a towel wrapped around his waist.

"Whoa! It's the middle of the afternoon! Go put some clothes on, dude!"

"Okay, Dad," he said as he gently pushed the door shut.

I started back down the hallway. Then suddenly little alarm bells went off in my head. Something wasn't right. I didn't know exactly what it was but something wasn't right.

"Hey Chase!" I started back towards his room. Suddenly he emerged, now fully clothed, and leaving his room door open. There was a sheepish look on his face.

"Chase. What's going on, buddy?"

"I forgot. I have something I have to go do right away. I'll be back in a little while," he said. Out the door he went in a hurry. Now I was getting curious. I heard Chase drive away and the wheels were turning in my mind. I walked into his room and pulled back the blinds. One of the windows to his room was wide open. Near Chase's bed I found a personal item that had to belong to some woman. By coming home early, I had caught Chase and this girl by surprise. She had hidden in the closet as they heard me coming in the front door and as soon as I went back down the hall, she had jumped out of Chase's window. Then Chase met her outside and drove her home.

When my wife got home later that evening, I told her what had happened. She went to Chase's room to confront him. "Who is she?" Kim demanded. Chase tried to pretend he didn't know what she was talking about. He finally gave her a first name, but that was all he would say. Kim asked where the girl lived. Chase refused to tell her. Kim went to Chase's car and looked at his GPS. She got the address of the last place he had been, then she started her detective work online. It wasn't long before she had confirmed the address and knew who the girl was. Off she went, like a mother on a mission. She might as well have had steam coming out of her ears as she pulled out of the driveway.

Kim arrived at the girl's home and knocked on the front door. The young lady's mother answered the door. Kim introduced herself as Chase's mother.

"OH Yes! Chase! He's such a nice young man," the mother said.

"Apparently your daughter thinks so, too. She was at our house a little earlier today in Chase's room. My husband came home and she climbed out the window. Fortunately he got there before anything happened."

"Oh! I'm sorry about that. Would you like to come in?"

"Yes. I would like to talk to your daughter if you don't mind."

"Sure! She's at the grocery store right now. She should be back in about ten minutes." Kim talked to Brianna's mother while she waited. She told Kim about some of the issues she had been having with her daughter. There had been a lot of other boys before Chase. Finally Brianna walked in the door. "Brianna, this is Mrs. Rodgers; Chase's mom."

"Oh. Hi."

"I heard you were at my house earlier today."

"Oh. We didn't do anything."

"I'm not stupid, so try don't that one on me! If my husband hadn't come home when he did, you would have done something. You better be glad I didn't come home and catch you in Chase's closet! I don't know what I would have done to you! I told Chase that when he sleeps with someone who is as easy as you, he is sleeping with everyone you've slept with and could wind up with their diseases. I want you to stay out of my house and stay away from Chase! Do you understand me?" With that, Kim was out of there, and we never saw or heard from Brianna again.

Chapter Six

COLLEGE DAYS

C HASE HAD DECIDED he would be a criminal justice major. He had no idea what he wanted to do. With the state crime lab being built right on the college campus he thought criminal justice would be his best choice for a major.

We packed all of Chase's clothes and other items into a couple of footlockers and we crammed it all into the back of my Yukon. Kim, Chase, Justin and I headed up the road to Belleville, about fifteen hours away including stops. The freshman dorms were in a converted motel. They were very nice. Each dorm room came with its own bathroom. Chase would be sharing the dorm room with two other football players.

We went into town and bought him a comforter and drapes that were the school colors, maroon, grey, and black. We also got him snacks and a small refrigerator that we packed with his favorite soft drink, Dr. Pepper. When the other players arrived, we met them and their parents. We attended a luncheon in the cafeteria with all of the football recruits, their parents, and the coaches. I was amazed at how big some of the guys were. We filled out more school paperwork and waited while Chase got a physical there on campus to clear him for football camp.

Finally when everything was done, we visited the St. Louis Arch together. Chase and I went inside and went through the museum again, but we decided to let Kim and Justin take the ride to the top while we waited down below. We walked through the park and observed people. There was a large group of Chinese students enjoying the park. We wandered over by the Mississippi River and looked around. Kim called us on her cell phone from the top of the arch. Chase and I were standing on a concrete pad near the river next to three flagpoles. Kim called me on the cell phone. She and Justin wanted Chase and me to lie down next to each other on the concrete pad spread eagle so that they could take our picture from the top of the arch. We were up to that challenge. A lady and her two children nearby were amused at our antics. It was a hot day, and the concrete was heating us up fast. Chase and I were lying on our backs, the fingers on my right hand and toes on my right foot almost touching the fingers and toes on his left hand and foot. We were laughing. Kim was taking too long to focus in and get the photo.

"Hurry up!" "We're cooking down here!" I told her. The lady standing nearby giggled along with her young daughter and son. They were staring at Chase and me. They couldn't believe we were acting like this in public and having so much fun together. The woman looked envious, as though she wished she could get in on the fun somehow.

We headed back to the hotel room to relax for a little while. The boys and I have often made fun of Kim for making up new words. When we were checking out of our hotel room, Kim was looking for a bag that she had picked up from the university gift shop earlier when we had bought some spirit wear. "Have you seen my Lindenbag?" she asked.

"Your what?" I asked. Justin and Chase roared with laughter.

She had combined the name of the school *Lindenwood* with the word *bag* to form a word that described the particular type of bag she was looking for. We teased her about it for a long time.

Chase wanted his car at school. By now we knew a lot of parents didn't let their kids have a car in their freshman year of college. That was good with us. We didn't think Chase was ready to have the car at school just yet. Everything he needed was right there on campus or within a short walking distance. If he needed to go somewhere else, he could ride the bus, Metro, or catch a ride with friends. The car wasn't the only thing Chase wanted that I didn't think he needed at college. He wanted his X-box 360 video game console.

"No, that's a major distraction you don't need right now, Chase," I said. "You're going to be too busy with classes, studying, and football to have time for X-box."

Chase sucked his teeth, but didn't say anything. It wasn't what he wanted to hear, but he knew I was right. I could see it in his eyes.

It's a long drive back to North Carolina, but I enjoy driving and the scenery both up there and back was pretty. I enjoyed the farms of Illinois and Indiana with their massive cornfields, the rolling hills and horse pastures of Kentucky, and the mountains of West Virginia. The drive through West Virginia isn't an easy one, especially at night. Even the four lanes are winding, with steep climbs and descents. It takes forever to get through the West Virginia mountains.

Once home, within a week or so I discovered that one of Chase's roommates had brought his X-box with him.

When we were getting Chase prepared for college, I bought him a brand new laptop. I also installed key logger software on his laptop and on his cell phone. This allowed me to keep track of his every move. Chase and I loved each other, but there was a part of our relationship that had become a competition. He was determined to get away with things he knew he shouldn't be doing, and I was determined to protect him from himself. If Kim and I were going to be paying for Chase's college, I expected him to put forth effort in the classroom and to stay out of trouble, and I had told him so. I no longer trusted him. I had caught him lying to me outright on several occasions.

When it came time for Chase's first college football game, we made another trip to Belleville. This was the first game ever to be played by the Lindenwood—Belleville Lynx football team. They were facing Avila University at Belleville. We could see Chase on the sideline across the field. It was an exciting game; high scoring, but close. Since Chase was small and a freshman we weren't surprised that he didn't start. We were hoping that he might come in late in the game for a few plays, but it never happened. The final score was Lynx 47 Eagles 37.

Even though Wendy had a new boyfriend and was hundreds of miles away, Chase stayed in touch with her via Facebook. I bought Chase some expensive masculine stationary and encouraged him to write her. He didn't. Chase wasn't much into writing. In the beginning back at Hargrave I had been skeptical about Wendy, but she had won me over. She

Chase poses with Justin for a picture after his first college football game.

encouraged Chase to keep his grades up when he was at Hargrave, and she had even asked him not to buy her a lot of gifts.

When we were going to go back to Belleville for another football game I asked Chase if he would like me to bring Wendy with us. "Yes!" I texted Wendy and she was really excited that we had invited her. Wendy was in her senior year at Chatham Hall, so we drove up to Chatham to pick her up on our way to Illinois. Wendy was the most excited I'd ever seen her. Justin had other things going on, so we left him at a friend's house.

I got tired driving and we stopped for the night. The next morning we arrived in plenty of time for the game. The Lynx were playing Robert Morris University. Again, we hoped that Chase would get in near the end of the game, but he never did. The final score was 45–6. The Lynx lost.

After the game Chase showed Wendy around the campus and introduced her to some of his friends. There was an Oktoberfest taking place in downtown Belleville that afternoon, so Kim and I suggested we might all attend. Chase had other plans. There was also a fall festival taking place in a nearby town and a lot of Chase's friends were going. He wanted to know if he and Wendy could go with them. I was a little concerned because I felt responsible for Wendy, but she was almost eighteen and Chase was eighteen. I decided to Let them have a little fun on their own. So Chase and Wendy went to nearby Collinsville. Kim and I went to the Oktoberfest.

Later that evening we texted Chase and found out where they were, and swung by and picked them up. We had managed to get a hotel room with a nice view of the St. Louis Arch. We got up the next morning and took Chase back to campus. Of course he begged us to stay a little longer, but we had to get back home. We went over to the football field and took a few photos of Chase and Wendy before heading back. I noticed that they were both wearing sunglasses that morning but I didn't think much about it.

As we neared Chatham Hall it was getting late and I was doing my best to get Wendy back at a decent hour. I wound my way through the Virginia mountains, around endless curves, Kim staying on me to slow down. Finally we made it, and as I helped Wendy with her bags, she gave me the biggest hug ever and thanked me for taking her to see Chase. She was glowing.

Not long after this, during a telephone conversation I asked Chase about an upcoming away game. He told me that he didn't travel with the team to away games. He explained that he had been redshirted. Why hadn't he told us earlier? Had no one explained to him what it meant to be redshirted? We had gone to those games thinking he might have a chance to play. When a football team redshirts a freshman, it means that he can practice with the team and dress out for games, but he doesn't play in the games. It gives him an extra year of eligibility. In Chase's case I was sure it was a combination of size and experience that brought about this decision. When I talked to his position coach, he assured me that Chase always gave everything he had on the practice field and that he fully intended to play him later.

While snooping on Chase I discovered that he was hanging around people who, I thought, were a bad influence. He was partying a lot. That apparently included smoking marijuana and getting drunk. I watched his Facebook posts, private messages, Skype messages, and internet searches. Was he posting anything on Twitter? I didn't find any tweets from Chase, but I did discover from one of Wendy's tweets that she and Chase had smoked pot when they went with his friends to the festival at Collinsville.

I told Chase that I knew what they had done that weekend. I also wrote to Wendy and told her that I knew. I made the point that Wendy's dad had trusted me to look out for his daughter, and I had failed him. I lit into Chase over that. When I wrote to Wendy she told me that she would tell her dad if I wanted her to. I told her that wouldn't be necessary. I wanted to think about it. I wasn't sure exactly of the best way to handle this. Then Wendy went into hibernation. She wouldn't respond to texts or any messages from me or Chase. Now I felt bad. Was I responsible for the breakup by not allowing Chase to attend Averett? Had I ruined his chance to rekindle his relationship with Wendy? I knew I was meddling and needed to stop.

I apologized to Chase for the meddling and promised to stay out of his love life. Chase told me not to worry too much about Wendy. He said that when she gets like this, you have to give her some space, and after awhile she will be fine. He was right. Eventually she began to talk to us both again.

This situation disturbed me to the point that I called up a pastor friend of ours and confided in him about the spying and the mess I felt I had created. He recommended I stop spying. I agreed. I definitely wanted to end that, but I was still worried about Chase. There were other signs of bad things going on.

In one private Facebook conversation Chase had encouraged a cadet at Hargrave to smoke weed. The cadet told Chase he was abstaining because he was worried about getting caught. The Hargrave staff conducted random drug tests and brought in drug dogs every so often. Chase then told this young man that he could use bath salts to get high because they aren't detected on drug tests. At the time bath salts were still legal in most states because of a loophole in the laws.

I had done some research online about bath salts, and I knew what they could do to people. These are not the kind of bath salts you put in your bath. They are labeled with a warning that states they are not for human consumption. They are dangerous synthetic drugs. By labeling them as bath salts, "not for human consumption" merchants were able to temporarily skirt the law. Sometimes Chase liked to talk tough, and maybe this was one of those cases, but I felt I still needed to keep an eye on him, so I continued spying.

From my snooping I had learned the names of a lot of Chase's college friends. I knew who they were and their relationships to one another, but they didn't know me. A girl named Molly I couldn't figure out at first. He only mentioned her a couple of times. I would only learn later what Molly's role was in Chase's life. Not long after I confronted Chase about smoking weed with Wendy, I could no longer get information from his cell phone. Somehow he had figured out that was where I was getting a lot of my information and he reset the phone. I continued to get information from the laptop.

Chase had the custodial bank account that we had opened for him when he was much younger. He had put money in it that he had earned from mowing lawns as well as birthday money from his grandparents and other relatives. He had saved up several thousand dollars by this time. We gave him a debit card, but he had no checkbook. We wanted to keep control of his spending. Chase still didn't have a good grasp on how to manage money. He hadn't been in Belleville long before he was hitting the ATM often. Our bank had a branch in Belleville, but it was some distance from the college. Chase was paying a lot in ATM fees because he was going to a nearby ATM, and there were extra charges for withdrawals. I called Chase and told him to take it easy with the ATM withdrawals. He began making fewer withdrawals.

After the football season ended, it wasn't long before Chase flew home for the Christmas holidays. His grades for his first term were terrible, and he was on academic probation. If he didn't pull his grades up over the next semester, he could be dismissed from the school.

I asked Chase if he wanted to go back to college. He assured me that he did.

"You're going to have to get your grades up or they're going to kick you out, Chase. College isn't for everybody, and it's okay if you don't want to go back."

"No. I want to go back," he said emphatically.

So I sent him back, but I didn't have a good feeling about it.

In my snooping I had discovered that Chase had a new idol; Wiz Khalifa, a rapper who loves weed and likes to rap about it. Chase was going to a nightclub in St. Louis regularly where a lot of bad things were happening. He went on with some of his friends about how Wiz Khalifa was scheduled for an appearance at the club. I was amused when Wiz didn't show up. There is no positive message in any of Wiz's ramblings which he calls music. To me it was a bunch of mindless drivel about getting high. Not a role model any parent would want his kids to emulate.

In some of his messages Chase bragged about how he had passed out on the dance floor one night at the club and woken up at some girl's house. Apparently a big fight broke out at the club about the same time and the police had been called. She must have thought he was cute so she rescued him. Somehow she got him to her car and into her apartment. He dated her for a while after that because he felt like he owed her something. Chase used the term "rolling balls" sometimes in his messages. "Man, I was rolling balls the other night at the club." I did Google searches on the term "rolling balls." "Rolling balls" is a term describing being messed up on Ecstacy or Molly. Hmmm. Then maybe Molly wasn't a girl. It must have been a drug.

Ecstacy and Molly are both forms of MDMA which is the acronym for the chemical compound methylenedioxymethamphetamine. The main difference between Ecstacy and Molly was their physical form: Molly is a white powder or crystal–like substance and Ecstasy describes the pill or capsule form. Chase also discussed buying something by the gram. All this scared me.

Chase posted on his Facebook timeline that he had taken a very long nap. I don't remember specifically how long. As I recall, he had slept for sixteen hours straight. That wasn't normal and must have been because he was coming down off of something.

I also read that a freshman girl asked Chase if he would sell her his

Concerta. Chase had been taking small doses of Concerta since he was a child for his Attention Deficit Disorder. It helped him focus in the classroom. He didn't like to take it because it had a negative effect on his appetite, and he wanted to maintain his weight for football. He agreed to sell it to the girl. She wasn't ADD but she thought it would help her concentrate in the classroom and get better grades. This was disturbing. I called Chase and told him that I had found out about the Concerta. I reminded him that it was a felony to sell such drugs. He could get in big trouble doing that. He agreed not to sell it.

I also discovered that Chase had ridden down to Mardi Gras in New Orleans with some of his "friends," who weren't the kind of people I was hoping he would choose as friends. I had hoped he would be spending his free time studying. After Mardi Gras Chase's ATM visits got more frequent. He began making as many as two or three withdrawals per day; $20–$40 at a time. It doesn't take long for that to add up to a considerable sum of money. I went to our local branch and put a stop on the withdrawals.

Chase was finally expelled from Lindenwood-Belleville during the second semester of his freshman year. His grades weren't up to par, and he was making no significant effort to improve them. On a Tuesday, after dropping out, Chase went to St. Charles, Missouri to out-process. The school headquarters are there. After he had out-processed I told him to pack his things and I would drive up to get him on Thursday.

"Can you come on Saturday?"

"Why? Aren't you ready to come home?"

"I need more time to pack. Besides I want to say goodbye to all my friends."

"Okay, Chase. I'll be there Saturday. Have everything ready."

"Okay, Dad."

I had a feeling Chase was up to something, so I used the key logger software to see what was going on. He had struck up an online relationship with a local girl. She was a couple of years older than him, but not a student. They had dated once and she was supposed to pick him up again Saturday evening. When Friday came around, Chase sent me a private message on Facebook.

"Dad. Can you come Monday to get me instead?"

"No, Chase. I can't. I've already made plans to pick you up Saturday! Why do you need until Monday, anyhow?"

"I still don't have all my things packed."

"Chase. Come on man! You're up to something. It's time to stop playing and come home. Either I come get you Saturday, or you can get home on your own."

"Just forget it, then!"

He hung up. I continued to keep track of Chase with the key logger software and his Facebook posts. Even though he was no longer a student at Lindenwood-Belleville, he continued to live on campus. He stayed in a friend's dorm room and ate in the cafeteria as if he were still a student. No one knew the difference other than his closest college friends and me. He must have been bumming alcohol and drugs off of his friends. The way he was going it was only a matter of time before he got into serious trouble.

After several days, I finally sent an email to the Dean of Students. I let her know that Chase was still on her campus even though he had been kicked out of school. At first she didn't show a lot of interest. We exchanged a couple of emails, but I didn't detect any sense of urgency on her part. She did finally talk to the student who was allowing Chase to stay in his room and told him Chase could no longer stay there. This young man was good friends with Chase but told him he had to leave because he didn't want to get in trouble.

With no place to go, Chase spent one night in the back of a friend's pick up truck in the dormitory parking lot. It was February. There was snow on the ground and it was very cold in Illinois. He spent another night in a mobile home with the father of the girl he'd just met. I wanted to rescue Chase, but I needed to teach him a lesson. I thought he would soon get tired of living like this and call me to come get him, but he was stubborn. The school had purchased houses across the street and converted them into dormitories for sophomores, juniors, and seniors. Chase was friends with some of the boys who lived in one of those houses. He had gone to Mardi Gras with them a couple of weeks earlier. He had convinced one of them to let him move in.

I skimmed through some of the videos on Chase's Youtube channel. The videos showed Chase and his buddies acting stupid, nothing dangerous or illegal. Then I stumbled across a video of Chase and his friends in the dorm room where Chase was now staying. One of them was showing off his shotgun. I grew up around firearms and have no problem with them when they are properly used by responsible people for self-defense and sporting purposes. A dorm room, however, full of teenaged boys who party 24/7 with alcohol and drugs wasn't a good place for a shotgun. I hoped this would get the attention of the Dean. I was right. I sent her an email about the shotgun with a link to the video. In the subject line I typed "Shotgun in Dorm Room!" She emailed me back right away and told me she would send security over to get Chase out of the room and off campus immediately. She would also make sure the shotgun was removed from the room. It wasn't long before Chase and I were talking on the cell phone. He didn't know I had anything to do with it, but he had been told to leave campus right away.

"Hey. I don't have anyplace to stay tonight. The school kicked me out of the room I was staying in. It's B.S.!"

"Chase, how long did you think they would let you continue to live on campus and eat in the cafeteria? You're no longer a student there."

"I don't know."

"Are you ready to come home now?"

"Yeah, I guess. So when are you coming to get me? Can you come get me tonight?"

"Chase, it's a fifteen hour drive! I can't come get you tonight."

"When are you coming, then? I don't have any place to stay tonight."

"I'm not coming to get you. Your mother and I are ready for you to come home, but since you didn't want to do it on our schedule I'm going to buy you a bus ticket. You can ride the bus home."

"WHAT? Ride the bus! Why?"

"Because, Chase. You need to learn to appreciate things a little more. You need to learn that you have to work for things in this life. Your mother and I aren't always going to be around to do things for you and you're going to have to learn how to do things on your own. When you have it good you need to show some gratitude to the people who are responsible for helping make things good for you. Now, if you want to come home, I'll go ahead and buy the bus ticket."

I gave him the address and directions to the bus stop. Chase packed up what belongings he could and began making his way to the bus stop.

In Belleville, there was a Metro; a train that went to the bus stop, and a city bus. These options were relatively inexpensive. I'm sure his friends would have given him a ride, too if he had asked. He chose, however, to walk for some reason. Chase had a small television he decided to take with him, but it must have gotten too heavy. So he decided to return to the campus to give it to one of his friends. By now the campus police were on the lookout for him. They arrested him for trespassing. He spent that night in jail. The next day he continued on his journey to the bus station. Here is what he wrote about his adventure which I found later on his laptop.

The last 48 hours was crazy for me............okay well I got arrested for trespassing which was bull crap. Then they let me out late that night I had nowhere to go so I just walked from the jail down the streets and met some crazy black lady that I could barley understand and she had a tattoo on her face. Well idk [I don't know] why but she gave me 4 dollars "I could not understand anything she said so idk why she gave me 4 bucks but I took it anyways" well she said she had to use the bathroom and I was like alright so she just pulled down her pants and went right there in front of me while still holding a conversation with me and I was like WHAT THE HECK. So I had nowhere to sleep so went to the video store and slept in the video return lobby part it was still cold in there but better than out in the snow... next morning I woke up to some dude leaning over me and returning his movie and I was like what the heck so I walked back to the apartments packed up all my stuff while avoiding the police because I was still on campus and then sat on the sidewalk for a good 4 hours.

Then some old nice lady gave me a ride to the metro and gave me 13 dollars and I was just like heck yea. So I got on the metro went to the bus station and just waited till six pm. In the meantime this blind dude was poking me with his stick trying to find a seat. So I showed him to his seat and then talked to him till my bus came. All he wanted to talk about was Judge Judy lol [laugh out loud] but it was pretty neat cause he could use his ipad with no sight. Well I got on my bus it was a boring 25-hour trip back to Cary, North Carolina, but half the trip I sat next to a drag queen and was just like me out of all people, really. But he was okay. I guess he made a lot of money dressing like a girl on stage. He got like 10,000 in one competition. Well I got home. Just my luck they lost my bags and now I'm in my bed finally.

Chapter Seven

AFTER COLLEGE

FTER CHASE CAME HOME I gave him a couple of days to unwind. Then we talked about his next move. "Chase, I'm happy to see you again, and I'm glad you're back home, but you have to start working on your future now. You're going to need to earn a living."

"I'll start applying for jobs," he said.

"Okay, that's a good start. One thing you should think about though is that it's a pretty tough job market out there now. The economy isn't doing well and most jobs you qualify for aren't going to offer you any kind of health insurance or other benefits. Most of them are only going to pay you minimum wage or a little better and give you only 30 hours a week. You're not going to be able to survive off of that if you move out on your own. There's always the military."

Because of his time in NJROTC and having been at Hargrave, Chase thought he knew what the military was all about, and he wanted no part of it. Besides that, it was my idea and not his.

"I'll think about it, Dad."

"You know Xavier and William joined the Marines. It's not what you think, Chase. For the most part, once you're done with your training, it's like any other job. You do your job and stay out of trouble, and they leave you alone. There will be the camaraderie that you enjoyed with football and Hargrave, and there's the teamwork like you had with football. There are a lot of similarities between the two. I think you would like it if you tried it. Besides, I know you want to get out on your own, and that's what your mom and I want for you, too. Joining the military would be the quickest way for you to do that. They provide housing, food, and most of your clothing. You get to bank most of the money you make and you learn skills that you can transfer to the civilian world when you get out."

"Okay, Dad. I'll look into it."

"Look, I'm not telling you that you have to go into the military. There are other options for you but I think it's one of the best options you have left in terms of getting out on your own the fastest."

"Okay, Dad."

Xavier was waiting to go to boot camp. He could earn extra rank and bonuses if he helped the local Marines recruiter sign up people. He didn't have Chase's cell number so he contacted me. I talked to him and mentioned that Chase had metal in his arm from his go-kart wreck. He told me that Chase shouldn't mention it but that he didn't think it would be a problem especially since he had played college football. I never told Chase about this call, but I gave Xavier his cell phone number, and Chase got a call from the Marine recruiter a couple of days later.

Chase told me that a Marines recruiter had called him.

"How did that go," I asked.

"Okay. I told him about my arm. He said they probably wouldn't be able to take me because of that."

"Hmmm. Okay, then." So the Marines wouldn't work. I decided not to mention anything else about the military. If he was going to do that, it would have to be his decision.

It was nice having Chase home, but I worried because Chase was twenty and not motivated to pursue anything. He lay in bed until noon. He seemed to have no ambition. When I pushed him, he would fill out job applications, but he didn't want a job. He went through the motions because I was on his case. He wanted his car, but I told him that if he wanted the car, he needed to get a job or attend a technical college to learn a skill, or both. I wasn't going to give him the car so he could go out and play with a bad group of kids and get in trouble. Sometimes in the evenings I would give him a ride to the mall. He was bored sitting at home all day. He met up with some of his old pals from high school who were still in the area.

I stayed on him about job applications, and even looked over his shoulder as he filled some out online. One time he joked with me. "I'm gonna marry me a sugar momma," he said with a big grin on his face. I laughed. Knowing Chase, he probably would find some pretty, sweet little girl who would support him. That would, in my opinion, be the worst thing that could happen to him. He needed to become the person he was created to be. I even got him to take a couple of different personality assessments online so we could figure out what kind of work he might enjoy doing and what he would be good at. Below is Chase's personality profile. It hit the nail on the head. Those who knew Chase will read it and marvel at how closely this profile describes him.

This report has been prepared exclusively for: Chase Rodgers

Your results indicate that your personality type is that of the:

Artisans (SPs) *are the temperament with a natural ability to excel in any of the arts—not only the fine arts such as painting and sculpting, or the performing arts such as music, theater, and dance, but also the athletic, military, political, mechanical, and industrial arts, as well as the art of the deal in business. Artisans are most at home in the real world of solid objects that can be made and manipulated and real-life events that can be experienced in the here-and-now. They have exceptionally keen senses and love working with their hands. Artisans seem right at home with tools, instruments, and vehicles of all kinds, and their actions are usually aimed at getting them where they want to go as quickly as possible. Thus Artisans strike off boldly down roads that others might consider risky or impossible, doing whatever it takes, rules or no rules, to accomplish their goals. This devil-may-care attitude also gives Artisans a winning way with people, and they are often irresistibly charming with family, friends, and co-workers. Artisans want to be where the action is; they seek out adventure and show a constant hunger for pleasure and stimulation. They believe that variety is the spice of life and that doing things that aren't fun or exciting is a waste of time. Artisans are impulsive, adaptable, competitive, and believe the next throw of the dice will be the lucky one. They can also be generous to a fault, always ready to share with their friends from the bounty of life. Above all, Artisans need to be free to do what they wish, when they wish. They resist being tied or bound, confined or obligated; they would rather not wait, save, store, or live for tomorrow. In the Artisan view, today must be enjoyed for tomorrow may never come. There are many Artisans, perhaps 30 to 35 percent of the population, which is good, because they create much of the beauty, grace, fun, and excitement the rest of us enjoy in life.*

Chase Rodgers *Tuesday, December 20, 2011*

Temperament Discovery Report Artisan Performer (ESFP)

One day I was out running some errands and I saw this skinny kid smoking a cigarette while riding a Rip Stick near downtown Cary. I had to do a double take. It was Chase! I didn't even know he smoked. He didn't look like Chase to me. A Rip Stick is like a skateboard but with inline wheels on casters. The board is hinged in the middle in such a manner as to allow the rider to tilt the front part and the back part of the board independently. This allows the rider to propel the board without ever putting his foot on the ground. It requires a serpentine motion. The first time Chase ever saw a Rip Stick in the store he picked it up and immediately started riding it around like he had been riding one his whole life. It was something he instinctively knew how to do. So there was Chase riding around downtown on his Rip Stick smoking a cigarette. I wondered what else he had been doing that I knew nothing about.

Chase spent more and more time away from home. He didn't have use of his car, but he did have his Rip Stick. We live in a suburban neighborhood with a lot of stores and other businesses very close by. Even the mall isn't that far away for a young man with a Rip Stick. Sometimes I asked Chase who he was hanging out with or where he went. He was always very vague. If he gave me someone's name it was only a first name. He wasn't open with his mom either. I eventually got the name Lilith. I went to Facebook and looked at his friends. Sure enough, there was a girl among his friends named Lilith. I didn't like the way she dressed or the posts she made. She dressed like a prostitute. Her hair was bleached blonde and looked frayed from too many perms. She wore a lot of make-up and revealing clothes that showed off her large breasts. She wore heels and black stockings with large runs in them. I could see from her photos on Facebook that she liked to smoke and drink and it looked as if she liked to do drugs, too.

Chase went out a lot with friends. Sometimes he walked or rode off on his Rip Stick. Other times a car stopped out on the curb, and he ran out the door and was gone before I could see who it was. He began going off for longer periods of time without telling us where he was going or when he would be back. Eventually he stayed away overnight, then for a couple of days. I would try his cell phone, but he wouldn't answer. When he did come home, he slept all day. Then he'd head out the door again in the evening. He had stopped filling out job applications. Kim and I stayed on him about it but to no avail.

Chase began losing weight and looking pale. I saw who else was in Lilith's list of friends on Facebook. I didn't like what I saw. Chase was headed in a bad direction fast. He was using drugs. I didn't know how much or what, but I was worried about him because of the company he was keeping.

Finally one day after Chase had been gone for two or three days without telling us where he was he showed up at the front door. He knocked on the door. He knew I was home because my truck was in the driveway. I didn't answer the door. It was one of the most difficult things I had ever done. It broke my heart not to let my son in the house, but I wasn't going to continue to enable his self-destructive behavior. He finally walked away from the front door, and soon after that, a green Honda Accord showed up in front of our house and picked him up. As they drove away, I wondered when I would see Chase again.

I kept up with Chase on Facebook by watching his posts, Lilith's posts, and the posts of some of the other people they were hanging out with. Chase was looking thinner and paler by the day. They appeared to be holed up in a hotel room some of the time. Lilith's best friend was a homosexual male who had blonde hair and was also very pale and thin. There was a wide variety of other people Lilith liked to pal around with, drug addicts, alcoholics, and gangsta wanna-bes. It was easy to tell what kind of people they were by looking at their Facebook timelines.

Lilith's gay friend, Ashton had a boyfriend who also had photos on Facebook. Ashton and his boyfriend were both extremely thin. If someone had told me that either of them had been diagnosed with AIDS, I wouldn't have been surprised. I wanted Chase away from them. What if those people were shooting up heroin? What if they were sharing needles? Chase had never been a mean kid. When he got in trouble, it was because he was clowning around when he shouldn't have been. He had always been kind and generous. He was naive. He had always taken everything at face value, and he trusted everyone. He never thought much about the potential dangers. If he wanted to do it, he did it. He never thought much about the future either. He lived in the moment. That was what scared me. Chase was vulnerable and I didn't know much about the people he was hanging out with, but I didn't like what I saw.

Two weeks had gone by, and Chase was still out there. I guess he thought he was going to prove to me that he could make it on his own. That was exactly what I wanted him to do; make it on his own. Every Facebook post looked scarier than the last.

Then Chase began wearing diamond stud earrings and tattoos. They weren't good tattoos either and looked cheap and amateurish. Chase knew that I wouldn't have approved of the tattoos or the earrings. He was rebelling against me. Tattoos, earrings, and piercings are more widely accepted in society today, than when I was young so I try not to judge people by their choices in such matters. I was raised not to do things like that to alter your appearance. I was going to have to accept these things for the present. The more stink I made, the more determined Chase would be to do more to upset me. That issue was the least of my worries.

I decided it was time to bring this whole episode to an end and get Chase back home before he ended up dead from an overdose or in prison. I dug more deeply into Lilith's Facebook timeline and found out who her mother was. I found her mother's Facebook profile, then I Googled her and found other information about her online. I learned exactly where she lived and where she worked. When I had her work telephone number, I gave her a call. "Mrs. Addington. My name is Darryl Rodgers. We've not met, but I'm Chase's dad. I'm calling because I'm very worried about Chase."

"Oh! I am too," she said emphatically. "How did you get my work number?"

"I'm pretty good at finding people using the internet," I replied. "Listen, I don't want to intrude on your work but I didn't know any other way to get in touch with you. Would you mind coming by our house and meeting with me and my wife sometime soon?"

"Yes. I would be happy to do that."

Lilith's mother, Angel, was a nice-looking lady. She had come straight from work. She was dressed professionally. She was polite and articulate. Nothing about her would suggest that she had a daughter who was dressing and behaving the way Lilith was.

"I don't know where Chase and Lilith are right now," she told us. "Chase lived in a tent in my backyard for a week. I asked him if he was sure he wanted to do that?" He said, "Oh, yeah. I'm used to camping out. I was a Boy Scout."

By this time we all knew that Chase and Lilith were moving from place to place. She didn't know exactly where they were.

"They were at the Motel 6 for a little while, but they're not there any longer," she said.

"Does Lilith have money for a hotel room," I asked.

"No. She doesn't have the money to pay for a hotel room."

"I wonder where Chase is getting the money?"

"I don't know," she said. "I'm an enabler. I'm sorry I let Chase stay there. I hope you're not mad at me."

"No. That's okay. I just want to find out where he is now. I need to keep up with him. I don't know how he's surviving; what he's doing for money."

"He and Lilith actually went looking for jobs the other day. He insisted that she go, too. I don't know what they're doing for money right now either. Lilith says he's different from the other guys she's dated. He's cerebral." She also told us, "Lilith is adopted. She started having trouble in her early teens, but she's always had a mind of her own and been rebellious. Her father and I were youth ministers at a church for a long time, but then they asked us to leave. After that he started abusing alcohol and drugs, and that's when Lilith got started on drugs. She was treated for heroin use at one point, and she spent some time in the mental hospital. She had a baby when she was fourteen and the baby was put up for adoption. I would advise you to do whatever you have to do to get Chase away from my daughter. She's like a drug all on her own. Boys are drawn to her. Do whatever you have to do to get your son away from her."

After Angel left, I remembered the custodial bank account. I had reinstated Chase's ability to make withdrawals after he came home from college, but when I locked him out, I had intended to go to the bank and have them put a stop to the ATM withdrawals. With everything else that was going on, I had forgotten. "That must have been where he was getting the money. I went to the bank the next morning. He had been going through the money fast. What had been over $5,000 was now down to less than $1500. I had them put a stop on the ATM withdrawals immediately. After Angel left I went back to perusing Facebook, looking at Chase's recent photos, looking at Lilith's timeline, and looking at their mutual friends. What could I do? I had to do something and I had to do it immediately!

I called our health insurance provider and asked what we could do to help Chase. They told me that, if he had never been in drug treatment in the past, they could not pay for treatment. If I could get a doctor to say that Chase needed to go to the mental hospital, they would pay for that. I kept making phone calls and running into dead ends. I was getting nowhere. I didn't know what to do. Suddenly the term *intervention* popped into my head. I had seen a reality TV show awhile back about interventions. I had never heard of an intervention before that. I began Googling the word *intervention*. The first thing I came across was a company based in Pittsburgh named Intervention Masters, Inc.

I talked it over with Kim and she gave me the green light so I gave them a call. I told them that I didn't know where Chase was and they told me that was no problem that when the intervention specialist arrives he would help me find him if necessary. They recommended a rehab facility for Chase in the Northeast, so I looked at their website and gave them a call. It was a crazy amount of money especially for a middle class family. It was around $20,000 –$25,000 for 30 days. We couldn't afford that. I called them back, and they recommended another place in Florida that would cost around $7,000 out of pocket after insurance. I could manage that. It was a 30-day program. I told them I would think about it and I began making more internet searches and phone calls to treatment centers all over the U.S. I was trying to determine what would be the best thing for Chase within our budget. Intervention Masters told me that they would take Chase wherever I wanted him to go but they thought Peaceful Plantation in Florida would be a good fit for him.

I called a friend whose wife is a psychiatric nurse. He then referred me to a lady who was friends with his wife and used to work in the rehab industry. This lady and her husband had worked in that industry for many years, and she recommended a place in Montana. I researched them online and gave them a phone call. Part of their training included a trip to the wilderness. I thought this sounded like something that would be right up Chase's alley. This place was in the middle of nowhere. If Chase decided to leave, there was no place to go—only miles and miles of wilderness. It was an all-male program, so there were no girls to distract him from the treatment. Furthermore there were no video games or internet.

I have a relative whose son had had a problem with alcohol. He went through a program called Teen Challenge, and it changed his life. She highly recommended it. It was a fifteen-month, Christian program and it cost less than $1,000. Teen Challenge had treatment centers all over the United States. I then called Intervention Masters and bounced that idea off of them. The young lady I had been talking with said "Oh, no. You don't want to send him there. There are a lot of people in that program who are right out of the prison system. He would learn a lot of bad things from them. Besides, they're really rough on the kids."

Then I asked what she thought about the place in Montana. She couldn't give me any specific reason why, but she was against it. She thought Florida would be better. When I wouldn't back down about the facility in Montana, Warren came on the phone. Warren acted like a sleazy used car salesman. Every time I shot down Warren's reasons why Chase should go to Florida instead of Montana, he came up with a new reason. When I pinned him down, he admitted that he didn't know anything about the program in Montana. "Look, we're familiar with the program in Florida. We *know* it's a good program. I can't say that about the program in Montana. I wouldn't wait too long to make a decision on this if I were you. Some people call us and while they're trying to make a decision, their child dies in a car wreck or from an overdose. We had a call like that just the other day. It was really sad."

After haggling a little longer, I agreed to send Chase to the rehab center in Florida. They had finally worn me down. Once the treatment location was decided, I signed a contract via email for their services and I sent them the money to cover their fees. Then they let me know that the intervention specialist was on his way. He was getting on the airplane to head to Cary because after all, we didn't have a lot of time. After thinking it over further I called them back and told them that I had made up my mind. Chase was going to the treatment center in Montana and that was that! "Okay," said the young lady on the other end. You're just paying us to get him there. Where he goes is up to you." Then I got a phone call from the intervention specialist, Aaron. He let me know what flight he would be coming in on and what the scheduled arrival time was. All of this was happening too fast.

"Where is he now?" he asked.

"I don't know."

"Does he have a favorite hangout?"

"Yeah. He and his friends hang out at the food court in the mall a lot."

"Go by there and see if you can find him. If he's there, entice him to come home. Tell him he doesn't have to stay. He can come home, get some food and take a shower. Tell him his mother would like to see him. How's he getting money to survive?"

"He had a custodial bank account with me and I meant to put a stop on it when I locked him out, but I forgot. I put a stop on it a few days ago. It was getting low anyhow."

"That's good. That means he might be ready for a hot meal and a hot shower. You'll need to begin assembling an intervention team that consists of a group of family and friends who are willing to help out with this. We don't have much time, so you need to start right away getting commitments from people."

It was early afternoon. I took Aaron's advice and drove over to the Cary Towne Center, our local mall, a few miles from home. I parked and walked into the food court. I looked to my right as I walked in, and there was Chase sitting at a table with Lilith and another girl I didn't know. Chase was sitting with his back to me. Lilith must have noticed me and got his attention. He turned in his seat and made eye contact with me.

"Oh, Hey Dad," he said with a big grin. His eyes were glassy and his pupils dilated. He looked dazed, pale, and weak. He got up from his seat to greet me. We embraced.

"Chase, I know you must be starving. Why don't you come home and get something to eat and take a shower. Mom and I miss you so much. You can come and go as you please. I'm not going to give you a hard time. We're just worried about you, Chase."

"Okay. Maybe tomorrow I'll come home then."

"Alright. Whenever you're ready."

"Okay, see you Dad."

I said goodbye and walked on into the mall, as though I had come there to shop and had only stumbled upon Chase and his friends. When

I left the mall I began making phone calls to assemble the intervention team. Of course, Kim, Justin, and I would be a part of it. I called my good friends, Les, Monte, and Bob. Les was four and a half hours away with a small business to run, so he couldn't make it. Monte and Bob live close by and were happy to help out. I was thinking that we needed some of Chase's friends too. Otherwise, I was afraid he was going to feel like he was being ganged up on by a group of adults. Kylie immediately came to mind. She's a good Christian girl; very smart, and she was good friends with Chase but not part of the drug scene. I knew this would be a difficult thing to do, though, so I got in touch with Kylie's mother to ask her permission to ask Kylie. She agreed that it was okay for me to ask Kylie. I did, and Kylie said yes. The team was coming together.

I was surprised when at 10:30 the next morning Chase showed up at the front door. I let him in. He wasn't supposed to be here this early. The interventionist wasn't here yet. How was I going to stall him? Chase was glassy-eyed. "Where's Mom," he asked.

"She's at work, Chase."

"Where's Justin?"

"He's at school." I was thinking Chase should know this. He made his way down the hall to his room and began digging through his things.

"What are you doing?" I asked.

"I'm looking for my camera. Do you know where it is?"

"No. I haven't seen it."

"How about my big knife?" Chase had a small knife collection, including a couple of large survival knives. I had hidden the big knives after locking him out. His behavior convinced me that it would be a bad idea for him to have large knives in his possession. I said I didn't know where the knife was.

He wasn't at the house long. He found his video camera, took a change of clothes and headed out the door. "I'll be back soon and maybe stay a little longer," he said on his way out.

"OK. I know Mom would like to see you. She's worried about you." I tried to get him to stay and get a bite to eat and maybe take a shower, but it was obvious he was on a mission. He had somewhere else he wanted to be. After he left it dawned on me that he was desperately searching for items to sell. I wasn't sure if that was so he could keep surviving on his own or if it was because he was desperate for drug money.

I drove to the airport at one o'clock to pick up Aaron. As I pulled up to the airport terminal in my SUV, there was a guy standing there with his bag in his hand. He looked to be of average build in his thirty's and was wearing a fedora hat. I rolled down the passenger side window as I pulled up. "Aaron," I shouted.

"Darryl?"

"Yeah! Hop in!" He threw his bag in the back seat and climbed in the front passenger seat. "So fill me in on Chase." I began giving him all the details about the latest developments with Chase as I drove away from the airport terminal. How he dropped out of college, began hanging out with Lilith, and how finally I had locked him out. I told him that I had taken his advice and found Chase at the mall and invited him home. I told him how Chase had come home and left again and how he was rifling through his belongings, probably looking for items to sell. Aaron asked if I knew of any good barbeque restaurants around. He said he had been to North Carolina one time before and he had never forgotten how good the barbeque was. I headed to Danny's Barbeque while we continued to talk about Chase.

Once we arrived at Danny's, Aaron began to work on a plan while we waited for our food. "So what's this about Montana?" Aaron asked.

"I think it would be a better place for Chase to go."

"Why is that?"

"Chase likes nature. He's an Eagle Scout. He has spent a lot of time in the woods with scouting and hunting and fishing with me over the years. Plus, we've done a lot of survival stuff together. I think he would enjoy the wilderness aspect of the program. Besides that, there are fewer distractions there. No electronics or girls, and if he decides to leave, there's nowhere to go, just acres and acres of woods and hills."

"Oh, that's not a good reason to send him there. There has to be a level of trust involved. He's almost twenty years old. He has to do this of his own free will. You can't force him or it won't work."

I smiled sheepishly "That's a good point. I can see that."

"And if you want him to go on his own free will, Florida is going to sound a lot more appealing to a young man his age than Montana. Besides that, I escorted a young lady out to a treatment facility in Montana one time and she wound up coming back home. She made it to the nearest town then bummed a ride with a truck driver. She eventually made it all the way back to the East coast, but in the meantime her parents were worried sick about her because they didn't know where she was. If an addict is determined to leave treatment, nothing is going to stop him no matter where he is."

So I agreed that we would send him to Peaceful Plantation in Florida.

"Don't worry too much about luring Chase back to the house right now. We'll get to that later." Aaron said.

"How is your intervention team coming along?"

I told him who had agreed to participate. "I'd like to find a few more," I said, but it's tough on such short notice."

"That's okay," Aaron replied. "We don't have much time. Let's go with what you have for now. We need a place to hold a meeting tonight." Aaron and I were finishing up with our meal. I managed to reach Kim on the telephone. She had Justin with her and they were hungry, so I agreed to bring Aaron with me to meet her and Justin at a Taco Bell near our house to continue with our game plan. I needed help working out some of the logistics. We found a hotel for Aaron just a couple of miles from our house. The hotel happened to have a conference room that was available. I called all the members of our team whom I could reach and told them to meet us at the conference room by nine o'clock.

Kim, Justin, and I arrived a little early. We sat at the conference table and waited for the other team members to arrive. Bob came in with a huge bag of bagels and some coffee from Brueggers. We all appreciated that. Justin was especially fond of the cinnamon-sugar bagels. Kylie arrived with her mother and step-dad. Monte had been working outside all day landscaping and had to come as he was because I wasn't able to get in touch with him until the last minute. Once everyone was there and settled in Aaron passed out workbooks and pens to everyone and began to explain to us how this would go down. It was already late, so Aaron had to rush through the presentation. We discussed the signs of drug and/or alcohol addiction. Aaron asked the question, "Who thinks Chase is an addict?" People slowly began to raise their hands.

Monte interjected, "I don't think we would be here tonight if he wasn't an addict, would we?"

"That's right," Aaron replied.

Kim expressed her doubts, "I'm not sure if he's technically an *addict* or not."

I talked about how fast he had lost weight and how pale he was looking. I also mentioned that the past two times I had seen him, he seemed to be dazed and glassy-eyed. We went on to discuss how and why addicts manipulate people. According to our workbook, addicts are always trying to escape uncomfortable situations. They will say or do anything to avoid those situations. We talked about how family members sometimes inadvertently enable the addict's behavior and we discussed how family members could get help through Al-Anon and other similar organizations.

Aaron then explained to us how we would each need to write a letter to Chase that we would read during the intervention. He explained to us why we needed to write these letters. An addict has an uncanny ability to talk his or her way out of just about anything. If we talk to him, he probably won't hear much or anything of what we have to say. The letters put the addict in the role of listener. We need him to listen. The letters would also prevent family members from speaking to the addict in a manner that might put him on the defensive. The first part of each letter would be designed to lift the addict up thus putting him in a more receptive mode. Reading the letters to him tends to have more of an emotional impact than just talking to the addict about his problem.

He gave us an outline for how the letters should be constructed. Section One would consist of three or four detailed stories which connected each of us with the addict in the past. Section Two would include general statements on the present drug or alcohol abuse, and Section Three would refer back to the positive qualities of Section One with a simple request to the addict to get help written with a gentle loving uplift. He gave us a little more detail about how each section of the letter should be written.

Then we talked about a "Bottom Line Letter." The Bottom Line Letter was a tough-love letter that we would have to read to Chase if he refused to go to treatment. It outlined exactly how things would change in his life on our end should he refuse to go. Aaron assigned Kim the duty of writing the "Bottom Line Letter." She was praying with all her might that she would not have to read it. Basically the Bottom Line letter said,

"You no longer live here. You no longer are a part of our lives. You can't visit us because every time you visit, we wonder if it will be the last. You can't call us because every time you call we wonder if the next call we get will be from the police or from the morgue. We can no longer lie for you. From now on when your friends and family ask how you are doing, we are going to tell them exactly how you are doing. We are writing you out of our will. So until you choose treatment, this will be the last time you will hear from us and the last time we want to hear from you." No mother wants to have to write or read this letter to her child. The final words of the letter say, "This is not us abandoning you, but rather you choosing drugs over us. We love you but this is goodbye."

We all exchanged cell numbers so that we could communicate with each other, including Aaron. It was a late night. We didn't leave the hotel conference room until around eleven. Kim and I didn't get much sleep. How could we sleep with all of this on our minds?

The next morning I was surprised when Chase showed up at our house around nine o'clock. He went to his room and looked around. "Did you find my knife," he asked.

"No, I haven't seen it, Chase."

"Oh, Okay."

I tried to act nonchalant, but inside I was going crazy. He was here much earlier than any of us anticipated. We thought he might not even show up for days. Now I had to get busy! How was I going to get everyone here before he was out the door again? I couldn't make phone calls because he was within earshot of me. He walked into the kitchen and looked in the fridge for a bite to eat. I reclined on the sofa and pretended to be looking at something on my phone while I began texting all of the team members one at a time. I tried to keep a conversation going with Chase to stall him and to keep him relaxed and unaware of what I was up to.

After Chase finished a snack he went to the master bath and started taking a shower. I was texting like mad. Everyone was responding except for Kylie. That had me worried, because I felt like she was such an important part of the team. Aaron was helping coordinate. He had everyone meeting at a coffee shop right down the street from our home.

Monte had to come from his home in Wake Forest, which is a good

45-minute drive away. Fortunately Chase was in no hurry on this particular day. Like me he enjoyed taking long hot showers and today was no different. The plan was that everyone would meet at the coffee shop and ride together in one or two cars to prevent spooking Chase with a lot of cars showing up at once. Monte drove straight to our house because he had so far to come and didn't know if he would make it in time or not. Aaron, Kylie, and Bob met at the coffee shop and rode together from there to our house. Kim had to come from work three miles away, but it would take a little while for her to get out of the building and through the parking lot to her car. They finally all made it to our house. I never was able to reach Kylie, so I was relieved to see she was there. I found out later the reason she wasn't responding to me when I was texting her was that she was in the bathroom throwing up because she was anxious.

Chase was getting out of the shower as the team members were walking in the front door. Everyone was quiet as they came into our living room. Chase was all the way at the back of our house with the door shut so he was still oblivious to what was going on.

We all took seats and got our letters out. We formed a rough circle in our living room. If you were standing in the center of the room facing the front door, Kylie was seated in the recliner next to the door. To her left in the other recliner was Bob. Monte was seated on the fireplace hearth next to Bob. Kim sat next to Monte in front of the fireplace. At the end of the couch was Aaron. I sat to Aaron's right and Justin sat to my right on the couch. We took a chair from the dining room and placed it at the top of the circle between Kylie and Justin. That was to be Chase's chair. I went back to the bathroom to check on Chase. He had finished his shower, dressed in jeans and a t-shirt, and was lying spread eagle on his back in the middle of our bed. "Chase, there's someone out here who wants to see you."

"Who is it?"

"I don't know. One of your friends, I guess. Come on out and see what they want." With that I walked out of the bedroom without looking back. Halfway down the hall I glanced over my shoulder Chase was following me at a distance. He followed me into the living room, walked straight over to the empty chair and plopped down in it exactly like he was supposed to. I made my way over to the couch and took my seat next to Aaron. Chase looked at me with an embarrassed look, like a little kid who had been caught doing something bad. Immediately Kylie began to read her letter to Chase exactly the way Aaron had instructed her to.

Dear Chase, you are one of my best friends and like a brother to me and I cannot even begin to explain how much I care about and love you. That's why I'm here today. I can honestly say that I have never had a bad time with you. Whenever we were together and it doesn't matter where we went, you always had me smiling. I remember the first time we met, we gave each other nick names, Chaseopher and Kaleisha. You're one of the funniest, most outgoing, caring people I know. One of my favorite memories of us together was when I came up with your family to watch you play football when you were at Hargrave. It was unbelievable! You were the fastest person out there and everybody called you "Speedy Chase Rodgers." I was so excited to see you play and it was amazing how good you were. Another one of my favorite memories was when we went on a double date. It was you and Shannon and Ethan and me; we all went to Olive Garden for dinner and acted like we were big and grown up adults. We thought it was so cool that we had the wine glasses on the table until the waitress took them away because we obviously didn't look 21. But one memory I will absolutely never forget was when we went to Biscuitville. You said you had never been, so we went there for the best breakfast ever early in the morning. We had to bring my crazy little brother and you guys became best friends. You always knew how to make me smile and brighten my day when I was upset. I can honestly say we never had a dull moment. But lately I've noticed a change in you. I used to hear from you almost every day. Now I'm lucky to hear from you once a month. We used to be so close and every day I feel like I'm losing you even more. About a week ago, your mom messaged me on Facebook, worried sick that something had happened to you. She didn't know where you were and who you were with. When I heard this, I began to panic. I messaged most of your friends after I had texted you and found out your phone was cut off. I was worried sick about you and I was so scared that maybe something really did happen. I started looking on your Facebook page to realize you were hanging around different people and that you had lost quite a bit of weight. You didn't look the same. You didn't look like or act like the old Chase that I used to know. Seeing those pictures broke my heart and from talking to your mom, I couldn't imag-

ine MY Chase ever doing drugs. When I heard about this, I stayed up the whole night crying and praying that you would get better and realize that life doesn't have to be that way. I think about you almost 24/7 and pray for you about the same amount of time. It came as such a shock to me that my Chaseopher had gone down this road knowing that I was only a phone call away. I don't want you to do this any more. I don't want to lose you. I don't want to lose my best friend, my big brother. I want to be able to reminisce with you at Biscuitville again. I want to go to the pool in the summer time and take long walks at my house like we used to do. I want your personality back. I want to be able to have deep talks again. What I'm trying to say is I miss Chase. I miss his smiles and his laughter and I will do everything I can to get that back. To get my best friend back. Will you please accept the help that we are offering you here today?

> *I love you.*
> *Kylie*

Next up was my friend Bob

Dear Chase, my earliest memory of you is from Boy Scouts. I remember a youthful kid running like a gazelle, climbing trees, and building and stoking a fire like a pro. At the end of each day, between the dirt and the soot from the fire on your face, you looked like a coal miner at the end of his work shift. Another pleasant memory for me is when we worked on shoring up that dock for your eagle project. Remember when your Dad was in waders and almost fell in? Then a snake came swimming at us? And finally your Dad got out the water and had a leech on him? That was fun! I am not sure if you know this, but over the years your dad proudly shared with me your physical accomplishments. He was always so excited to share with me how you bench pressed so many pounds or ran the 40-yard dash in so many seconds. He also joyfully shared with me many of your football accomplishments. Every time he told a story, I could always see how proud he was of you. But over the last couple of years, I have begun to see your dad's hope and joy for you turn into despair and distress. The thought of how to deal with your drug addiction has taken a real toll on your family. I don't know if you realize this, but your Dad's hair has gone through 4 shades of grey over the last year and although your Mom still looks twenty-five years old to me, she does not laugh nearly as much as she used to. It has also forced your little brother to grow up quicker than he should have to. My hope is you accept this opportunity presented to you. Always remember that you are loved.

Then Came Monte

Dear Chase, Obviously, I have not had an opportunity to get to know you personally, but I feel like I know you because of all the conversations I have had with your father. You were about thirteen when he and I reconnected and many of our earliest conversations were about you. I know about your athletic accomplishments, I am aware of your competitive nature, and I am also aware of the schools that wanted you to come play football. It is no secret that you are reserved and quiet. Based on what I know of your aggressiveness on the football field I have always considered you the kind of person who let their accomplishments do their talking. I can say with genuine sincerity that I have always respected a man who conducted his life that way. I can also honestly say that during many of those talks with your dad I have come to the conclusion that you were in fact that kind of person. He was obviously proud of you and I loved hearing the story of you, the quiet young man who kicked butt on the field. Chase, when I played high school football I was a lot like you. I was quiet and shy, but I became something totally different in the game. That is another reason I have enjoyed hearing you father brag on you. It has always been apparent to me that both your parents loved you and wanted what was best for you. I have strong recollections of the earliest times I saw you and your dad together. It was obvious that you guys loved each other. It was also obvious that you trusted him and knew that he had your back. Chase, I kind of envy you because I have never had a father to love me. My father never saw me play football. In fact, he left when I was five and I never ever saw him again.

As my long-time good friend Monte read this part of his letter I began to cry uncontrollably. This caused Monte to begin to cry also as he finished reading his letter.

Because of that I have a special appreciation for a father who fights for his child, and I know that is what your father is doing for you now. I frequently tell my boys that they are "easy to love." Sometimes I will qualify that by telling them that I would love them regardless of their actions, but then encourage them by bragging on their good behavior. Chase, you were "easy to love" when I first met you. You were respectful, goal-oriented, courteous, and motivated. You have to know that you have changed late-ly. If you are not aware of that then you are the only one that is unaware. All the people who love you know who you used to be, and know that that person still exists. He is just camouflaged by something that you need help with. That brings me to another reason why I envy you. Your parents are still fighting to get their "easy to love" son back. In spite of the fact that you have made it so tough they still love you and want to help you. Chase, PLEASE, PLEASE, PLEASE take advantage of their offer to help you. They know who Chase really is and are willing to help him find his way back. Your challenge is not gonna go away on its own. You need help, and help is being offered to you because you are loved. Please let them help you.

Monte

Kim's Letter

Dear Chase, I am writing this letter to tell you how very precious you are to me and how much I love you. How special that day on Nov 22nd was when I heard your cry when you took your first breath and when I saw your beautiful face. I was so thankful for God blessing me with you. You have a wonderful loving spirit about you and a sense of humor that is in-fectious where others enjoy being in your presence. As a child you would wrap your arms around me and tell me guess who I love most? I knew the answer but would always ask. Who? You'd say God then I'd ask who next? You would always quickly reply "Dad then you" and I'd tickle you for say-ing Dad before me. It was always "Rock Paper scissors shoot..." I love you more. You could always make me laugh. I still owe you a prank for putting that rubber frog on my breakfast plate at Grandma's house. How everyone at the table was cracking up laughing when you made me scream. I en-joyed spending time with you, just you and I like watching the scary mov-ies or having you crawl up next to me and hear you say "I love you, mom." I used to dream and imagine what type of man you would grow into. You were always trustworthy, even when you did something you should not have you always owned up to what you did. I admired that about you. But somewhere, sometime, something changed. You began telling lies, sneaking to do things, hanging out with people who encouraged you to do things that are not in your best interest. The past three weeks I have felt like a grieving mother who has lost her precious son. I so want you to get the help you need so you can have a happy and fulfilling life, so you can be a part of your family who deeply cares for you and is concerned for you. Please accept this help that is offered to you today.

Before I started reading my letter I glanced around the room. I looked at Justin and he was crying. Even Chase's eyes were red and he wiped away tears.

Dear Chase, I love you so much. When you were a little toddler the first word you said was Da Da. I also distinctly remember the second word you said and it wasn't Mama. It was BALL!. I was driving and you were in your car seat. You saw some kids kicking a soccer ball around and you pointed and said, BALL! It wasn't long after that you were playing soccer, baseball, and then football. Do you remember the time when you were playing soccer and your team was down 4–1 at half? You scored 4 goals in the second half to win the game and your coach made a huge deal out of it. He told you repeatedly that YOU won that game for our team because you were relentless! You literally wore the other team down. You came at them time and time again until they couldn't take any more. You played with heart and determination! Do you remember the time when you made that game-ending walk-off interception on the JV team at Cary High when you played Apex in a very close game? All night long you had your man covered, and when they finally went to him you picked it off as the clock ran out and your entire team rushed onto the field and carried you off. You played with heart. Coaches can teach players a lot of things, but they can't teach anyone to play with heart. That is something rare that has to come from within and you had it. Remember how you used to call me in your room at night when it was time to go to bed and you would beg me to throw you passes? You would lie on your back in the bed and I would zip the ball to you underhanded, fast and from every conceivable angle. I would deliberately make the passes difficult to catch. You would lie there on your back and catch pass after pass with a big grin on your face. Sometimes we both laughed. When I got tired and wanted to quit, you would beg me to throw you more passes. Sometimes I would throw you 200 passes or more like this. I loved every minute of it. Remember the time we went deer hunting together and you got your first deer? You made a great 100-yard shot, got a huge grin on your face, and gave me a high five. Then there was the time we went shark fishing not too long ago and you caught the biggest shark of anyone on the boat. Chase these were fun times, and I want to have a lot more fun times like that together, but I've noticed some changes in you recently. I was disappointed when you dropped out of college. I love you so much, and I only wanted to help you move on to the next phase of your life. You said you wanted to get a job and get an apartment and live on your own. I wanted to help you do that, but you stayed out late every night and slept late every day and hardly ever filled out a job application or turned one in. For weeks now you have said you want a job, but you still don't have any steady work. I'm worried about you because you look pale and very thin to me. You never come around any more so even if I wanted to take you hunting or fishing or do something fun with you I couldn't. I miss you. I don't seem to see that spark in your eye that I once did. Sometimes I feel like someone else has moved into your body. I look in your eyes and I look for the old Chase that I knew but he is nowhere to be found. I want the real Chase back. I love you, Chase. Please come back to me, son.

Dad

Justin's Letter

Dear Chase, you are my bother and I love you very much. I am here today because I love you. I have always looked up to you and you were always making me laugh. I'll never forget the time when we jumped in a cardboard box and slid down the bed. I remember at first I was afraid to go but you kept pushing me to go, so I finally went. I had so much fun and me and you kept going back down in the box. Then mom came in and took a picture of us going down in the box. That day was so fun. You have always managed to make anything fun. Just being around you is fun. But lately I've noticed a change in you. You stay out late and never come home. You promised Mom and Dad you would change, but you never did. You said you stopped with the drugs but you didn't. You said you wouldn't stay out late, but you did. I think your condition has gotten out of hand. You are my brother and I don't want to lose you. I want the old Chase back, the one that was fun to be around the one that didn't sneak around. I want the Chase that I love back.

From: Justin

When Justin was finished reading his letter to Chase, Aaron took over and began asking Chase if he was ready to go to treatment.

"I'm not a drug addict," Chase shook his head slightly. Aaron continued to talk with Chase as the rest of us listened and watched. It went back and forth. Chase kept shaking his head. I got a lump in my throat as I thought about the increasing possibility that Kim was going to have to read the "Bottom Line Letter" to Chase. I kept thinking that we might never see him again after this day, at least not alive. "Today? You want me to leave today?" Chase asked.

"Yes," Aaron replied.

"But Lilith's birthday is today. She's not going to like it if I leave today, especially without telling her what I'm doing or where I'm going. Why don't we do it tomorrow?"

"Your parents have already purchased the plane tickets and made reservations at the treatment center."

"Where is it," Chase asked.

"It's in Florida," Aaron knew how to say all the right things, ask all the right questions, and push all the right buttons. He knew how to keep the pressure on and answer all of Chase's objections.

Chase finally caved. "All right, but the only reason I'm doing it is for you guys. I'm not a drug addict." I breathed a sigh of relief. Aaron instructed me to go get my laptop and let Chase use it to look at the website for Peaceful Plantation. I had a brand new Macbook Pro. I was surprised when Chase used it with ease, as though he had done it a million times before. After handing the laptop to Chase and getting him to the website I sat back down next to Aaron. I began to get this sinking feeling that Chase might be messaging someone on Facebook. I whispered to Aaron, "He may be using Facebook to contact friends."

"Go look!" Aaron whispered back. I walked back over to Chase and glanced over his shoulder. He was looking at the Peaceful Plantation website, but I could tell that he had seen me coming and closed another window. "Okay, Chase," Aaron said in a commanding voice. Go get your bags packed. The plane leaves in a few hours. We need to get to the airport."

"We who?" Chase asked.

"I'm going with you," Aaron said.

"All right then." With that, Chase headed down the hallway to his room.

"Follow him!" Aaron whispered to me.

I went to Chase's room. When I got there, he was standing a few feet inside the doorway with his back to me. He was hunched over as if he was trying to hide something. When I moved to where I could see, Chase put away a pen. I caught a glimpse of some writing on his forearm. He had written a telephone number on his forearm. I wasn't sure what that was all about, but I didn't like it.

I stood there while Chase stuffed clothes into his suitcase. He turned and walked out of his room towards the master bath. I thought he was going to get his toothbrush and toiletries. He closed the door behind him and I heard him turn on the water. Then it hit me that he might be going out the window. I reached for the knob. He had locked the door! I ran around to the sliding glass door that leads from our dining room onto the back deck. From the deck I could see that the bathroom window was open. It's a long jump from that window to the ground, with a gas meter and heat pump in the way to make the landing even more challenging. I ran back into the living room where all of the team members were still sitting. "He went out the bathroom window!" I yelled. Everyone gasped.

"Go after him!" Aaron ordered. During the planning phase my friend Monte had been tasked with going after Chase if he were to decide to run for any reason.

"Oh my God!" Monte exclaimed, looking panicked. He bolted out the front door and began sprinting down the street.

"Monte!" I yelled, "you're never going to catch him like that! He runs like a deer! Plus, we don't even know which way he went!" I got Monte to slow down and take a breath. "Let's get in my car and drive around Cary. Maybe he went to Lilith's house. Maybe we'll spot him. He couldn't have gone far."

"Okay," Monte tried to catch his breath. The two of us got in Kim's Toyota Camry and began driving around Cary, looking for Chase in places we thought he might turn up. The rest of the team stayed behind at our house in case Chase came back home. We made our way over to Lilith's mother's house. This was my worse nightmare. I thought Chase was gone for good. We parked around the corner where we could observe the house from a distance without being spotted. We waited for Chase to show up, but nothing happened. We decided to cruise around town and keep looking.

Then my cell phone rang. It was Aaron. "Come on back," Aaron said. "Chase will come back eventually. We all need to be here when he does."

Monte and I drove back to the house and walked in the front door. Kim was on the telephone with Chase. He asked if Kylie was still there and Kim assured him that she was. Chase wanted to speak with Kylie, but Aaron didn't think it was a good idea so Kim told Chase Kylie couldn't come to the phone right then.

"Can Kylie go with me to the airport," Chase asked. After getting Aaron's approval she told him yes.

Then Kim covered the phone and whispered, "He says that if he goes he wants me to promise him he can have the car when he gets back."

"Tell him yes," Aaron said. Kim hung up and we all waited for Chase to make his way back home. After he finished packing his bags he got in my truck with Aaron and Kylie. Monte drove them to the airport. Kylie told me later that she read him the riot act on the way over. She told him that he looked terrible, thin and pale. She told him he looked gay.

"What?" Chase had chuckled. He was wearing skinny jeans and a diamond stud earring. "Don't cramp my style," he told Kylie. He took out a pack of his favorite chewing gum, Wrigley's Cobalt Peppermint, pushed a stick of it into his mouth, and offered Kylie a piece of gum. Kylie thanked Chase.

"Be sure to keep the wrapper," he said.

"Why is that," Kylie asked.

"Because. I'm going to be famous some day and you'll be able to tell everybody about the day Chase Rodgers gave you this chewing gum. You know I'll probably meet some movie star while I'm in rehab and become famous." Kylie's eyes were still red and swollen from all the tears she had shed during the intervention. "You know, crying doesn't look good on you," Chase told her. All Kylie could do was smile. Chase had a way of making people smile and laugh even under the worst of circumstances.

Several other letters had come in. One written by Coach Tanner, one by Kim's brother, Eric, and one written by his wife Clare. Kylie took them along with her in the truck. She gave them to Chase on the ride to the airport so that he could read them when he had time.

Chapter Eight

TREATMENT

C HASE GOT SETTLED in at Peaceful Plantation in Delray Beach, Florida. He was not allowed to have any contact with the outside world for the first week. After several days had passed I got a phone call from the lady who was in charge there, Madelyn. She told me they had run drug tests on Chase and had asked him questions about his drug habits. They weren't sure what Chase might not be telling them, but they had confirmed that he was using marijuana, alcohol, and molly. MDMA, short for 3,4 methylenedioxymethamphetamine, is most commonly known as "Ecstasy" or "Molly." It is a manmade drug that produces energizing effects similar to the stimulant class amphetamines as well as psychedelic effects, similar to the hallucinogen mescaline. MDMA is known as a "club drug" because of its popularity in the nightclub scene, at "raves" (all-night dance parties), and music festivals or concerts. MDMA is a Schedule I substance, which means that it is considered by the U.S. Federal government to have no medical benefit and a high potential for abuse.* Molly, was probably partly responsible for his rapid weight loss.

Kim later asked Chase how and when he had started using drugs. I had always thought he started with marijuana at Cary High School because of the sudden change in his behavior, but he told her that the first time he ever tried anything was at Hargrave when Brice smuggled in some spice. "Spice" refers to a wide variety of herbal mixtures that

*From the website, teens.drugabuse.gov. National Institute on Drug Abuse.

produce experiences similar to marijuana (cannabis) and that are marketed as "safe," legal alternatives to that drug. Sold under many names, including K2, fake weed, Yucatan Fire, Skunk, Moon Rocks, and others —and labeled "not for human consumption" — these products contain dried, shredded plant material and chemical additives that are responsible for their psychoactive (mind-altering) effects. He told her that he also used alcohol for the first time while he was there.

Several days after Chase had moved in to Peaceful Plantation, Justin called my attention to the fact that Chase was signing in on X-box.

"What?" I checked and he was right. Chase was signing in every fifteen to twenty minutes. I was furious!

When I had first talked to Madelyn I'd asked her if Chase would have access to any video games. Video games could be a huge distraction that Chase didn't need while going through treatment. She had assured me that he would not have access to any video games while he was there. I called Madelyn and discussed it with her. She told me there were two houses and that the patients are at one house for part of the day and at another house for the other part. It was the second house that had an X-box, but she said Chase wasn't supposed to be playing it and that she didn't see how he could be online because it wasn't connected to the internet.

"He's very resourceful, Madelyn. I'm telling you that he's using it, because I can see him signing in and out."

"Okay. I'll look into it and get back to you."

I didn't hear anything back from Madelyn that day or the next. Meanwhile I was growing very angry as Justin kept me posted that Chase continued to sign in. I left messages for Madelyn, but she didn't return my telephone calls. I talked to other people there, but I was getting the run-around. Finally I talked to a young man named Logan. I tried to explain the situation to him, but he kept cutting me off. He threw it all back in my face. "Have you ever considered that your way of handling things isn't working, sir?" he asked indignantly.

I slammed the phone down. I'm not proud of the way I behaved. Sometimes my temper gets the best of me. Logan had told me that he was a recovering addict. That's often the way it works in the rehab industry. People who have been through treatment can wind up employed in the industry. I understand the need for that, because people who are going through treatment feel they can relate to people who have already been there and people who have already been there understand better than anyone how to get through to the addict.

One thing I've noticed though is that addicts, recovering or not, are master manipulators. They know how to lie, cheat, whine, deflect, or do whatever is necessary to get what they want or feel they need. I'm not saying they all do that all the time. What I am saying is that many of them are naturally or through their experience good at manipulating others.

When Logan called me back, I hung up on him again. I then called Intervention Masters. I was angry with them. They had pressured me into choosing Peaceful Plantation in Florida over the program in Montana, and now Chase was playing video games while on vacation in sunny Florida on our dime. I began recording the conversations I had with the staff at Intervention Masters. "Is your company compensated by Peaceful Plantation or any other treatment centers for referrals," I asked Warren, one of their staff members.

"We're not directly compensated by Peaceful Plantation," he said. I kept asking the same question. I knew the answer to the question, but I wanted to hear him say it. "You coerced me into choosing Peaceful Plantation because your company gets a kick back, didn't you?" Finally they had Aaron call me.

"You were free to send him anywhere you wanted to," Aaron said. "We didn't force you to send him there."

"You pressured me Aaron," I said. "You and the entire staff at Intervention Masters ganged up on me and you would not let up. You knew I was in a vulnerable position and you took advantage of that to manipulate me into the decision that was most lucrative for your company. How many parents do you people do this to in a month? How do you sleep at night?"

I hung up and discussed the situation with Kim. Then I called an attorney.

He told me that he had two teenage daughters, so he could empathize with me. "At this point, the most important thing is what is in Chase's best interest." he said.

I thought about it. He was right. I thanked him for his help and said goodbye. Aaron called me back and offered to accompany Chase to Montana for an additional fee. "Let me think about it," I told him. "I shouldn't have to pay out of pocket for any more of your services, since you folks talked me into Peaceful Plantation in the first place, when I wanted to send him to Montana. In the second place, he has continued to get online with X-box."

"Even now," Aaron asked in disbelief.

"Yes. Even now."

The next day I talked things over with Kim. I asked Justin more about the gamer tag that showed Chase was signing in to X-box Live. What Justin and I discovered was that some of Chase's buddies back at Lindenwood-Belleville University were using Chase's gamer tag. It wasn't Chase at all. Then I called Aaron and told him my mistake.

By this time I knew Chase was very resourceful and sneaky and capable of doing some amazing things. I wished he would put all of that creativity and energy to use doing something productive. I told Aaron that we had decided to leave Chase at Peaceful Plantation and let him finish his treatment there. I apologized to Aaron for giving him and the other staff members such a hard time. I made it clear, however, that I thought it was a shady way to do business not to disclose to customers up front that their company gets kickbacks for referring clients to certain treatment centers. I had felt pressured into choosing that center which did pay a kickback.

Over the 30 days that Chase was at Peaceful Plantation, we heard from him only a few times. In those conversations Chase repeatedly told me that he was not a drug addict.

"Chase, the staff at Peaceful Plantation told me they found Molly in your system."

"Yeah, but, Dad, most of these people I'm in here with are hardened drug addicts. They're older than me and they have all these horror stories; years of heroin or cocaine abuse."

"Chase, you lost a lot of weight in a short period of time. You were getting pale and looking thin, and you were running with a rough crowd. I know Lilith has used heroin. We need to treat this now before it gets worse."

Finally Chase was in his last week at Peaceful Plantation. I requested a conference call with Chase and his therapist. She agreed to conduct the session via Skype. She was off camera but was working with Chase on his relationship with me. I was very open and apologized to Chase for spying on him. We were talking about rebuilding our relationship; rebuilding the trust. Chase didn't say a lot. His therapist had to dig to get responses out of him, and usually the responses consisted of very few words. Words weren't always Chase's strong suit and he wasn't comfortable in such situations. I asked her about Chase's ADD and how much of a factor she thought that was with his addiction.

"I don't think it's much of a factor," she said. "I haven't noticed a lot of ADD symptoms." There was a pause. Chase had a little yellow squeeze toy in his hands that he had been rolling around and squeezing during the entire session. Every time he squeezed it the eyes would bulge out. His therapist giggled. "Maybe you're right. I guess the ADD is a factor." Chase's preoccupation with the squeeze toy had finally registered with her. I can only guess that it was given to him to use as a stress-reliever.

The session didn't go as well as I had hoped, but it was a start. Chase was quiet and reserved, but it had always been difficult to get him to open up to me about his deep feelings. It wasn't comfortable for me either, but I knew we had to go down this path. Improving our communication and understanding of each other was part of helping Chase get better. I was scared I was going to lose him so I was doing everything in my power to reach out to him. I wanted him to understand how much I loved him and how scared I was that I might lose him. I wanted him to know this is what drove me to do some of the things I had done. I only wanted to protect him.

When Chase finished his thirty days at Peaceful Plantation, they recommended a halfway house for the next phase of his treatment. While living in the halfway house, Chase would attend two Intensive Outpatient sessions per week. IOP was group therapy. Peaceful Plantation had a halfway house close by that they recommended Chase move into. It was a new option they had started. Chase had other ideas, though. He had his mind set on another halfway house in Deerfield Beach, south of Boca Raton. I didn't understand why at first, but then I realized he had met someone at Peaceful Plantation, a friend who was going to the halfway house in Deerfield Beach. Kim and I didn't think it was the best idea. We would have preferred he go to the halfway house run by Peaceful Plantation, but he seemed determined. We finally agreed to let him go where he wanted. It wasn't long after Chase moved into the halfway house at Deerfield Beach that he was calling to say that he wanted his car. He was relentless. He called me every day to beg for the car.

"Chase, what do you need a car for," I asked.

"We have to get a job here. That's part of the recovery program. If we're going to stay in the halfway house, we have to have a job."

"Okay, Chase. I get that, but can't you walk to your interviews? I can look at the map and tell there are businesses close by."

"No! I can't walk to my interviews! It's hot outside! I would be drenched in sweat by the time I got there!"

"What about the bus?"

"It takes forever for the bus to get to the stop and in the meantime I'm sweating out there. It's hot, here!"

"Okay. Well, let me think about it, but I don't think so." Every time he called and asked about the car, I stalled him. Finally I called Aaron. He had told me that I could call him if I needed anything. I explained the situation to Aaron.

"No! He doesn't need a car! Tell him to take the bus!"

"He says he has to wait too long on the bus and by the time it gets there he's soaked in sweat."

"He's lying. It doesn't take that long for the bus to get there. A car is the last thing he needs right now."

"Okay. Thanks, Aaron. I appreciate the advice."

Not long after Chase moved into the halfway house, I saw on his Facebook timeline that he had a new friend named Grayson. He looked like trouble with a capital T. Within a very short period of time Grayson was able to talk his parents into letting him have a car at the halfway house. Chase began riding around and hanging out with Grayson. One day I got a telephone call from the manager at the halfway house. Chase had broken one of the cardinal rules. He tested positive on the weekly drug test. Grayson liked to use cough syrup to get a cheap high and he had talked Chase into using it with him. Normally breaking this rule would have resulted in expulsion from the halfway house. The management decided to give Chase and Grayson another chance especially since they hadn't been there long. They sent them to detox for the night as a formality.

There is an interesting mix of people in the West Palm area. There are many ultra-rich people and many drug addicts. One day while Chase was riding around with Grayson, they pulled up to a traffic light and spotted a Lamborghini close by. Chase decided he wanted to take a photo of it so he opened his door to step out of Grayson's car. When he opened the car door, a man on a moped slammed into it and flew off of his moped. When it was obvious the guy was okay, Chase got back in the car and he and Grayson drove off.

Pretty soon Grayson had talked his parents into his renting an apartment. The management at the halfway house was concerned that Chase might leave and move in with Grayson, but that didn't happen. Within one week of moving into his new apartment, Grayson had relapsed and was back at Peaceful Plantation for treatment.

Chase had picked up a job working as a telemarketer. True, there's a lot of turnover in that industry, but I was proud of him that he had found work. He said he was doing well with it. Most of the guys at his work place were considerably older than he was. They pitched in and gave him some clothes. He had left here in a hurry to enter rehab and didn't have room to pack a lot of clothes or time to pick out the best things.

He never let me forget about the car, but he backed off. He must have realized that I wasn't going to give in. He bought himself a bicycle at Target with his first paycheck. One day while he was riding the bicycle back from work, a car with several guys in it pulled along side of him and started yelling at him. They stopped the car and one of them got out to start a fight with him. Chase rode off, but not before one of them spit on him. He didn't understand what any of it was about. He made it back to the halfway house and called the police to report the incident. Chase was upset by the whole thing, but the police never arrested anyone and that was the last he heard or saw of those guys. He thought the police weren't taking him seriously, because he lived in a halfway house.

One Sunday afternoon I got a phone call from Brian, the manager at the halfway house. He sounded upset. "Hey. I'm calling to let you know Chase is missing. He didn't make curfew. I'm so sorry. I'll keep you informed. "

"Thanks for letting me know, Brian. I'm sure he'll show up soon."

"Do you have any way of getting in touch with him?"

"I'll try his cell phone. I'll let you know if I'm able to get in touch with him." I called Chase, but didn't get an answer.

A few minutes later I had a call back from Brian. "One of the guys who lives here said he saw Chase ride off on his bicycle earlier. Have you heard anything from him yet?"

"Not yet, Brian. I tried his cell phone, but didn't get an answer. I'll keep trying."

A few minutes later I had another call from Brian. "Chase called. He's on his way back. He rode his bicycle to Ft. Lauderdale, which is twenty miles to the south! That's probably an hour and a half bicycle ride!" Chase made it back to the halfway house before dark, but was miffed as to why anyone would be upset about what he had done.

I asked Chase if he had a lock and chain for his bicycle.

"Nahhh. No one is going to bother it here," he said.

A couple of weeks later he called to tell me that he had left his bicycle parked near the front door of the halfway house and came out one morning to find it was gone.

After the bike went missing, Chase wanted another way to get around besides walking and the bus, so he bought himself a skateboard, a long board, to be exact. It was very flat there with few hills to ride down, but then there aren't any to have to walk or push up a long board either. This solution seemed to work for him for awhile.

I was proactive in Chase's treatment. I called his therapist at IOP to find out how he was doing. I shared everything with her about Chase and our relationship in an effort to help her understand us and treat him, as well as possible. I was happy with Sharon, the new therapist. I could tell she cared about Chase, and she listened intently as I talked. She told me that Chase was making progress, but that it would take time. Over a period of several weeks I had two or three telephone conversations with Sharon. Then Sharon moved to a different organization, and I lost contact with her.

About this time Chase decided he had had enough of this halfway house. He said it was constantly in turmoil. They kept firing managers and hiring new ones. There was no stability there. For example, at one point Chase had a mentor; an older gentleman who spoke with me on the telephone about getting Chase involved in church there. Less than two weeks later this gentleman had relapsed. A previous manager, a twenty-four year-old man, had been fired for embezzlement. Even before Chase could move, the halfway house closed down. The owners called to tell me they were working hard at finding a new manager, but that they were going to have to close this one temporarily while they looked.

Chase moved into a new halfway house, which he said, was in a better part of town. A few days later, he called me to complain that the people at the old halfway house had stolen his Xbox video game console. He had used what little money he could scrape up to buy an Xbox, and now it was missing. He said that he had left his Xbox behind, and when he went back to retrieve it, the temporary manager would not let him have it. He was furious! I tried to calm him down. "I'll go back there and break in and steal it back" he exclaimed.

"No, Chase. You're not going to do any such thing. It's only an Xbox. You can get a new one. It's not worth getting in trouble over. Now go back to your new halfway house and forget about the Xbox."

Pretty soon I got a phone call from one of the owners of the old halfway house. "Chase came back to our house and fell through the ceiling!"

"Fell through the ceiling?" I asked in disbelief.

"Yes. My manager has his Xbox. We told him he can have the Xbox back when he pays to repair the ceiling."

"How did he fall through the ceiling?"

"I don't know. He was up in the attic for some reason. I'm not sure why. We think he may have been looking for a stash of drugs up there." I had several phone conversations back and forth between the lady who owned the old halfway house and Chase.

"Chase, you did at least $200–$300 worth of damage to the ceiling. It's a wash. Let them keep the Xbox and move on."

He kept calling me wanting to argue about the Xbox for a long time.

I refused to argue with him. Instead, I calmly explained the facts. After a couple of weeks he finally let it go.

Chase liked the new halfway house a lot better than the first one. The people there were closer to his age, and the management seemed stable. I talked to one of the managers, Mitchell, on several occasions, in order to arrange payments. Insurance didn't cover everything, and I had to pick up the rest. Chase had to go to a new IOP because his new halfway house was too far from the IOP he had been attending. Mitchell gave me the telephone number of Chase's new therapist at IOP. After several attempts, I was finally able to talk to the new therapist, Reverend James Thurmond. I had hoped for a family counseling session, but instead I only had a one-on-one with the therapist.

"I understand addicts and what they are going through," he said, "because when I was young, I did drugs myself. I spent twelve years in prison, and I've even been shot. If it hadn't been for God looking out for me, I'd be dead."

Was he bragging about the misconduct of his youth? He told me he was a licensed therapist and went down his list of certifications and accomplishments in the field. He also had a reverend in front of his name, but I suspected he was no bona fide reverend.

"Chase has a lot of resentment towards you," he said, "because you made him do a lot of things he didn't want to do when he was younger."

I listened intently as he told me that Chase was "co-dependent."

"I'm going to have him write you a letter explaining exactly how he feels about your relationship."

"That's great, James," I said. "He has a tendency to bottle things up. It will be good for him to let all of that out, and I think it would help me to understand him and communicate with him better if he would write the letter." I later found where Chase had started the letter, but he didn't get far. I'm not sure why he never finished it.

There was some merit to what Chase's therapist was saying, but it wasn't spot on. The way he approached it let Chase off the hook; absolved him of all personal responsibility. No one can make us do anything we don't want to do. Only when we accept personal responsibility for our own lives and stop blaming others can we make real progress in our relationships and careers. I admit that I sometimes manipulated Chase into doing things he didn't want to do. My intentions were good. He wanted to play football, but sometimes he didn't want to workout or run sprints with me. I would cop an attitude with him, and he would go along. Why would he go along if he didn't want to? Chase knew I wasn't going to punish him for not participating in these activities. Chase went along, I think, because, like me, Chase had a phlegmatic personality. He avoided conflict at all costs. I was exactly like that when I was his age, but I had overcome that to a large degree. Chase was quiet and easy-going, and he would do anything not to have to deal with conflict. When Chase didn't want to do something and he knew I wanted him to, he either clammed up or told his mother. He was afraid to confront me about it.

I had already become aware of this dynamic in our relationship, and I tried to change over time. Getting him to talk to me about his feelings, however, was extremely difficult. I also did things for Chase that he was capable of doing for himself and should have been doing for himself. Why did I do this? There were several reasons, but one was that my parents did a lot for me when I was young, and I let them. Now that I had the responsibility of parenting, I wanted to make up for my laziness and selfishness in my youth. I enjoyed cooking for him and washing his clothes. As he got older, I realized he needed to learn to be more self-sufficient. He got good at keeping his room clean and when he was in college he had to do his own laundry and had no problem with it. As far as co-dependency goes, I fully accepted the fact that I had done some things wrong, but I didn't feel that allowing Chase to cast *all* of the blame on me for this was going to help him get better. Chase needed to learn to say *no*, and he needed to learn how to communicate better. He also needed to accept personal responsibility for his decisions if he was ever going to get better.

Mitchell called me one day, very excited. "You need to get Chase on a football team somewhere," he said. "He raced a kid that moved here from Nigeria. They had a five-dollar bet. This kid was fast, but Chase smoked him!" Mitchell had no idea that Chase had played high school football and had earned a scholarship.

When I explained, he said, "Well, I'm telling you. You got somethin' there, man! He could play football!"

I chuckled. It did give me an idea, though. There are two arena football teams in Florida. I got information about the one closest to where Chase was living, and told him when they were going to hold their try-outs. I thought he was so out of shape, that there was no chance, but maybe it would give him some hope; something to shoot for. When I told him, it sparked a little interest, but not enough to cause him to do anything.

A few weeks later, Chase called to tell me he thought he had broken his foot. He told someone at the halfway house that he had competed in the long jump in high school. On a dare he jumped over the swimming pool at the house. He made it, but when he landed he hurt his foot. I told him I would pay for him to go to the doctor and get it checked out, but he never went. He told me it got better on its own. Chase was living too far to commute to the old telemarketing job, so he began to search for work. One of the first job opportunities he came across was a one-night gig working at a haunted house. He got paid to scare people. By the time he paid for his costume, he barely broke even, but he didn't care. The way he looked at it, he got paid to scare people. What could be better than that?

By this time, Chase had been in Florida for several months. He missed us and we all missed him. It was time to drive down for a vis-it. Kim, Justin, and I piled into the Yukon and headed south down I-95. It's an 11- hour drive, but shorter than the one to Belleville, Illinois. We drove past Charleston, South Carolina, Savannah, Georgia, and on down the East coast of Florida, also known as the Space Coast. We ar-rived at our hotel room in Deerfield Beach rather late and told Chase we would meet him the next day.

We awoke late the next morning, got dressed, and drove over to the halfway house to pick up Chase. He had a big smile on his face as we met. He gave us all a big hug. The first thing I noticed was his crazy hair-do. He had it spiked straight up similar to a Mohawk and died orange. Had he done this because he knew I wouldn't like it? I pretended not to notice. Chase, Justin, and I are all very fair-skinned. Chase had the best tan he had ever had and was proud of it. He directed us towards some restaurants near the beach. We ate at Burgerfi. Chase had a burger and some ice cream. He loved ice cream.

After lunch we went for a walk on the beach. As we walked past some shrubs next to the sidewalk, Chase reached down and snatched up a green anole; a lizard. He put it on his shoulder and it seemed content to ride there as we walked along. Eventually it jumped off of his shoulder into the bushes nearby. Chase explained to us that there were a lot of lizards in the area, particularly one type that is brown which we don't have back home. He had become very good at catching them. He always was good with animals.

We drove back to the hotel and rested for a while. Chase played with his hair constantly with a little smirk on his face. I did my best to ignore his behavior. Kim wanted to go back out for dinner and then for a moonlit walk on the beach. Chase wanted to know if his "friend" could come along with us.

"Does your friend have a name," I asked.

"Samantha," he said.

I tried to suppress my smile, but I couldn't. The corners of Chase's mouth slowly turned up until he was grinning from ear to ear. I knew then that he had conquered the fear of talking to girls which he had once had. No matter where he was or what he was doing pretty girls seemed to be drawn to him like a magnet. When we drove back to the halfway house, Samantha was waiting for us. She was petite with red hair, bright blue eyes, and a pretty smile.

We all went to the beach and took a walk. I brought along a flashlight and occasionally shined it around looking for hermit crabs. Samantha and Chase were fascinated by tiny organisms on the beach that glowed in the dark. They tried to single one out by scooping a handful of sand and sifting through it. It proved to be a difficult task, but they were finally successful. Samantha especially seemed curious about the tiny luminescent creatures.

Later we went through the drive through at Arby's. Justin ordered chicken fingers with honey mustard dipping sauce. I pulled into a parking spot and we discovered that Justin didn't get his honey mustard. I told him to run inside and ask for some. He didn't want to do it. I insisted. He was perfectly capable of doing it himself. Samantha bounced out of the back seat before I knew what had happened. She reappeared a few moments later with Justin's honey mustard. I was impressed that she was so quick to do that. We sat there and ate in my truck while we got to know each other better. Kim asked Chase what he would like to do the next day. She wanted us to all do something fun together. Samantha quickly spoke up and mentioned that there was a Lion Country Safari at West Palm Beach. We talked it over and decided to go check it out. We made our plans for the next day and dropped Samantha off at the half-way house. Chase went with us back to the hotel.

The next morning we drove over around nine o'clock, picked up Samantha and headed to West Palm. We entered the Lion Country Safari and began to drive through. There were signs everywhere warning customers to keep their windows rolled up at all times. We pulled up next to some rhinos and marveled at how close they were to my truck and how big they were. They grazed casually as though we didn't exist. The rule about the windows quickly went out the window. Bzzzzzzzp. Chase's window zipped down and he took photos with his cell phone.

We moved on to an area where there were ostrich. An ostrich approached our car and Kim got brave enough to roll down her window and take photos. The ostrich began to get a little too close for comfort. "Roll the window up Kim," I exclaimed. No sooner than she had it rolled up, the ostrich began to peck at her window relentlessly. Kim screeched and we all roared with laughter as the ostrich made a spectacle of himself, his beak hitting our window over and over. It must have been fed from cars before.

We looked at zebras, kudus, and all types of herd animals. Finally we entered an area that was fenced in. At the entrance to this area there were more signs that warned visitors to keep their windows rolled up. The signs had bigger and brighter warnings. Only one car could pass through the gate at a time and then the gate would close behind it. Each car waited a minute or two at the gate. The line was moving slowly. We crept into the area where the lions were. There was still another fence that separated the lions from the cars, but we were able to drive by them, a few feet away. They lounged around in the shade as we looked on.

After we completed the entire tour we parked and headed into a separate area on foot. There were a wide variety of animals there, and we meandered through, taking them all in. There was a petting zoo where Chase and Samantha had fun feeding the goats. Then we discovered the giraffes. There was a tall tower with stairs that allowed a large number of people to be on eye level with the giraffes. Some attendants were selling leaves of romaine lettuce. They were expensive, but it was a special time and Samantha loved animals. We all did, but she seemed to be enjoying this time more than anyone.

I bought some leaves and we split them up amongst us. Then I went back and bought more for Samantha. She would hold out the leaf and a giraffe would walk over, stick out its long, dark tongue, circle it around the lettuce leaf and pull it into its mouth. Being up there on eye level with the giraffes gives one a new perspective. They're huge animals, but so gentle. Then we dropped Samantha off at the halfway house and Chase spent one more night with us. We dropped him off the next morning and he gave us each a nice, long, tight hug.

A few weeks later Chase called to ask if he could come home. I told him I didn't think he was ready. He begged me. Finally I told him I would think about it. Over the next few days he kept calling me, asking to come home. Kim thought maybe it was time to let him come home; maybe he had been there long enough. I found a local therapist who specialized in addictions and made an appointment with him. He was experienced, in his mid to late 40s. The degrees on his wall didn't impress me nearly as much as his experience in this field. He had been at it for close to twenty years. Kim and I told him everything we could think of about Chase.

After listening to us for some time and asking questions, he looked concerned. "I don't recommend that Chase come home right now. I don't see how it's going to help his situation. I hope he gets better. You know, very few of them do. I hope he's one of the ones who will beat the odds. You never know." I got a big lump in my throat. I left that man's office feeling sick. Was it that bad? Was there a chance Chase might never recover from this?

Chase finally quieted down about coming home, but it didn't last long. A few weeks later he was asking again. He also wanted to know if we had a tent he could borrow.

"Chase, why do you need a tent?"

"Samantha and I want to go camping at a park in Maryland."

I barely knew Samantha, and Chase wanted to go on an extended camping trip with her using one of my tents? I told him that everything was a mess up in the attic and that I wasn't sure if I could find the tent.

"How is Samantha going to go camping with you if she's in treatment?"

"She already left. She's back home in Delaware."

Now it made sense. Samantha had left treatment, and Chase was ready to get out of there. I had visions of Chase and Samantha running off with the tent and living out of it while they got their hands on drugs any way they could. It was reminiscent of the time he had lived in the tent in Lilith's back yard.

Samantha had purchased a guinea pig while at the halfway house. When she flew back to Delaware, she took her guinea pig, but left its cage behind. Chase thought it was a waste to have a guinea pig cage with no guinea pig, so he went out and purchased a black and tan guinea pig of his own. He named it Little Buddy.

Chase continued to call and ask about coming home. It would soon be Thanksgiving and Kim was hoping he could be home by then. I kept stalling, trying to keep him in treatment as long as I could.

One day I got a call from Mitchell, the manager at the halfway house. He was irate. Mitchell and his wife worked together managing the halfway house. Mitchell's wife didn't like the smell of the guinea pig and complained about it to Chase. Chase said he gave Little Buddy a bath and cleaned out his cage, but Mitchell's wife complained again a day later. The conversation got heated and Chase said some mean things to Mitchell's wife.

Mitchell told me that he was going to kick Chase out right away and that I needed to make arrangements to pick him up or get him into another halfway house. I apologized to Mitchell for Chase's behavior and asked him to pass on my apologies to his wife. Not long after I hung up with Mitchell I got a call from Chase. He had a friend from Peaceful Plantation who had his own apartment. He was going to let Chase stay with him until I could get there to get him. He was coming home. The situation with the guinea pig seemed to be a convenient way for him to bring the situation to a head, so he could get what he wanted. Either way, he would be home soon.

I booked a hotel room and packed my things as quickly as I could. I told Kim what was going on and she agreed that I should go pick Chase up. I left around two p.m. on a Friday afternoon. Since I was driving down by myself, I drove straight through. I was in Florida, less than thirty miles from the hotel when I began to get sleepy. I've been in this situation before and I know what my limitations are. I knew I could push on a little further and if it got too bad I would pull over, but I felt confident I could make it to the hotel safely. A few miles later blinding blue lights suddenly began flashing in my rear view mirrors. I immediately pulled over to the side of the road. Okay, this is going to be easy, I thought. I'm going to be nice to this officer and he is going to realize that I have not been drinking and let me go on my way. The officer approached the passenger side of my vehicle, which I found rather strange. Over the course of my lifetime I've been stopped a few times and I've never had an officer approach the passenger side. I hit the button to roll down the window on that side.

He shined his flashlight in my face. "Do you know why I stopped you," he asked.

"No, officer. Why did you stop me?"

"You were swerving all over the road!"

"Really?"

"Yes, *really*! How much have you had to drink tonight?"

"I haven't had anything to drink." I don't drink, sir. I chuckled.

"*Is something funny?*"

"No sir. I was only trying to lighten things up a bit."

"There's nothing funny about any of this! Do you know how many people I see get killed out here from driving and drinking or driving while fatigued?"

"I'm sure you see that a lot, officer." He demanded that I hand over my driver's license and registration card. By now I was nervous. This guy was young and gung ho. I knew I hadn't done anything wrong, but his demeanor was making me nervous. I quickly pulled out my driver's license and handed it to him. I continued to dig for my registration. I knew I had it, but I couldn't find it. The more I dug for it the more nervous I got. Now I was fumbling. Finally I found the registration and handed it to him. "I'll be right back," he said.

I watched in the mirror and noticed that another officer had pulled up behind the first cruiser. I was glad we have officers who take their job seriously and help keep us safe, but I was also thinking this guy needed to chill out. I watched in the side view mirror as he approached this time from the driver's side. The other officer approached from the passenger side. The young officer shined his flashlight in through the driver's window.

"I need you to step out of the vehicle please." He gave me a field sobriety test shining a red penlight in front of my face and asking me to follow it with only my eyes, as the other officer looked on. He tested me for a long time. I was getting tired, but I forced myself to concentrate on the red light.

Finally he said to me, "You're free to go. How much further do you have to drive tonight?"

"Only another 15 minutes."

"Okay. Be careful."

"I will, officer." I made it the rest of the way to the hotel with no problem. I was in bed by two a.m. I'm glad we have police officers out there who help keep us safe. I could appreciate that this young police officer was a little nervous. They never know exactly who they're pulling over. There is no such thing as a routine traffic stop. Every one could literally be their last. They can never let down their guard.

The next morning I drove over to Chase's friend's apartment. Chase met me downstairs with his suitcases, his guinea pig cage, and last but not least, his guinea pig named Little Buddy. I met Chase's friend. He was an older guy, probably early 30s. He was very polite. I thanked him for giving Chase a place to stay for the night.

Chase and I started our journey home. As we were leaving Florida, Chase pointed out mopeds. "That's what I need to buy when I get back home," he said. That's the last thing you need, I thought. A lot of addicts drive mopeds because most of them have lost their license due to DWIs. You don't need a license to operate a moped. They're also relatively inexpensive and don't use much gas. Addicts tend not to have a lot of money because they can't keep jobs, and if they do have a job, they spend their money on drugs or booze, not cars.

"Chase, do you remember that time I was driving mom's car and you and Justin were riding with me? I was sitting at the traffic light at the intersection of Harrison and Maynard in Cary and a guy plowed into me from behind in a large pickup truck."

"Yeah. I remember."

"Do you remember what happened?"

"Yeah. It pushed us into the middle of the intersection and we T-boned a minivan and they sideswiped another car. There were four cars involved in the wreck and the trunk of mom's car was gone."

"That's right, and do you think there is anything I could have done to have avoided that wreck?"

"No."

"What would have happened to me if I had been on a moped or a motorcycle at that traffic light?"

"You would be dead."

"That's right. I would be dead." Chase never said anything else to me about mopeds.

On the ride home I set the ground rules for Chase. "We're happy to have you back home, Chase, but there have to be ground rules if you're going to live in our house. First of all, no earrings." He sucked his teeth. "Are you going to give me attitude or are you going to abide by the rules?"

"Okay, Dad. No earrings. I got it."

"If you go out, you have to let us know where you're going and when you'll be back. No more overnight stuff when we don't know where you are. I know you want the car. You can have it, but only after you get a job and hold it for long enough that I'm confident you can keep it. You will also have to enroll in IOP at home and go twice per week."

"Okay. I can do that," he said calmly.

"No more hanging out with Lilith and that bunch either."

"That's no problem. I don't want to be around any of them any more." Something about the look on his face and the tone of his voice made me think he really meant it. I was happy that Lilith had also moved on. While Chase was in Florida I had seen on Facebook that she had a new boyfriend named Freddy.

Chapter Nine

HOME SWEET HOME

WE WERE ALL HAPPY Chase was back home. We celebrated Thanksgiving together at home, and we were all thankful Chase was doing better. It was a good day together as a family. We found a place for him to attend IOP in Raleigh and we started helping him look for work. There was a new Bass Pro Shops going in three miles from our home and they were hiring. I drove Chase over for an interview. He had his hair cut short and it looked normal. His hair was naturally dark brown, but the Florida sun had lightened it. He was sporting a well-trimmed beard.

Bass Pro Shops never called, but we kept Chase looking, filling out job applications, and going to interviews. It was difficult to get him out of bed in the morning. He liked to sleep late. I kept a tight leash on him about staying up playing video games. He didn't go out either. I attended IOP with Chase on family nights once per month and I requested family counseling sessions. Chase and I learned a lot about each other through these exercises, and he began to open up to me. We were making progress with our relationship.

Chase kept Little Buddy in his room in the cage that Samantha left behind in Florida. After a couple of weeks, he thought Little Buddy was lonely and needed a friend. I wasn't convinced, but Kim was sympathetic so I took Chase out to the pet store, and we bought another male guinea pig. This one was white and black, like a dairy cow and was smaller than Little Buddy. Chase named him Piggy Smalls. Soon we determined there wasn't enough room for Piggy Smalls and Little Buddy in the small cage, so Kim got Chase a larger cage. He connected the two cages with a passageway between them. This took up a lot of space in his small bedroom. Little Buddy bullied Piggy Smalls by growling at him. One thing was for sure; they didn't smell good. It didn't take many days after cleaning the cage and giving them a bath before they smelled bad again. I began to sneeze and cough a lot; probably due to the hay Chase fed them.

A few weeks later, Chase had a phone call from both a pet store and a grocery store near our house. He went in for the interviews. I drove him over to a place where he was screened for drugs prior to employment. The grocery store called and offered him the job. Before he could actually start work, however, the pet store called. He felt like he would enjoy working at the pet store more, so he called the grocery store back and respectfully declined the job offer. He went in for training at the pet store and he soon began to learn the job. He was good at it. He liked the animals, and they liked him. I'm sure most customers liked him, too. He seemed to get along well with his manager and the other employees.

My good friend Les had smoked for a long time. He was able to replace his smoking habit with E-cigs. It was a God-send for him. Back in the early days of E-cigs when most people were buying the cheap store brands and before the vapor shops came onto the scene, Les was already ahead of the curve. He had done a lot of research online and had found the best combinations of e-liquids, cartomizers, and batteries. He was light years ahead of everyone else. A few years earlier, when Chase was seventeen, we went to Greenville, South Carolina for Christmas. We had stopped in to visit with Les. I've never smoked, but I was curious about the E-cigs. Les had one he let me try. I played around and blew a few smoke rings. Chase wanted to test it out, so we let him. We were both amazed that he immediately blew perfect smoke rings. I began to think Chase had smoked before and was covering it up.

Now that he was back from Florida and his smoking habit was out in the open, he wanted to smoke E-cigs. It was apparently a fad. I told him I would pay for him to get started but that he would have to get a job so that he could sustain his habit with his own money. I would rather he had not smoked at all, but I was happy he was smoking E-cigs and not cigarettes or pot. We went down to a vapor shop that had recently opened just around the corner from our home and I got him set up. They had a nice room in the back with paintings on the wall by local artists. There was a pool table there. Chase and I played a friendly but competitive game of pool. It was good to have him back and to be spending time together. I got lucky when he scratched on the eight ball.

In early December, I received an invitation to a conference I wanted to attend. I was able to bring along guests, so I asked Chase if he would like to go with me. He was eager to go.

I explained: "Chase, this is going to be an event where people are going to be speaking all day long. There isn't going to be much to do there except sit, listen and socialize during the breaks. Are you sure you want to go?"

"Yeah. I wanna go," he answered confidently. I got him a ticket to the conference, and planned for him to go. I expected him to back out at the last minute, but he didn't. We drove down to Greenville, South Carolina, and spent the night with Les and his wife Joyce and their large family of dogs and cats.

We had to get up early the next morning to drive to Atlanta. Les wasn't feeling well, so Chase and I went on without him. We were supposed to meet another friend of ours, Jack, but he wasn't there yet. He called to say that he was on his way but would be late. We pulled into the closest parking spot we could find and headed to the restored older home where the conference was to take place.

Chase and I went inside and looked around a little at some of the materials. I had brought my video camera with me but someone already had a tripod set up in the only good spot. We put our coats on a couple of seats to save them while we met some of the speakers and guests. I talked with them as Chase listened in. There were a few younger people close to Chase's age in attendance as guests and speakers. Chase was taking it all in. I was surprised that he seemed content to sit there and listen. There were several breaks during which we met quite a few interesting people, at least one college age young man whom I had seen on television before.

Jack eventually joined us. The event organizers had pizza delivered for lunch and there was plenty of it. I bought a book from one speaker who I liked and picked up a couple of free books. I hand-held my video camera to record some of the speakers from my seat, but it was difficult with people's heads in the way. Jack left early, but Chase and I stayed until everything was over. We headed back to Greenville, South Carolina, to spend another night with Les and Joyce. By this time, Les was feeling better.

I'm from the Columbia area of South Carolina, originally and lived in the Greenville-Spartanburg area between 1982 and 1988. I met my wife Kim in Greenville in 1986. We both have family and close friends there. Kim's brother Eric lives in Greenville with his family, and he heard that Chase and I were in town. He called me and asked if Chase and I would like to go to lunch the next day. We met Eric for lunch at a Mexican restaurant that he suggested. We had a good visit with him, and then we headed back to Les's to grab our bags, say goodbye, and head home. As I was pulling out of the parking lot, Chase picked up my video camera and started to record me. It was a spontaneous moment of joking back and forth between father and son, a contest of wit and humor. It went something like this:

Chase asked, "Who would win in a fight; a cheetah or a leopard?"

Using my best Russian accent, I said, "Of course the cheetah because cheetah's know how to cheat."

Chase laughed.

"Who would win in a fight, Wolverine, the character from the X-Men movies, or Darth Vader?"

"Darth Vader because he is ruthless."

"He's ruthless?"

"Yes, I said, he will do anything to win."

"Mmm Hmm, but Wolverine has healing powers"

"Darth Vader has Storm Troopers."

Chase snickered. "Yeah, but Wolverine can tear through the Storm Troopers."

"No. They have weapons. I like weapons."

"Wolverine has done very well against many different types of weapons."

"He cannot defeat the Death Star," I said, "Besides that, Darth Vader has the power, the force. And he has the light saber."

Chase argued, "Wolverine's pretty powerful."

I countered, "But he does not have a light saber and the force." "The first thing Darth Vader would do is use his light saber to cut off Wolverine's hands and then Wolverine...would be...finished."

Chase said only, "Oh."

He had put up a good fight, but I won that round.

I wanted to get Chase something special for Christmas, but I found Christmas shopping difficult. A new hobby shop at the mall had caught my attention. I wandered in one day and looked around. They had large-scale remote control trucks that were made for off-road racing and would hit top speeds of 60 mph! I bought one for him.

On Christmas Day Chase had the truck out in our front yard right away jumping the curb and chasing cars down the street. He was driving it very well right from the beginning and having a blast with it.

Samantha came down from Delaware to visit us for a week over the Christmas holidays. She went with Chase and Ross to downtown Raleigh to watch the ball drop on New Year's Eve. When Samantha's dad had called ahead to ask if it would be okay for Samantha to come down, he told me Samantha was crazy about Chase. That didn't surprise me. A lot of young ladies were attracted to Chase. He was handsome, charming, and funny.

After Christmas Chase continued working at the pet store. He was still going to IOP regularly and once he had a job I let him have his car. A branch of the place he was going to for therapy in Raleigh opened in Cary. He moved to that branch so he wouldn't have so far to travel for IOP. By now his manager at the pet store was probably wondering why he had to be off by 5 p.m. every Tuesday and Thursday, but according to Chase, she never asked.

The insurance money was running out. They were only going to pay for a few more sessions of IOP and I sensed that Chase was drifting back to his old ways. He began to get back his old attitude because a lot of the kids who were attending IOP were leaving there and immediately going to light up a joint. Some of them were only there because they had had a DWI and had to attend to be able to keep their license. Chase wasn't happy that the insurance company was about to cut off funding for his IOP sessions.

I tried to explain to him that they couldn't fork over an endless supply of money. "Chase, I'll help you find another place to go even if I have to pay for it out of pocket. Don't worry about it," He came to me one day and asked if he could go to a North Carolina beach for the weekend with some friends. It was a couple of hours drive from home. He was going to pay for a hotel room and provide the transportation. He wasn't forthcoming about who these friends were.

"Chase, I'm not too sure that's a good idea," I said.

"Why not?"

"How can you be sure your friends will pay you back? What about gas money? You haven't been working long. You need to start saving your money for a deposit on an apartment."

From the time Chase got back home from Florida, he had made it clear that he wanted to get an apartment and get out on his own. I thought it was good he was thinking this way since he was twenty years old and not going to school. Chase didn't have a clear understanding, however, of what it costs to live independently. I tried to explain it to him on numerous occasions, but he didn't get it.

I arranged a meeting with his therapist at the new IOP location. I told her the situation and she began to go over the numbers with Chase about what it would cost for him to live on his own. Finally, he could see some of these harsh realities. "Chase, I know you have a goal of getting out on your own, and your mother and I want to help you do that. I believe you *can* do it. You have to understand that it's going to take a little more work, planning, and time than you initially thought it would."

He nodded in agreement, but I could tell he didn't like what he was hearing. Chase approached me again days later about going to the beach with his friends. I told him again that I didn't think it was a good idea. Then he tried to book a hotel room and found that he couldn't because of his age. He wanted me to book one for him in my name and then he was going to pay me back. I refused to do it, and he got angry with me.

He eventually found a rental house at the beach that the owners were happy to rent to him for the weekend. The closer the time drew for Chase to go on his trip, the more it bothered me. I could see him slipping away and I didn't know what to do. I was scared. I initiated another conversation with Chase about his planned trip to the beach. We argued, and I told him he couldn't go. He told me that he was going to go any way.

I told him that he couldn't because my name was on the title of his car. "That car belongs to me," If I say it doesn't go, then it doesn't go! In fact, I'm going to take the car back!"

"That's it! I'm moving out today," he shouted. With that, he went out the front door, jumped in his car and drove off. I knew he had to be at work soon. I began thinking how I could repossess the car. After all, it was legally mine, and he took it without my permission.

I contacted an attorney and she told me that I should call the police and tell them Chase was an unauthorized driver of that vehicle. I did call the Cary Police and they sent an officer by to talk to me.

"I can go with you and make sure that the situation doesn't get out of hand while you repossess the car," he said.

The only problem was that I no longer could find my key for the car. Without the key it was going to be difficult. I told him I would think it over and call him back if I decided to go take the car back. After I had some time to cool down, I decided to let it go for the time being. Chase didn't come back home that night or the night after that. We finally heard from him a few days later and he told us he had moved in with a friend, but that was all he was willing to share. I assumed he had discontinued his IOP sessions. He only had a couple more left that insurance would pay for. I decided to let the situation run its course. I had a feeling Chase and his new roommate, whoever he or she was, would soon get tired of each other, and he would want to come back home.

My friend Bob was concerned that my name was on the title and the insurance, while Chase had the car. The car made Chase a popular person among his circle of friends. Most of them didn't have a car due to drug and alcohol abuse. They had either lost their driver's licenses, or they didn't have a steady job so as to be able to afford a car. The car made Chase feel important because his friends needed him. He gave them rides everywhere, and they took advantage of it. Chase was generous and never wanted to deny anyone a ride if he could help it. These things didn't bother me as much as the fact that he might let other people drive his car. If someone asked to drive it, I didn't think he would tell them no. Who knew who might be driving the car? If another person was involved in a collision in that car, especially while under the influence, with my name on the title, I would be liable. I could get sued!

When I brought this up with my attorney and my friends, they all agreed that I needed to take action and fast. I called Chase and told him that I had decided to sign the title over to him. I said that I would help him get his own insurance. He agreed to meet me at our bank where we could have a notary public witness our signatures. I went to the bank as planned that day, but Chase never showed up. I called him, but he didn't answer his phone. For several days I tried to get in touch with him, but he did not return my telephone calls. Now I was getting angry. I was finally ready to give Chase the one thing he wanted more than anything—the car. Yet he wouldn't meet with me so I could sign it over to him.

Several days later I went to the pet store to confront Chase about the car. There was only one customer in the store and I tried to be discreet. Chase was busy stocking shelves, and I thought it would be simple for me to discuss this issue with him. One of Chase's coworkers could hear us talking. Chase didn't want to talk about it, at least not right then, but this was the only place where I could find him. I got him to agree on another time for us to meet to take care of the title transfer. I had noticed that the car was not in the parking lot. His explanation was, "I was out of gas money and I walked to work today."

"That was a long walk," I said. It was a good three–four mile walk. I didn't believe him for one second. "Chase, I don't believe that. If someone else is driving that car, you need to put a stop to that right away. Your mother and I are at risk if they are involved in a collision, because my name is on the title."

He didn't say anything. I told him I would see him in a few days at the bank to take care of the title transfer and I headed out the door. When I got home, I thought the situation over. Maybe Chase would not show up again to take care of the title transfer. He could be letting someone else drive the Corolla.

I decided to drive Kim's car back to the parking lot where the pet store was when Chase would be getting off from work. I then waited to see who would show up driving his car. I parked far enough away that

I wouldn't be spotted. I brought along my video camera to capture the moment.

I didn't have to wait long. A blonde girl showed up driving Chase's Corolla and parked near the pet store. I began shooting video while keeping a low profile. It wasn't long before Chase came out and got into the passenger side of the car. I could only see the back of the young lady's head. I assumed it was Lilith. Her hair looked bleached blonde to me. It was full and long, like Lilith's hair.

The car pulled out of the parking spot and I followed from a distance. It didn't take long for them to catch on that I was behind them. The driver began to speed up and tried to time a light so that I would be caught by it. I ran that red light. I knew there was a delay between my light turning red and the other light turning green. I glanced both ways before I zipped through the intersection. I continued to follow them across town and she made all sorts of maneuvers to try and give me the slip. My cell phone rang. It was Chase. "Dad! What are you doing? You're ruining my life!"

"No, Chase. I'm not ruining your life. *You* are doing that! All I want is my car back. Either that or you let me sign over the title, but I don't want anyone else driving that car with my name on the title, especially Lilith."

The young lady grabbed the cell phone away from Chase. "I'm *not* Lilith," she screamed.

"I don't know *who* you are, but you have no business driving *my* car!"

"I know I shouldn't be driving it. I only have a permit."

"Why don't you pull over and we can talk about this?"

"Why don't you just leave us alone?"

"You know, this isn't going to work out between you and Chase. He doesn't care about you. He's only using you for a place to stay right now."

"What do you know about our relationship? It's none of your business!"

"If you weren't driving my car, with my name on the title, without my permission right now, we wouldn't be having this conversation." She screamed obscenities at me. I later learned her name was Tatyana.

"Chase has a drug problem. This isn't going to last."

She cursed at me again. "Wow! You're using beautiful language for such a sweet, innocent little thing. You're a little tramp, just like Lilith." It started to rain hard. The shower seemed to come out of nowhere. Chase pulled up to a traffic light, and the girl jumped out of his car. I could imagine the steam coming out of her ears as she stomped away in the rain. Chase drove off and I continued to follow him. He only drove a couple more miles before he pulled over. I pulled up beside him in a convenience store parking lot. He got out of the car.

"Chase," I said, "all I want to do is sign the car over to you. Why is that so difficult? In the meantime, please don't let her or anyone else drive it!"

"All right Dad. I could meet you at the bank on Thursday at noon."

"Chase, I love you, buddy, and I'm sorry for all of this."

"I love you, too, Dad, and I'm sorry too," he replied. He gave me a tight hug.

"All right then. I'll see you on Thursday and we'll get this whole thing worked out."

Chase called the next day and begged me to apologize to Tatyana. "She's going to kick me out if you don't apologize," he said.

Yes, I owed her an apology even though she was driving my car without a driver's license. I wasn't ready to apologize. I politely refused.

Thursday came and Chase was there at the bank like he had promised. I signed the title over to him, and he followed me back to our house where I got on the telephone and got him a good deal on auto insurance. I promised to pay for the first 90 days. He would be on his own after that. When I signed over the title he got a new tag, not quite as fancy as the last one. He wasn't happy to be giving up his old "SPEEDY34" tag. I promised to save it for him. He thanked me for getting him such a good deal on his car insurance and headed out.

I did some research on Tatyana and discovered that she was from the Ukraine originally. That information was easy to find on Facebook. I thought she must have moved to the states when she was young because she had no detectable accent. The cover photo on her Facebook page was a sign that read, "Why not hugs AND drugs?" Great. Just the kind of girl Chase needed to be around. I found her Instagram account titled, "Angels on Drugs", and last but not least, she had tweeted a Charles Manson quote, "I am the devil and I am here to do the devil's work."

What was even more disturbing to me were some video clips that she had uploaded to Facebook in which she, Chase, and a young Hispanic man, named Ferdinand, were goofing off in the woods at a nearby park in the middle of the day. They seemed to be impaired. Ferdinand tried to start a fire in a fire ring in the park. Chase thought it was a bad idea and stomped the fire out. They all laughed and Tatyana said something strange about the fire pit being a portal to Hell.

Ferdinand looked close to Chase's age and his Facebook profile picture was a photo of a premature infant with a tube in its nose. Ferdinand must have fathered a child he was unlikely to be supporting. He was too busy playing around to have time to take care of a child. He was still a child himself. That made me angry.

Several days after I caught Tatyana driving Chase's car, I chatted with her via text.

She wrote, "I don't appreciate you calling me names the other day. You don't even know me. The least you could have done was apologize."

"I don't owe you an apology."

"You called me a tramp."

"Are you?"

"I'm not like Lilith and those other girls, Chase knows."

"To begin with, you were driving my car without a driver's license. Secondly, why would you want to be around Chase if you're not using drugs? Chase has a drug problem that I'm trying to help him overcome. He doesn't need to be around people who are a bad influence on him like you. For your information, I've already been to your Facebook wall and I noticed that your cover photo is a sign that reads, "Why Not Hugs AND Drugs?" So don't try and tell me you're not like those other girls. You're *exactly* like Lilith and those other girls."

"It's nice to know that you are so attracted to me that you went to my Facebook wall and snooped around."

"Trust me. You're not my type. I also noticed that you're a big fan of Vladimir Putin. That's surprising, considering you come from the Ukraine and he is taking over your homeland right now."

"That's right! I do like Putin and I hate the United States of America with a passion! I hope he crushes this country! It sucks!" She hung up.

I was lying in bed at six a.m. on a Saturday morning when the telephone rang. Kim answered it. It was Chase calling to say that he had run out of gas and needed help. He gave her an address, so I got up, dressed, punched the address into my GPS and headed down the road. I stopped at a station on the way to fill a gas can. The GPS took me to downtown Raleigh among the high-rise buildings. I drove past the address and looked for Chase's car but didn't see it. The street was one-way so I went around the block thinking I had missed his car somehow. I still didn't see the car so I went around the block again. Then it dawned on me that Chase had walked to this hotel. He must be inside, and the car someplace else. I began to pull into the circle drive when I spotted Chase coming out of the front door under the awning.

He got in the front seat of my truck and said, "I have a friend who needs a ride too." A young man emerged from the front door of the hotel. His head was down as he walked towards my truck, looking at the ground. His long brown hair draped in front of his face, obscuring it. He got into the back seat of my truck on the passenger side right behind Chase. I drove away from the hotel.

"This is Dylan," Chase said.

"Nice to meet you, Dylan."

"Where's the car, Chase."

"Uhmmm, I think it's that way," he pointed. I began to drive away from downtown in the direction Chase indicated. "This doesn't look right," he said.

"You don't remember where you left the car, Chase?"

"Not exactly."

"I think it's that direction." His friend pointed from the back seat.

"Okay." I began to follow his directions.

"Those trees. I remember those trees," he mumbled.

"Yeah. I do too," Chase said. I finally spotted the little blue Corolla on the side of the road. I pulled over and asked Chase for the keys. I put the gas I had in the tank and got in the car to try and start it. The battery was dead. Chase admitted to me that after he ran out of gas, he had desperately tried to restart the car until he had killed the battery. I pulled my truck in front of Chase's Corolla nose to nose with it. I pulled out my jumper cables and connected them to the two batteries. It was dark, rainy, and chilly out. The traffic was beginning to pick up. I gave the battery time to charge a little, and tried to start Chase's car, but to no avail. I tried to make sure the cables had a good connection and tried again—still nothing. So I told Chase I would have to come back for his car later.

I took Chase's friend, Dylan, home first. On the way he began to hiccup. I'd never heard hiccups like that before. He was extremely drunk. I thought he was going to throw up in the back seat of my truck. I followed his directions to his home and as I pulled up, it looked familiar. I remembered picking up one of his siblings, or so I thought, a few years earlier when I took Chase and a truckload of Cary High School football players to see a movie. Chase's friend Dylan piled out of the back seat of my truck and ran as hard as he could to the front door. I knew he was going to throw up. I said something to Chase later about his friend being drunk.

"Oh, no, Dad. He wasn't drunk."

"Chase. Come on, man. I wasn't born yesterday." I went back later and got Chase's car when it wasn't so rainy and cold and there was plenty of daylight to help me see what I was doing. I thought I had connected the cables to the battery, but I obviously hadn't made a good connection. I was able to get it started and drove it home. I kept it a few days before letting Chase know I had it running again.

I still kept track of Chase on Facebook. Aside from Tatyana and Ferdinand, I had noticed another young man named Freddy who was in Chase's circle of friends. Freddy was Chase's age. He was a black kid who was somewhat light-skinned. He had a mustache, a beard, and was of medium build. His arms were tattooed and he frequently posted photos of his drinking, marijuana, and drug parties. When Chase left to go to Florida for treatment, Freddy had become Lilith's new boyfriend. I didn't know much about Freddy other than what I saw on Facebook, but I didn't want Chase to have anything to do with him. Chase was going to get in serious trouble if he kept hanging out with Freddy.

A few weeks later I had a call on my cell phone from a number I didn't recognize. The voice on the other end said, "You can come get your son!" It was Tatyana. "You were right about him," she exclaimed.

"Where is he?" I asked.

"I locked him out of my apartment, and he's sitting outside my front door."

I hopped in my truck and headed over to the apartment complex where Tatyana lived. I drove around for quite awhile looking for Chase because I wasn't sure exactly which apartment she lived in. I finally spotted him sitting on the landing at the top of a flight of stairs, outside the door to her apartment. He was sitting on his footlocker. It was the same footlocker we had bought him when he first went to Hargrave Military Academy. I didn't criticize him or say, "I told you so." I helped him load his footlocker into the back of my truck and headed home. I was glad Chase was coming back home.

The next day, Tatyana called me to tell me that Chase had a necklace that belonged to her, which she would like to have back. I told her that I would see what I could do. I talked to Chase about the necklace. He admitted that he had it. I told him he should return it to her. One day I spotted it among some of his things which he had left on the kitchen counter. It had a crystal in it and the design was new age. I thought about taking it to Tatyana myself, but decided it would be better to get Chase to do the right thing. I told Chase again that he should return Tatyana's necklace. "She has a lot of things that belong to me in her apartment," he said. "She's not letting me back in to get my things, so I'm going to keep her necklace until she lets me back in to get my stuff." I called Tatyana and told her what Chase had said.

"He doesn't have anything here," she said. He's only being vindictive. He's looking for any excuse to get back into my apartment. He's mad that we broke up."

"Okay. I'll talk to him."

I mentioned the necklace to Chase again. "Chase, do you have things in Tatyana's apartment still?"

"Yes."

"What specifically does she have of yours?"

"I don't know, but I know there are things there that belong to me. I only want the chance to go look through the apartment and get anything that is mine."

"Chase, you don't own anything of much value. Do the right thing.

Let this go and return her necklace." He pursed his lips and shook his head.

Two days later, Tatyana called me again. "Chase sent some people to my apartment to scope it out and to intimidate me. I barely know them. I wish I hadn't let them in. They wouldn't leave. After I threatened to call the police, they finally left."

"What makes you think Chase knows these people or had anything to do with them?"

"It's too much of a coincidence that they would come by now. I barely know them and I know he has connections to them. It was two guys and a girl. They acted strange. Chase has been acting so aggressive towards me. He keeps saying he has things in my apartment, but I don't have any of his stuff. He came here the other day and tried to force his way in. He broke the chain on the door. I had to call my step-dad to come repair it."

"Tatyana. I'll talk to him, but he's a grown man. I can't *make* him do anything. If you're that scared, I suggest you go to the courthouse and file a restraining order." Chase denied knowing anything about the people Tatyana said came to her apartment. He still had her necklace and he still wanted to get into her apartment to get his things back. I told him again that he needed to drop it and move on.

Tatyana called again the next day. "I heard noises outside my apartment window last night. I heard voices. I know Chase sent people over here. They're going to try to break in. They're going to do something to me. I couldn't even sleep last night I was so scared."

"Did you file a restraining order yet?"

"Not yet. But I'll get my mother to go to the courthouse with me tomorrow to do it."

"You need to do that Tatyana. In the meantime, I'll keep trying to talk some sense into Chase. I've told him he needs to drop all of this and return your necklace. I'm sorry you're going through all of this. I can only do so much. Chase is a grown man."

Thirty minutes after I got off the phone with Tatyana, I had a call from her mother. "Mr. Rodgers?"

"Yes."

"My name is Inga Barnett. I'm Tatyana's mother." She spoke fluent English with a Russian accent. She seemed very nice. "Can you please talk to Chase," she asked politely. "Tatyana is scared to death that he or some of his friends are going to do something bad to her."

"Mrs. Barnett, thank you for calling. I will talk to Chase. Please understand that he is a grown man and that I have no control over him. I will do my best. I told Tatyana that she should go to the courthouse and file a restraining order against Chase. I'm sorry she is going through this. I've never known Chase to be the type to hurt anyone. I don't think he would, but tell her to get the restraining order to be on the safe side."

I did talk with Chase again and he still wasn't willing to let it go. After a couple of weeks, he finally returned Tatyana's necklace to her and she let him in her apartment to recover a few small items. There was nothing of real significance, as I had thought. Chase settled back in at our home and things seemed to be going along okay.

Several weeks passed. Early in May of 2014, Chase told Kim and me that he had decided to move back to Florida. I thought it was probably an idea that would pass. He soon announced, however, that the pet store where he was working had a chain store in Florida close to Deerfield Beach and that they had approved a transfer for him. He hadn't even left, and I already missed him. I was also afraid for him.

"Chase, why are you going to Florida?" I asked.

"Dad, all of my friends from high school are either in college or the military. The only people my age that still live here are addicts. The people I've been hanging around with here are a bad influence. I need to get away from them."

"Chase, you need to let me help you get back into IOP. There are some things *you* need to change. You can't run from your problems. Until you change some of those things about yourself, you will attract people who are a bad influence wherever you go."

Chase looked dumbfounded as he always did when he couldn't quite grasp what I was saying.

"Go back to church with us, Chase. You can get involved with the youth group. You will find people your age. You can find messed up people everywhere, but church is at least a good place to start looking for better people to be around. Stay here and we'll go fishing together. We'll go hunting and go to the range and target practice. We'll have fun! Don't leave."

"I've already done the transfer. I've already made arrangements for a place to stay. I have it all worked out. You can come visit me down there and we can go fishing in Florida. He had made up his mind, and I knew I wasn't going to change it.

"Okay, buddy," I said, "Be careful and remember that your mother, Justin, and I love you. If you need anything, let me know."

Chase loved movies and super heroes, and movies about super heroes were his favorites. Spider Man was among his favorite super heroes. The intro to his football highlight video we'd made years earlier had consisted of music from the original Amazing Spiderman. Chase rounded up Kim, Justin, and me one evening. He insisted that we all go together to see the latest Spiderman movie. I couldn't tell you much about that movie now, but I enjoyed going because we were all spending time together as a family and doing something Chase wanted to do.

A few days earlier I had ordered identical medallions for Chase and Justin. You may recall that when Chase was thirteen, I read a book titled, "Raising a Modern Day Knight." My friend Bob and I went through the Raising a Modern Day Knight study together and I had discussed the principles with both of my boys. I had asked for their input and we had designed a manhood crest that we felt represented the men in our family. I had gone through the first ceremony with Chase, but that was as far as we had made it. Sometimes we let life get in the way of the most important things. Bob and I even purchased a sword to be used in the manhood ceremonies, which we had never used. I had intended to have our manhood crest printed out and framed for each of my boys, but I never got around to it.

I wanted to send both Chase and Justin a message and to give them something that would be a reminder of their faith. Soldiers know what a challenge coin is. It is a special coin the size of a silver dollar. Soldiers sometimes are given these coins to commemorate a particular battle or campaign they have fought in. I found challenge coins on a website that showed on both sides, a knight in armor.

A verse from Ephesians 6:10-13 was on the coin. Finally, my brethren, be strong in the Lord, and in the power of his might. 11 Put on the whole armour of God, that ye may be able to stand against the wiles of the devil. 12 For we wrestle not against flesh and blood, but against principalities, against powers, against the rulers of the darkness of this world, against spiritual wickedness in high places. 13 Wherefore take unto you the whole armour of God, that ye may be able to withstand in the evil day, and having done all, to stand.

The passage goes on to describe each piece of armor that a Roman soldier would have worn in that day. There is an analogy made between the pieces of armor of the soldier and the things a person needs to do to protect themselves from evil. We all struggle between good and evil at times. This verse reminds us of the struggle and teaches us how to be victorious in the struggle against evil within ourselves as well as that outside us. I ordered a chain with a special piece that holds the challenge coin so that it could be worn around the neck, used as a key chain, or without the chain, it could be displayed on a stand. I presented Chase and Justin with these medallions and ordered one for myself later. Chase was planning to leave for Florida within days. About that time, I came home to find a couple of small packages on the dining room table.

"Dad! What's in the packages," Justin asked excitedly. I teased him a bit before I gave him and Chase their packages and let them open them. I explained to them what they were and the significance behind them. "I'm not superstitious," I said. "You boys know that. There is no power in these medallions. The medallions are symbolic. They are there to remind you of some very important principles." I read them the scripture verses from Ephesians 6.

It was late on a Thursday afternoon, May 29, 2014 and I was talking on my cell phone with my buddy Bob. He travels on business regularly to a town a couple of hours away. He likes to call me on his drive back into town sometimes and chat. He asked what I had been up to and about Justin and Kim. Finally he got around to asking about Chase. I told him that Chase was supposed to be moving to Florida. In fact, he had told us he was leaving this very day, and he had told Kim that he would stop by and see us before he left.

It was getting late, and we still hadn't seen him. Kim was upset about that. Justin and Kim were in the living room watching television, and, as I often do while talking on the phone, I was pacing around. I went outside so my conversation wouldn't disturb the two of them. I was under our carport at first, then pacing around in the driveway near the carport. Bob and I continued to talk about Chase.

A police cruiser pulled up on the curb and stopped near our driveway. I didn't think much of it. Over the years, I had often seen police cruisers stop at that very spot and seen the officer doing paperwork for a few minutes before pulling away. There is another street that dead-ends right into our driveway. I'm not sure why they stop there. It's a convenient place to pull over, I suppose. This time, however, the officer got out of the car. He had a clipboard in his hand and he looked down at the clipboard as he slowly took a few steps. He made his way around the front end of the cruiser and began to walk up our driveway. "Bob, I need to go," I said. "Chase must be in some kind of trouble. A police cruiser pulled up and the officer is coming up my driveway."

"Oh, okay." Sensing that I needed to go right away, he hung up. I started walking down our driveway to meet the officer half way. As he approached, he was still looking down at his clipboard. Standing right in front of me, he looked up.

"Mr. Smith?"

"Uh, no sir."

"You're not Mr. Smith?"

"No sir. I'm Darryl Rodgers."

"This is xxx Kingsland Drive, right?"

"Yes it is."

"How long have you lived here?"

"Twenty-four years, sir."

"And you're not Mr. Smith," he asked again as he fumbled through the papers on his clipboard.

"No sir, I'm not."

"Oh. You said you're Mr. Rodgers, right?"

"Yes sir."

"Mr. Rodgers. There's been a wreck on I-40. Chase's car ran off the road and hit a tree. He died at the scene. I'm so sorry." I stood there and looked at him for what seemed like an eternity. For me, time had stopped. I had expected him to say that Chase was in jail or in some other kind of trouble. NO! He couldn't be dead! My shoulders slumped, and it felt as though all of my energy went out of me at that moment.

"What happened?" I asked.

"Chase wasn't driving. There was a young lady driving his car. I believe her name was Tatyana. There was a Dylan Michael Smith in the back seat. Both of them were taken to the hospital with serious injuries."

"He's dead?" I asked in disbelief.

He looked down. "Yes, sir."

"This must be a very difficult part of your job. I'm so sorry you have to do this."

"It's okay, Mr. Rodgers. Is the rest of your family inside? Would you like me to go in and tell them?"

"No. That's my job. My wife and other son are sitting in the living room."

"Would you like me to go with you for support?"

"Yes. That would be good if you wouldn't mind."

My heart was racing as I turned and headed for our front door. The officer followed close behind. I already knew where they were sitting. When I opened the door, I turned to my right and there was Kim sitting in our recliner. Justin was across the room in the back corner reclining on the sofa. In the past any time I have had bad news, Kim has urged me not to beat around the bush, but to come straight out and say it. "I have something I have to tell both of you," I announced. I glanced at Kim then over at Justin, then back to Kim quickly. I looked her right in the eye.

"Chase was involved in a wreck. He was killed." My wife's mouth flew open. She gasped and her hand immediately went to her face, her palm covering her mouth. It seemed as if all the blood drained from her face. When she was finally able to gain her composure, she asked, "When did it happen?"

"Around five o'clock, I believe, ma'am," said the officer. "It was during rush hour traffic. She apparently tried to change lanes and there was a car in her blind spot. Eyewitnesses reported that the other car blew the horn and she lost control of Chase's car when she tried to move back into the other lane. They ran off the road and hit a tree. Chase was pronounced dead at the scene." I heard a sob from the other side of the room.

"It hurts so bad," Justin cried out.

"Oh, Justin!" Kim had forgotten he was in the room. He was up from the sofa now and she went to embrace him. We all cried uncontrollably.

"Why wouldn't he listen to me? Why wouldn't he listen to me," I asked over and over.

"I know honey," Kim tried to console me.

"I tried to warn him," I sobbed.

"You did everything you could." I felt sorry for the police officer. He stood there motionless. There was nothing he could do but try to comfort us and wait for us to ask questions. It must have been awkward for him and horrible to have to deliver this kind of news.

"Chase didn't do anything wrong," he said. "He wasn't driving. This is not his fault." I asked him about the condition of Chase's body. "There's very little damage to the body. It looks like he's sleeping, so I don't know what your family's beliefs are, but if you want an open casket, I think you will probably be able to have one."

Ironically, we learned that Chase was the only one wearing a seatbelt and the only person who was killed.

"We suspect that she was impaired," the officer said. "We found two marijuana cigarettes in her purse. We're investigating. These things usually take some time. Please be patient with us. Dylan and Tatyana are both at Wake Med on New Bern Avenue. Dylan was in the back seat and broke both of his legs. She broke her back, her pelvis, some ribs, and punctured both lungs." He stayed with us awhile longer and gave us his card before he left. The officer told us he would be in touch, and that we could call if we needed anything or had any questions.

I began to make phone calls to family and friends. Kim did the same. I went to Facebook to notify some people via private message. Most of our local friends on Facebook already knew. They knew before we did. I went online and found a news report with photos of the wreck. It looked bad. There were a lot of rescue workers in the photos and according to reports the wreck had traffic backed up for miles on I-40. It happened in a curve right past the Wade Avenue exit. I looked through the list of contacts in my phone and found Wendy's number. She answered right away. I didn't know what to say. "Wendy?"

"Yes."

"This is Mr. Rodgers. Where are you?"

"I'm in Georgia right now."

"I have something I have to tell you. Chase was killed in a terrible wreck a couple of hours ago." The other end of the line was silent. "I'm sorry to have to tell you this. Are you okay?"

There was a long pause. I knew she wasn't okay. Neither was I, and telling her this was just about as difficult for me as telling Kim and Justin. I told her that I would try to keep her informed of the funeral arrangements. Wendy told me later that she had been visiting friends and was on her way to our house to see Chase. She got tired and had to stop in Georgia for the night. Chase had told her to try and hurry because he had to leave for Florida soon.

I looked at Dylan's Facebook wall. Already the fights had begun. People were leveling different accusations at Tatyana. Her friends were coming to her rescue. One of her friends named Eva posted this:

"She wasn't even high. She smoked earlier in that day. I know the actual story because I went to the hospital and heard it for myself."

The Raleigh Police charged Tatyana with Misdemeanor Death by Motor Vehicle, Operating a Motor Vehicle Without a Driver's License, Provisional DWI—pending the toxicology report, and a minor possession charge for the few marijuana cigarettes they found in her purse. She would only get the Felony Death by Motor Vehicle if they could prove she was impaired which would be nearly impossible in North Carolina because there is no legal limit when it comes to marijuana. It's difficult to believe this, but apparently operating a motor vehicle without a driver's license and then being at fault in a fatal collision is not a big deal as far as the law is concerned.

We contacted the funeral home and set up a time when we could go by and talk to the director and begin to make plans. Things were happening very quickly. In the midst of making and receiving phone calls, I went to our bedroom and fell face down on the bed and cried like a baby for an hour. I've never felt emotional pain that intense before. After twenty years, my precious Chase, my little buddy was gone from this earth forever. If only I could have found a way to get him to listen to me.

Chapter Ten

SAYING GOODBYE

I CAN REMEMBER THIS DREAM VERY VIVIDLY. Chase came to me. I don't know exactly where we were. There were no objects or other people around. There was only Chase and me. There was a partition between us. It was clear and I could see Chase through it. I don't believe it was made of water, but it had properties very similar to water. Imagine a wall of clear water a foot thick but with no top or bottom. I could see his face right up next to the partition. The water-like substance seemed to have a ripple effect that sometimes distorted Chase's face. We stood there and looked at each other. Neither of us spoke. It's as if we both knew there was no point in trying to speak. Neither of us would be able to hear the other. Chase was somewhere I couldn't go at least not right now. It was upsetting that I could see him but not talk to him or get to where he was, but at the same time it was comforting to see him and know he was okay. I think that is what it was all about. Chase was letting me know he was okay.

Kim and I hardly slept a wink that night. The next morning I was up early and I went online. I was looking through Facebook trying to see what Chase's friends were saying; trying to think of anyone I still might need to notify.

I got a private message from Susan, Ross's mother. Ross had been one of Chase's best friends from Hargrave Military Academy. He had played on the Hargrave football team with Chase and was now playing at Presbyterian College in South Carolina. Susan wanted to know if we needed anything or if they could come over and bring us breakfast. It was 5:15 am. I couldn't believe anyone else was up besides me. "Sure! That would be fine," I wrote her back.

In less than an hour, Susan, Ross, and Ross's sister, Madison were at our front door. They brought bagels and coffee with them. We all sat at the dining room table and talked while we munched on bagels. We told Susan how much we would like to have a Hargrave #34 football jersey for Chase to be dressed in. She said she would take care of it for us. Ross is a quiet young man, but it was at that point that I realized how close he and Chase had been. I could tell he was hurting.

All that occurred over the next few days are a blur for me now. Everything happened so fast. Family began to show up. Friends and neighbors came by. People who were friends with Chase but whom I didn't know came by. The telephone rang. Friends and family from all over were calling. News reporters called and asked questions. Kim and I had to meet with the funeral director several times and with the preacher. We decided to put David in charge of the ceremony. David, is the father of Alex, one of Chase's childhood friends who had lived next door for many years.

My niece, Amy is married to Doug who is a preacher. We asked Doug to speak. Susan contacted Chase's high school football coach from Hargrave for me. She got him to agree to speak at Chase's funeral.

We were going to have a visitation and a memorial service. I had never planned a funeral before. I kept busy. I wanted people to know who Chase was. I wanted them to discover things about Chase that they never knew. I pulled his Boy Scout uniform out of the closet along with his merit badge sash and some of his sports trophies. I dragged out two pairs of his football cleats. On one pair he had used a black marker to write the word ZOOM down the side along with some flames. I took some of these items to the funeral home to be displayed where people could see them as they walked in. Chase's senior year football highlight video would be playing on a T.V. monitor overhead. We borrowed a #34 jersey from Cary High to display and Lindenwood-Belleville University sent us a jersey with 48 on it, the number he wore there.

Family soon began arriving. First, Kim's brother Eric, his wife, Clare, their daughter Erica, and Kim's mother, Jean drove in from Greenville, South Carolina. Eric helped me put together well over 100 photos for the funeral director to use in a slide show that would be displayed on other monitors. Clare is great at organizing and is always eager to serve people. She jumped in, answered the phone, and greeted people at the door when we couldn't be home. She worked hard at making our lives easier during a very difficult time. She went to the store and bought us a football that was placed in an area at the funeral home where Chase's teammates would see it and be able to sign it.

More family and friends arrived. People brought food. We had a lot of food. I didn't feel much like eating, but what food I ate was good. I appreciated people bringing it as it helped feed us all, including our extended family. A sense of calm came over me from the moment the police officer told me of Chase's death. I felt no anger toward anyone. I kept telling people that I only wanted to make something positive come of this, and I meant it.

On Sunday Justin rode with Susan, Ross, and Madison out to the crash site. I was not far behind them. Ross had made a cross that he wanted to leave there. He already had it pushed into the ground by the time I arrived. It was about three feet tall and painted white with Chase's football number, 34 at the top, his initials, CMR, a football, an orange tiger paw for Hargrave, and a heart underneath that. On the horizontal piece was a scripture verse: "So we are always confident, knowing that while we are at home in the body, we are absent from the Lord. For we walk by faith, and not by sight. We are confident, yes well pleased to be absent from the body and to be present with the Lord. —1 Corinthians 5:6–8." Ross is a quiet guy, but there is a lot going on inside of him. I could feel his love for Chase. Susan helped me secure pallbearers. Ross, Brice, David, and Nathan, all from Hargrave; Gavin and Ethan, from Cary High. All of the pallbearers were former high school football teammates of Chase's except for his friend and former Hargrave roommate, Brice.

The police called several times over the next few days. They told me they had found $200 cash in a pocket of a pair of jeans that belonged to Chase. They also found his wallet. Monte rode with me to the place where they instructed me to come, and we met the officer in charge of the investigation. He turned those items over to me. He asked if there was anything else that I would like for them to look for.

I told him I had given Chase a medallion a few days before the wreck. "Don't worry about it too much. I know you guys are busy with way more important things right now. It's of very little monetary value but it would mean a lot to me to know that he had it with him."

"Okay. We'll look for it," he assured me.

My sister-in-law, Clare had asked if there were any people we didn't want to see at the visitation or the memorial service. I told her I didn't want to see Lilith or any of her friends. I didn't want to talk to any of the drug addicts right then. I wasn't angry with them, but I wasn't ready to see them either.

The lead investigator with the Raleigh police called and told me that Tatyana's mother, Inga wanted to know if she could have my telephone number. I told him that was fine. Somewhere during all the confusion I had missed a call from her. I got the message later, but by that time I wasn't sure I wanted to talk with her. I didn't want to say anything that might somehow jeopardize the investigation. I decided to wait and maybe call her later.

The funeral director approached Kim, Justin, and me, and asked if we would like to spend some time alone with Chase before people began arriving. We told her we would like to. We walked into the room where people would later stand in line to view the body and then greet us. There was the casket, open, Chase's body inside. The three of us walked up to the casket together. They had shaved his beard as we had requested. His hair looked nice and he was dressed in his #34 Hargrave football jersey. I stood there and looked at him for a little while. Then I placed my hand on his chest. It felt hard as a rock. I looked at his face. Of course his eyes were closed and his face expressionless. They had done a good job with the makeup, but I could see some slight bruising around the cheeks.

None of us cried. I think we were all cried out. For some reason viewing the body wasn't as emotional for us as it apparently is for a lot of people. I think that was because we knew that wasn't Chase. Without

Chase's spirit, his lifeless body didn't look like him. The big smile, the twinkle in the eyes, the infectious laugh, and the kid who was always wired up and on the move was no longer present.

"This isn't Chase," I said. "This is only the body that housed Chase for 20 years. The real Chase is no longer here. He's in heaven now." I firmly believe Chase is in heaven because he accepted Christ as his personal Lord and savior when he was a little boy. Based on the questions his pastor asked him and how Chase answered those questions, I believe he is in Heaven. Certainly he made some decisions that I did not approve of and that I don't believe God would approve of. Haven't we all?

Steve, One of my friends and neighbors, a guy I used to duck hunt with, showed up early at the funeral home for visitation. We invited him in to chat. Steve had made a point a few years earlier of stopping by to take Chase and me with him for a boat ride on Jordan Lake. It was a pre-season duck-scouting trip. He pointed out bald eagles, and we found pottery shards left behind by American Indians. Chase always enjoyed getting out and exploring.

Then Pete and his wife Sherry, whom we met at a church where we were once members and where Chase was baptized, came in. Pete had edited Chase's football highlight video for me a couple of years earlier. This video was playing on the TV monitor as he and Sherry walked in the front door of the funeral home. We embraced.

Kim and I made our way to an area where we could wait to greet people. We were unable to see the casket from where we stood unless we took a few steps forward. A line formed. Someone approached me and told me we needed to keep the line moving. I took that to mean we should spend a little less time with each person. That was difficult because there was such an outpouring of love from the people arriving. I wanted to spend as much time as possible with each one.

Someone else told me the line was all the way out the front door. I found myself working my way forward down the line to try to speed things along. The casket came into view to my right. Suddenly I noticed Lilith and Ashton approaching the casket. As she saw Chase's body, Lilith put both hands over her mouth, and her face turned red. Ashton stood motionless, his eyes huge. He looked like a scared little boy. I had a sudden change of heart. I felt like I needed to approach them, but Clare didn't see me coming and quickly stepped in and asked the two of them to leave.

One of Chase's old soccer coaches came by, then his Boy Scout leaders and other Boy Scouts, football teammates, Kim's co-workers, friends, and family. Then I spotted Viktor. I hadn't seen him in a long time, so it took me a few seconds to recognize him. He was a Russian kid who had played football with Chase on the JV team his freshman year. He was in the U.S. Navy now and had driven all the way from Norfolk, Virginia.

Then another young man approached me. Before he ever got to me I could see he was in pain. His face was beet red, and tears streamed down his cheeks. He was a friend of Chase's from Boy Scouts. They were the same age. Their high school football teams had played against each other. I never knew this young man had such deep feelings. I hugged him and tried to comfort him as he sobbed. Finally, the visitation was over. We went home to rest. Later I found out that some people who came left because the line was so long. Many elderly people can't stand for that long.

The next day the memorial service was held at the church we had been attending for the past ten years. It had a large sanctuary, so we felt confident it would hold everyone. Dylan Smith's mother approached me before the service, along with Dylan's uncle, Carter. They wanted to view the body. The funeral home staff was about to seal the casket. At this point they were only allowing family to view the body. I asked for permission and quickly escorted the two of them down front.

My friend, David conducted the service. There were several other speakers, including Luke, one of Chase's teammates from Cary High, Coach Tanner, Chase's coach from Hargrave, and Doug, the husband of my niece Amy. All of the speakers had very good things to say. I was particularly impressed with how poised Chase's friend Luke was for his age. Like Chase, he was twenty years old. Standing in front of such a large group of people and delivering a eulogy for his friend had to be difficult. We used recorded music to keep things simple. Kim did a good job of picking out the songs. The service closed with the playing of Taps.

The family left first. I stopped to embrace Dennis, an old coworker and good friend of mine, as I headed out the door. It had been a long time since I had seen him. I wept in his embrace. We got into the limousine that was waiting for us and the motorcade began its drive across town. All of the funeral home staff was friendly, kind, and professional. I especially took a liking to our limo driver who talked with us during the drive. Timing dictated that we drive across town during rush hour traffic to the only cemetery in Cary. The Cary Police did an outstanding job with the escort. We were amazed to find out how many off-duty officers had come in on their day off to help.

We left the limo at the cemetery and made our way under the shade canopy to take our seats. Other people gathered around as David and Doug spoke the final words. After the service, we spoke with family and any others who approached us. The crowd had thinned when David approached.

"Lilith and Ashton are here. They'd like to speak to you. Is that okay now or should I ask them to leave?"

"It's okay now. Tell them to come on over." Lilith and Ashton stood at a distance. I watched as David went to them and told them they were welcome to come speak with me. They had both looked as they had the day before. Lilith was red-faced and teary while Ashton had that frightened look.

"I'm so sorry," she sobbed.

I hugged her and tried to comfort her as she cried. "I know, Lilith. I know."

"You probably hate me, and I can understand that. I loved Chase. He was such a sweet kid."

"I know you did, Lilith. I don't hate you. I'm not even mad at you."

"He's the fourth boy I've dated who has been killed in a car wreck," she said, as she wiped away her tears.

I had gradually released my hug with Lilith. I put my right arm around Ashton's shoulder. "I only want the two of you to learn from this. Ultimately, it was the lifestyle that killed Chase. It was the choices he made, the people he associated with, and the drugs and alcohol. God loves you and I love you. I only want to see you change for the better. I want to see something positive come of this. I want to see you stop with the drugs and alcohol."

Lilith and Ashton stared at me. They seemed to be at a loss for words.

I smiled, "Thanks for coming by to talk with me. Have a nice after-noon." I shook hands and chatted briefly with all of the pallbearers. I thanked them for serving.

Brice approached me. I strained to hear him. His voice was soft, barely above a whisper. He smiled gently. "I'm sorry for your loss."

I shook his hand and pulled him in for a hug. "Brice, Chase loved you. I'm sorry I gave you such a hard time when you two were room-mates at Hargrave. I know I was out of line, but I was only trying to pro-tect Chase. I was trying to prevent something like this."

"It's okay. I realize now how much you loved him. You did things that no other dad would have cared enough to do. As far as the drugs go, I'll never touch the stuff again." He broke eye contact with me and looked at the ground. "Chase was under a lot of pressure while he was at Hargrave."

"I know." With that, I released him and moved on. I never quite un-derstood that. I never intended to put any pressure on Chase. He was a playful kid who never grew up. That's part of what made him so much fun to be with. I didn't want to change that, only temper it so that he could make it on his own one day.

A few days later, I ordered Justin a new medallion and I placed his around my neck. Then I drove to the hospital and went up to Dylan's room. When I got to his room, the door was open and the light was off. He was asleep and by himself. There was some light in the room from the window, but it was close to sunset and even the light from the win-dow was growing dim. I sat down in a chair at the foot of his bed and waited for him to wake up. Heavy metal music screamed from a radio on the window ledge. I couldn't make out any of the words to the music. It was only screaming and horrible-sounding guitar chords. It sounded as if the music were coming straight from Hell.

I bowed my head and prayed. He kept sleeping. I asked God to give me strength and the right words to reach Dylan. I asked him to speak through me. I prayed for Dylan's healing and that the wreck might be a wake up call for him to change his life. I texted Doug and asked him to pray with me. Doug is my niece, Amy's husband. We have what seems to be a spiritual connection because Doug is a godly man. He's a preacher like my dad was, and he looked up to my Dad a lot. We both had served in the military and loved the game of football. It was comforting knowing I had him in my corner as I prayed. The covers were over Dylan's legs, so I couldn't see them. After awhile one of the nurses came in to tend to him. He rolled over and went right back to sleep. I stayed in my seat.

Finally he stirred a bit and sat up partially in his bed. He saw me sitting there and tried to focus, rubbing his eyes. "Who are you?" he asked. He looked confused.

"I'm Darryl Rodgers."

He scratched his head. "Oh! You're Chase's dad! Oh, my God! I'm so sorry." He looked like he was going to cry. He turned the radio off and sat up the rest of the way. I pulled my chair over next to his bed. We talked for a while about Chase and him. I talked about the boys' camp that I ran at one time. Dylan was raised by a single mom. I told him that it must be difficult growing up without a dad around. He nodded. He pulled back the covers and showed me his legs. Metal rods poked through the skin. It was a mess. He described his injuries to me in detail. His legs were badly broken. I told him about the medallion I had given Chase. He said Chase wasn't wearing it when the wreck occurred and he had never seen it before. Before I left, I pulled Justin's medallion from around my neck and I gave it to him.

"No. This belongs to your son," he said with a hurt look.

"It's okay. I've already ordered him another one. Keep it." Tatyana was in a room on another floor above Dylan. She was in a neck brace and she would use a wheelchair to come down and visit him every so often. I thought about visiting her while I was there, but I wasn't ready for that yet, and I didn't want to do or say anything that might jeopardize the police investigation.

I said a short prayer for Dylan, gave him a hug, and left. I later called Dylan's mother. Dylan seemed to be in desperate need of more positive male role models in his life. Maybe it was a little late for that, but I thought it was worth a try. She had been attending the same church we had attended. I asked her if anyone from the church had been to visit Dylan and she told me they had not as far as she knew. I contacted a gentleman who was on the staff at that church and asked him if he could get someone from the church to visit Dylan. He said he would, but it never happened. I felt like it was an opportunity missed.

The medallion I gave to Chase had become a symbol for me—a way to remember him. The police hadn't been able to find it. I had been out to the crash site and tried to find it. I sent one to each of the pallbearers as a token of my appreciation along with a thank you note. Each note was different and tailored to each individual pallbearer. I had hoped the medallion would also be a symbol for them; something to remember Chase by, that also would remind them to be men of character.

Kim and I went to the cemetery on Father's Day. She took with her a new arrangement of flowers along with a small plaque she had made with a football on it and Chase's jersey number. While we were there, I wandered around the cemetery and noticed another footstone that belonged to a young man named Timothy. I looked him up online. The initial report stated that he had died when he took LSD that had been offered to him by another young man. I found out later that he had been given a synthetic drug called, 251-NBOMe. Another young life wasted, all because of drugs.

It was quite a way to spend time on Father's Day, visiting our older son's grave. No one should have to bury their child. It's not the way things are supposed to be, but we live in a broken world. Often things are not as they should be. Father's Day should be a time when fathers celebrate with their children, doing something fun together. It didn't seem real that Chase's body was in that casket buried six feet down or that he was no longer with us, cutting up and making everyone laugh. I felt numb.

In the days that followed Chase's death I could hear his voice calling to me, "Dad. Dad." Lest you think I've lost my marbles, let me add that I'd never heard nor ever thought I heard an audible voice. Yet I felt as though Chase was trying to tell me something, trying to get my attention. I don't know exactly what to make of this experience. I can only tell you what happened. I'm confident that one day I will understand what Chase was trying to tell me.

We were left with Chase's two guinea pigs, Little Buddy and Piggy Smalls. We didn't have time to take care of them. There had to be someone who would love to have them. I ran an ad on Craigslist. At first I was asking for a little money for the Guinea pigs and the cages, but then I decided to give them away. I had an email response from a young lady named Kylie. At first I thought she might be Chase's friend Kylie. I gave her my number and she called to get more information about the guinea pigs and cages. It wasn't Chase's friend. This Kylie was a twelve-year old girl. Her mother also called to confirm everything. She asked where I lived. When I gave her my address, she couldn't believe it. This Kylie's grandmother, her mother, was my neighbor across the street. Kylie lived a forty-five-minute drive away. Her father came by the next day after work and picked up the cages along with Little Buddy and Piggy Smalls. My neighbor informs me that Kylie feeds the guinea pigs well and gives them a lot of love.

It was late June, 2014. Kim and I were at home one evening when I spotted someone through the blinds coming up our walk. She was a blonde and a stranger. When I opened the door to see who it was, this attractive woman standing there with a strange look on her face said, "Mr. Rodgers? I'm Inga Barnett, Tatyana's mother." She stood there awkwardly. I could see the pain in her eyes. She looked scared to death of how I might react.

"Ohhh!" I said. "Please come in!" She sat down in one of our recliners while Kim and I sat next to each other on the sofa.

She told us over and over how sorry she was about Chase. She cried. "I can't imagine what you must be going through. I don't know what I would have done." She told us that Tatyana said she had not smoked any marijuana the day of the wreck. In fact, Tatyana had told her she hadn't smoked any marijuana for two or three weeks.

I didn't believe what Tatyana had told her, but I did want to comfort this woman. She hadn't done anything wrong. I could easily have been in her shoes. It could have been Tatyana who was dead and Chase who was behind the wheel and being charged with a DWI. I wanted to comfort her, but I hesitated. I was afraid I might say something that would let Tatyana off the hook. "We'll have to wait and let the police complete their investigation," I said.

She told us how volatile Tatyana was at times. She said that she had been suicidal in the past. I didn't think much of that. A lot of teenagers go through rough times and contemplate suicide. Most teens get through those tumultuous years when the hormones are raging and they are so self-conscious of their appearance.

I was shocked when Kim told Inga firmly how much the funeral services cost us.

"Our finances aren't the best right now, but we'll see what we can do to help out with the money," Inga said.

I felt bad for her. I wanted to tell her not to worry about the money, but I didn't say anything.

She told us that Tatyana's past had been turbulent. She was born in the Ukraine. Tatyana's father had abandoned them when Tatyana was young. They had moved to the United States when Tatyana was six years old. It was when she was in middle school that Tatyana's mother and stepfather began to have problems with her. She moved out and into her own apartment when she was sixteen. She never finished high school. When Inga left our house, I ached for her. That poor lady. She was so nice. It wasn't fair that she had to go through this.

Chapter Eleven

SOMETHING POSITIVE

FREDDY WAS ONE OF CHASE'S FRIENDS whom I believed had been
a very bad influence on him. I had never met Freddy in person, but
his Facebook posts gave me a negative impression. He made what I
considered to be lewd and rude comments in his posts. He liked to post
emojis of little pistols to make people think he was a tough guy. Emojis
are tiny cartoon-like drawings that can be used in text messages and on
social media. He posted a lot of photos of drunken orgies with Lilith and
her friends. The photos were taken at various locations, some of them
at a mobile home. Freddy's eyes were half-shut in all of his photos. One
of the boys in the photos who likes to go by the alias, Jamal, on Facebook looked scrawny and pale. He posted this on Facebook: "I created a
messed up reality in which I live every day." Judging from his posts and
photos, I had to agree with him.

I believed Freddy was a big and very bad influence on Chase. The
more I thought about him, the angrier I got. I set out on a mission to find
Freddy. I looked at Facebook to find out who his friends were, where
they hung out, where they lived, where they worked. I gathered as much
information about him as I could. I narrowed down the area where I
thought that mobile home might be and started riding through trailer
parks to find it. It was frustrating. I knew I was close, but it was like
finding a needle in a haystack.

I am a law-abiding citizen. Other than breaking the speed limit once
in awhile, I can't think of another law I've broken. I wasn't sure what I
was going to do when I found Freddy; I might simply gather more infor-

mation on him to hand over to police, or I might beat the living crap out of him. I wasn't sure, but I was going to do something.

I sent a text to Lilith's mother. "I know Lilith is dating Freddy. I need to know where he is."

"I don't know where he is," she wrote back.

"It's okay. I'll find him." The truth was, I couldn't find him. I probably didn't need to find him, but I couldn't let it go.

A few days later, I went back to the hospital to visit Dylan. This time Kim went with me. We passed a nurse standing in the hallway working at a laptop. The door to Dylan's room was open and the lights off. I peeked in and his bed was unmade. There was a rollaway bed in the room that was also unmade. There was no one in the room. I was puzzled. Kim and I started back down the hall. We were walking past the nurse when she asked if there was anything she could help us with.

"We're here to see Dylan Smith," I said.

"You just missed him. He checked himself out an hour ago."

"*Checked himself out?*"

The nurse smirked.

I shook my head and walked away. Dylan had complained about how the nurses treated him. He also had complained to the whole world on Facebook. His drug-addict friends had been up to his hospital room hanging out. They definitely weren't a good influence. Without his mother's permission, they took Dylan out of the hospital. He was only beginning his physical therapy and had metal rods sticking out of his legs, but he had rolled right out of there.

I later visited Dylan several times in the split-level home of his grandfather. He was living in a room downstairs. This was the same place where I had picked up one of Dylan's relatives who had played football with Chase to take him to the movies years earlier. It was the same home where I had dropped off Dylan when he and Chase had run out of gas and he was so drunk.

This was a large, closely-knit family. Whenever I stopped by to visit, several of them were usually standing around outside the front door. I chatted with them and they were all very friendly towards me. They seemed like good people.

In my visits, I was trying to get through to Dylan, to let him know that people cared about him. I gently urged him to change his lifestyle so that he wouldn't end up like Chase. He wasn't interested in hearing it.

One day he told me, "Marijuana is nothing, man."

I felt sad. Everything in Dylan's life was telling him that it was time to change. Yet he refused. I felt frustrated with Dylan, but I didn't let on. I wanted to help him, but my thoughts began to turn more to getting information out of him. He always played dumb. It seemed a natural role for him. "Uhhhh. I don't remember much about what happened that day, man. It's all a blur to me now." He seemed to be protecting his own skin and maybe Tatyana's, too.

Dylan's grandmother told me there was a big going away party for Chase the night before the wreck.

"Who threw the party?" I asked.

"I'm not sure. I think Chase threw it himself."

"That wouldn't surprise me."

"It was in a hotel room. That seems to be the trend. There were a lot of different drugs present from what I hear, including Xanax. Chase and Dylan stayed up really late. They slept in the morning of the wreck. They were both messed up on Xanax. Chase nearly overdosed. His friends had trouble waking him up. He and Dylan slept until early afternoon, then went over to Godbold Park in Cary and smoked weed."

"Was Tatyana with them?"

"I think so. They all went to McDonald's after that and then they were headed to the Crabtree Valley Mall in Raleigh when the wreck occurred."

On July 7th, I had another dream about Chase. The paragraph that follows is the post I made about it on Facebook: *While I took a 30-minute power nap this morning, I enjoyed an epic journey with Chase in a canoe. We were in the most beautiful translucent blue water I have ever seen. There was a slow current and in places where the water was shallow enough I could see the white sand on the bottom. I was sitting in the front and Chase was in the back. We paddled around and, much to my dismay, Chase almost flipped us over on several occasions. We were drifting toward an island that we were getting very close to when I was suddenly transported back to planet earth.*

I have had other dreams about Chase, and most of them were very vivid. When I woke, usually I was aware that I'd just had a very vivid dream, but if I do not immediately tell someone or write it down, I quickly forget it. There have been a few night terrors as well. My wife tries to wake me carefully knowing how physically volatile I can be during one of these episodes.

It can take a long time to get a toxicology report back these days. The crime labs in most states have a backlog. I read about a family in Florida who waited for nearly two years to get the results of the toxicology report in a DWI case. According to a report I saw, the long waits on toxicology reports are due to several factors. For one, DNA technology has improved so much over the years that DNA evidence is being used in more cases now. This creates a bigger demand for the crime labs. The states are on a tight budget and can only afford to pay so much for scientists and lab technicians. According to a news report I saw, the state of North Carolina is understaffed at their crime lab.

Tatyana had a court date, but it got pushed back several times. It was partly because the police were waiting for the toxicology results. Finally I got a call from the lead investigator on Tatyana's case one day in mid-July.

"Hi, Mr. Rodgers. Officer Mancuso here."

"Hi, Officer Mancuso. Thanks for calling. How are you today?"

"Fine. Just calling to let you know we got the toxicology report back from the North Carolina Crime Lab."

"Okay. What does it show?"

"Tatyana had morphine in her bloodstream. Tatyana was administered that in the hospital, of course. The only other thing that showed up was a THC metabolite. (THC, or tetrahydrocannabinol, is the chemical responsible for most of marijuana's psychological effects.) The North Carolina Crime Lab doesn't quantify the THC because there is no legal limit in North Carolina for marijuana in the bloodstream while driving. They only report whether it was present in the bloodstream or not."

"Right. So what you're saying is that you likely won't be able to get a conviction on the Felony Death by Motor Vehicle charge, because you can't prove impairment due to the way the law is written."

"Correct. Usually a DRE (Drug Recognition Expert—a police officer who has been specially trained in the recognition of drugs and their affects on the body) can make an assessment at the crash scene and his assessment will carry a lot of weight in court, but Tatyana's injuries were too serious to allow that. She had to be transported to the hospital as soon as possible."

"From what I've heard, Tatyana was a regular smoker. I would be surprised if she wasn't impaired. Dylan's grandmother told me they smoked weed the same day of the wreck."

"We know without question that they smoked within two hours of getting in the car. There is absolutely no question about that."

"Of course you mean they smoked marijuana."

"Yes. I've considered sending the blood to another lab that would quantify it for us. Then we could look at what other states have established as a legal limit and try to build a case upon that. I'm willing to try just about anything, but I'm not sure a judge would even allow that in court. I'm about to go out of town to teach at a conference. I'll be back in two weeks. I'll get in touch with you when I return and give you an update."

"Okay, Officer Mancuso. Thank you so much for all your help."

I gave it about three weeks, but when I had not heard from Officer Mancuso, I sent him an email and then left a message on his voice mail a day or two later.

He called me back. "I called the NC crime lab today and they told me that the THC metabolite they found in Tatyana's bloodstream was inactive, okay?"

"Inactive? What does that mean, exactly? So you didn't get the THC quantified?"

"The THC has not been quantified, but there's no way she could have been impaired. If the THC metabolite was inactive, then it had been awhile since she last smoked. Otherwise it would be an active metabolite. There's no point in sending the blood to another lab to be quantified."

"Wait. That's not consistent with what you told me before. You said that you *knew* without question they had smoked weed within two hours of getting in the car."

"Well, we weren't sure that *she* was included in that *they*." I didn't like it. Something about this didn't seem right. In my opinion, he didn't want to go to the trouble or expense to send the blood work to another crime lab, so he made something up to try and pacify me. After all, one of Tatyana's friends posted on Facebook the day of the wreck that she had been to the hospital and heard for herself that Tatyana was not drunk, but had only smoked pot earlier that same day. If she had indeed smoked pot earlier that same day, then she would have likely been impaired and the THC metabolite would certainly not have been inactive.

Still, it would have been practically impossible to prove impairment in court, because there is nothing in North Carolina Law that defines impairment by marijuana, and we wouldn't have the testimony of the DRE officer because of Tatyana's medical condition at the time of the wreck. Spending money to send Tatyana's blood to another lab to have it quantified would have been a waste of the taxpayer's money. Even if it showed a high level of THC in the blood, the Felony Death by Motor Vehicle charges would never stick.

By this time, I didn't care about getting a conviction as much as I cared about knowing the truth. I wanted the blood sent to another crime lab and the THC quantified so that I would know if Tatyana was impaired or not. I needed to know. But there was no point in arguing with the detective.

Once the police had completed their investigation I had several telephone conversations with the Assistant District Attorney who would be handling the case. He was a good guy, young, but competent and sympathetic to my feelings about the case. The law, however, made it practically impossible for him to deliver any justice. It was becoming painfully obvious to me that Tatyana was not going to be held accountable by the law for the role she had played in Chase's death. This made me angry. I kept thinking, "This is not right! This is not right! God, you need to make this right."

Every day I fought a battle inside my own mind. My anger with Tatyana grew, and I wanted to take matters into my own hands. I was growing more and more impatient with God. How could he let this injustice stand? I knew where Tatyana worked because she put it on her Facebook profile. I drove by, thinking I might happen to catch her on camera driving without a license even after the wreck. I hoped if I could gather this information that it might help the judge decide to come down a little harder on her. I wasn't persistent enough in my efforts to be there when she was getting off of work. I think because a part of me didn't want to succeed. A part of me was saying, "Let it go."

I thought about what I might do to her if the judge let her walk. I fought those thoughts and tried to put them out of my mind. They would come back, and I would battle with them again and again. I thought about what I was going to say to her and what I was going to say to the judge when I went to her court hearing. This whole thing wasn't fair. This life never is. I remember Chase complaining to me when he was a little boy about something not being fair. "Life isn't fair, Chase. Get used to it. It's not supposed to be fair. You have to adjust. You have to learn how to deal with it and overcome the circumstances. That's part of what life is all about," I'd said. Those words were ringing in my ears, but I still desperately wanted to even things up. I knew it wasn't right to think that way, but I did.

I contacted an attorney about bringing a wrongful death lawsuit against Tatyana. Maybe I could get justice that way. Maybe that would make me feel better. I probably could have won a wrongful death lawsuit against her, but there was no money to go after. She had no insurance, and she had been driving Chase's car covered by *his* insurance. She had no money, and her family had no money, and even if they did, I wouldn't have wanted to hurt *them*. I only wanted teach her a lesson. I wanted to hold her accountable.

If I won a lawsuit, I could possibly have garnished her wages for the rest of her life, but I would have to pay the attorneys, and I would likely never recoup what I spent to sue her. Where was the justice in this world? How could she operate a vehicle without a driver's license, cause a wreck resulting in a death, and then walk away from it as if nothing had happened? This is the world we live in today. There is very little justice. There is very little accountability or personal responsibility, but if I took matters into my own hands, I would be the bad guy. What a messed up world!

Some friends of ours who had moved from Raleigh to the coast of North Carolina years ago, invited us to spend a weekend at their beach house in late July. They had heard about Chase's death and wanted to offer us a place to relax for a few days. We took them up on the offer. Aside from the beach house, they lived in a very nice home in an upscale, gated community. We had dinner with them and the youngest of their three sons. Afterwards we went by their house and chatted.

The next morning we attended church with them, and then my friend gave Justin surfing lessons. I was surprised at how quickly Justin picked it up. I tried a few times but I couldn't stay on the board. I did enjoy watching Justin. This family's oldest son, who was college age was in treatment at the time at Teen Challenge. His problem started with marijuana and went from there. I'd heard that story over and over again. I mention this story to point out that drug problems among our youth affect all socio-economic groups. In Cary, where we live, in an affluent area, there is a growing problem with drugs simply because a lot of teenagers can afford them.

I wish now I had not been in such a hurry when I sent Chase for treatment. Teen Challenge would have been a much better alternative than Peaceful Plantation. Intervention Masters had steered me away from Teen Challenge. They argued that a lot of people coming through Teen Challenge had come out of the criminal justice system. They warned me that Chase would learn bad things there. Probably the main reason they steered me away from Teen Challenge, was because they had no financial incentive for referring people there.

Teen Challenge is a fifteen-month program compared to Peaceful Plantation's thirty-day program, followed by a halfway house. People don't change those kinds of habits in thirty days. Teen Challenge is very inexpensive compared to most treatment centers. It costs $750 to get in, depending on which center you go to. They have centers all over the United States. Peaceful Plantation was a rip off.

I was on Facebook on August 6th, when one of Dylan's posts came up in my news feed. Dylan had gotten a tattoo in Chase's memory. Until then, I had not been angry over Chase's death, but when I saw that tattoo, I went ballistic. One of Chase's own tattoos was of a diamond and it had been poorly done. Dylan got a diamond tattoo on his forearm. I don't think my anger had anything to do with the tattoo. Now I was angry that my son was dead. I had reached out to Dylan, and he had rejected me and my message. I shouldn't have taken it personally. I had hoped he would miraculously change his ways, yet I hadn't been surprised when he didn't.

I was angry though. I tore into him on that post. "If you want to do something to honor Chase's life," I wrote, "why don't you stop smoking the crap that killed him? A tattoo does not honor my son. The only reason he ever got any tattoos was because he was addicted to drugs and hanging out with the likes of that street urchin, Lilith Addington. I don't see you as being a whole lot different from her."

That started a firestorm, and the debate raged back and forth between me and Dylan and some of his Facebook friends. Even Dylan's mother got in on the act. She wrote the following in the comments. "PLEASE jump off Dylans balls for smoking weed. It's already legal in 1/3 of the states and it will be legal here pretty soon so the doctor can and probably will prescribe it to him! There are so many worse things he could be doing...was doing with Chase."

Tatyana also came up in the discussion on Facebook. I insinuated that she may have even wrecked the car on purpose because Chase was leaving for Florida and she was angry because she was still in love with him. She and I never communicated directly, but I could see her comments and she saw mine or was told by her friends what I had written. I felt she owed us an apology for her role in Chase's death. She had never said one word to me about it. Her attorney had probably told her not to talk to me or my wife and I understood that. I didn't expect her to apologize to me in any case. She was much too proud for that, but it was a matter of principle with me.

The next week, I was at the mall and speaking with one of Chase's old football teammates. We were in the food court when I mentioned that Tatyana had never told me she was sorry. "Someone told me that she said she has nothing to be sorry for; that it was only an accident."

He looked at me in shock. "That's your son," he exclaimed. "Even if it *was* an accident, that doesn't matter. If we were sitting at a table here in the food court and I accidentally spilled my drink on you, I would immediately apologize to you! How much more should I apologize to you if I killed your son, even if it *was* by accident?"

I was taken aback by this young man's analogy. I had never thought of it that way before.

"Her attorneys have probably told her not to talk to me," I said.

"I don't care!" he said. "If I had done something like that, you better believe I would be apologizing to you!"

The word accident is something we need to use sparingly. I corrected myself many times in the days following Chase's death. It was no accident that Tatyana was driving Chase's car without a driver's license. She broke the law, and the day of the wreck was one of at least two times that I'm aware of that she drove without a driver's license. I'm sure there were many more instances. If she was impaired at the time the crash occurred, that also was no accident. It's time for people to stop using language to deflect blame. People need to accept responsibility for their actions and make positive changes.

I haven't made any more trips to visit Dylan. I later read somewhere that there are five stages of grief. The first stage of grief is denial and isolation. The second stage is anger. I was now apparently entering the anger stage, and I was doing it online for the whole world to see. Some of Dylan's family members came to my defense on Facebook and thanked me for putting Dylan in his place. Tatyana and Dylan both made their cover photos diamonds that looked exactly like the tattoo. I wasn't sure if it was to pay tribute to Chase or to antagonize me; probably both. It didn't matter. I had finally moved on.

The day after I had the Facebook blowout with Dylan something unusual happened. Out of the blue, Freddy contacted me on Facebook via private message. It seems that, between my angry outburst on Facebook and my text to Lilith's mother, Lilith was beginning to get worried that I might become a problem for her. She told Freddy about my Facebook tirade, and he apparently thought he could get me calmed down. He told me he didn't like Dylan and some of the other people who claimed to be Chase's friends but who didn't know Chase at all. Freddy claimed he and Chase were very good friends. He said he loved Chase and that he was very upset about his passing.

I asked Freddy if he would like to meet for lunch soon. He agreed to have lunch with me the next day at a place called The Mellow Mushroom. It sounded to me like a place where you'd find a bunch of sixties era doped-up hippies hanging out.

I arrived at the Mellow Mushroom the next day around noon. I drove around the parking lot and scoped things out. I didn't see Freddy. I parked and walked in. Of course, I was on high alert. I didn't trust Freddy. I got a table. The waiter came to my table, and I asked for a glass of water. I thought it was odd that the waiter was wearing a ball cap with a line drawing of a diamond on the front. It looked exactly like the tattoo Chase had that was now emblazoned on Dylan's forearm. That was unnerving. I now think in this case, it was a logo for a skateboard manufacturer.

My first impression of the waiter was that he was an addict, but he gave me good service. He kept my water topped off and kept coming back to check on me. I sat where I could see the front door. I waited, but I didn't see Freddy. That figures, I thought. He's a coward. Then I thought I saw him walk past the front door. I only caught a glimpse as he walked by. I walked outside and looked around, but I didn't see him anywhere. I decided to leave, but by the time I had arrived home a few miles away, Freddy had messaged me. He was there! I went back to the Mellow Mushroom. As I drove up I could see him sitting outside on a bench by himself. I walked up to him.

"Freddy?" He stood up to greet me and we shook hands. We went inside and got a table. We ordered and while we waited for our food we talked about Chase. Freddy had met Chase at Cary High School. He told me funny stories about Chase. I realized that Freddy did know Chase because he described an impulsive and funny kid with a unique sense of humor. He called Chase naive because he didn't always understand the ways of the world.

"I didn't go to the funeral," he said, "because I didn't want to see some of those people. They pretended to be friends with Chase after he died, but they barely knew him. That made me angry. There were a lot of people who only used Chase for a ride. They used him because he had a car and they didn't. I tried to tell him they were only using him."

He also told me how angry he was with Tatyana. "I feel bad, because he was looking for a place to stay, and I told him about Tatyana. I warned him that she was unstable. She had been through a lot of roommates in a very short period of time. I think she did it on purpose."

"Did what on purpose? Wreck the car?"

"Yeah."

"Nahh, I don't believe that. I'm angry with her, too, but I don't believe she intentionally ran his car into a tree."

"I do. She said she was going to ruin his life before he left this state. She can't get away with this," he said.

"She probably will." "The police have told me that it's going to be a very difficult case to prove, because there is no legal limit in North Carolina when it comes to driving while under the influence of marijuana. There is nothing in the law that defines impairment by marijuana. She's not going to get much time if anything, a slap on the wrist most likely."

I could see the anger burning inside of him. "That's not gonna happen."

I took that to mean that he intended to take matters into his own hands. I sensed that Freddy was the kind of guy who wouldn't do something like that himself, but he may have had connections to get it done. A part of me wanted to get even, too. The law wasn't going to hold her accountable.

It wasn't fair that Tatyana could drive Chase's car without a driver's license, probably while impaired, and wreck it, killing him, and then walk away to live a normal life. I never discounted the fact that Chase bore responsibility for his own death. Chase knew Tatyana didn't have a driver's license, yet he let her drive his car. Why?

Chase made the decision to use marijuana and other drugs. Chase associated with people who regularly used drugs and alcohol and who engaged in other illegal activities. Yes! Chase was responsible for his own death, and I was responsible, too, for failing to communicate the dangers to him in a way that he could understand. Chase had paid the ultimate price for his decisions. He got the death penalty. What price had Tatyana paid for the role she played in Chase's death? Yes, she had injuries she would have to deal with, but she would be able to go back to a normal life. I agreed with Freddy. She had to pay! Because of my spiritual upbringing, however, I was constantly reminded that it wasn't my place to get revenge. Romans 12:19 King James Version —Dearly beloved, avenge not yourselves, but rather give place unto wrath: for it is written, Vengeance is mine; I will repay, saith the Lord. If Tatyana had truly done anything wrong, God would make it right in either this life or the next, regardless of how fair or unfair the law may be. I had to have faith in that. Otherwise, everything I had based my entire life on was meaningless.

"No, Freddy," I said, "We can't seek revenge. As much as I would like to, we can't do that. It's wrong, and besides that, we would spend the rest of our lives in prison." He reluctantly agreed with me. I could see it still bothered him. It bothered me, too. But for now we agreed to let it go.

"You know, Chase wanted you and your wife to understand that he was only smoking weed. He wasn't doing anything all that bad. Weed is nothing."

"Freddy, I don't agree that weed is nothing. I think it's a dangerous drug and I believe that it killed my son, but I know Chase also used other drugs." I had ordered the jerk chicken hoagie. It was one of the best sandwiches I had ever had. The Mellow Mushroom may sound like a hippy paradise, but they make good food.

"It was mostly marijuana and alcohol," he said. "He experimented with other stuff, but it was every now and then, not a daily habit. Any time we had a party or were hanging out, Chase just wanted to know where was the weed." I mentioned to Freddy the possibility of going to treatment.

As we were walking out the door he turned to me, "You said something about treatment. What kind of places do you know about?"

"I'll send you some links to websites in a Facebook message."

When I got home I called the Mellow Mushroom and bragged on their service and their jerk chicken hoagie. "Please pass my comments along," I said. The young lady who answered the phone assured me she would.

I sent information to Freddy about Teen Challenge. We met again a few days later and got to know each other better. One day he asked me to pick him up at the trailer where he was staying. I drove up and I couldn't believe my eyes. It was the trailer I had seen in the Facebook photos, the same trailer I had searched for.

Freddy told me the trailer belonged to Lilith's Dad. Lilith's Dad was in his fifties, he had had his bouts with alcohol and drugs, but he was sober now. He was a diabetic, and one leg had been amputated at the knee. According to Freddy, he had been employed by a large computer firm at one time.

Sometimes I bought Freddy lunch and even cigarettes. I sincerely wanted to help him, but I knew he wasn't going to quit smoking cold turkey. I wanted to earn his trust and his friendship. If nothing else this would be the one positive thing that would come from Chase's death. Freddy going to treatment and turning his life around was a long shot, like Dylan Smith had been a long shot. I'm a person, however, who believes in miracles.

By this time I had made several calls to Teen Challenge to gather information. They told me that Freddy would have to call himself and get on the waiting list to get in. It was difficult to get them on the phone. Freddy or I usually got an answering machine and had to leave a message. We seldom got a return phone call, but we kept trying.

They finally sent Freddy a manual via email which he had to study. He called them again, and they quizzed him about the manual. They told Freddy he was accepted into the program, but first he would need a physical that included a TB (tuberculosis) test, and he would need a state-issued photo I.D. Freddy had lost his wallet with his identification in it. I helped him get a new ID. As part of the physical he also needed a copy of his shot records. They asked Freddy about his criminal convictions history. He told them about a couple of misdemeanors.

Freddy had violated probation once by leaving the area where he lived without notifying his probation officer. He had never checked back in with her. According to Freddy, she knew where he was but was too lazy to come and get him.

"It's all about the money," Freddy said. "If she can make some money out of the deal, she will come and find me, but if there's no money in it for her, she's not going to make the effort." I was impressed with Freddy's reasoning. He seemed capable of doing well financially without breaking the law. He was not only intelligent but had street smarts. He was however, stuck in a quagmire of his own making. He was still associating with people who kept bringing him down, and he didn't seem to know how to escape them. Maybe he didn't have the will power to do it.

He was also trying to avoid the consequences of some bad decisions in his past. These consequences he was going to have to deal with sooner or later. "I want to have a normal life," Freddy would say. "You know, with a wife and kids, a house and cars, nothing extravagant, just a normal life." Sure, he wanted it, but did he want it enough to do what it would take to change?

Freddy went online and filled out a form to have a new state identification mailed to him at the trailer. I kept asking him every day if it had come. The answer was always no. It seemed to be taking a long time. He finally explained to me that Lilith's Dad had probably picked it up with the mail, and the trailer was very disorganized. It was probably buried in the mail, paperwork, and other junk.

Finally I took him by DMV and dropped him off. A couple of hours later he had his new I.D. Next I took him to Cary High School where he put in a request for his shot records. I don't know what happened there, but that plan wasn't working. I took him to the local Health Department, but they didn't have his shot records either. They were able, however, to give us the address of the place that did have them. Freddy called ahead, and they told him they would be closing for lunch soon and that they would leave his shot records at the front desk. We barely made it in time. The doctor's office was about to close for lunch. Freddy flashed a big smile and begged at the front door for the lady working at the front desk to let him in. She did, and he picked up his shot records.

We were making progress. I took Freddy to an urgent care facility to get his physical. I had to come out of pocket to help pay for it. They gave him the TB test and there was a window of time during which he was supposed to come back for his TB results. We missed the window because we misunderstood and he had to redo the test.

When we finally had everything together, we faxed it all to Teen Challenge. They were ready to take him in except for one obstacle. Freddy needed to clear up his criminal record. That meant that he was going to have to turn himself in and spend fifteen days in jail. Teen Challenge wanted people to clear up any legal matters before coming into the program so they wouldn't have the situation of the police showing up and pulling a participant out during the middle of treatment.

Freddy did a few things around my house to repay me for feeding him and buying him cigarettes. He cleaned and organized our storage room and our hall closet. He did a great job. My friend Bob also hired me to spread some dirt and mulch for him out on his hobby farm near Pittsboro. I paid Freddy to help me, so he could raise some of the money he needed to pay for Teen Challenge. I didn't mind paying for it, but I thought it would give him some ownership if he paid for part of it himself. I'm used to hard manual labor, but Freddy had to stop often for smoke breaks and something to drink. Freddy made about $100 working with me on the farm. While he stayed with us, Freddy gave me a GPS and a nice microphone. He had found out that I like to shoot and edit video and thought the microphone might come in handy. I suppose these gifts were his way of repaying me something for helping him out.

I had known right away that Freddy knew Chase. If you have a close friend you spend a lot of time with, you tend to pick up some of his habits. Chase had picked up a certain laugh in the last year of his life. Freddy had the same way of laughing. As a result I knew the two of them had spent considerable time together. When Freddy and I were together, we talked about Chase. He told me things about Chase that I didn't know, and vice versa. Freddy also filled me in on Tatyana. He told me that Chase was only living with Tatyana for two to three weeks before the relationship was over. After that they went through the motions for a while before she kicked him to the curb.

According to Freddy Tatyana had a large stash of marijuana in her apartment which she was selling. She was out one day when Chase was alone in her apartment. Some guy came to the door wanting to buy weed. Chase called Tatyana and asked her how much weed to give the guy for $20. Tatyana was often moody. She hung up on Chase without telling him how much weed to give her customer. So Chase gave him the entire stash. That guy must have thought he hit the jackpot. According to Freddy Chase did it out of spite, but then played dumb about it. Tatyana was furious! Freddy also told me that Tatyana liked to use and sell Molly. He said that Tatyana had candles and a pentagram set up in her apartment. I don't know if any of this is true or not. This is what Freddy told me. I had heard from other sources that Tatyana liked to buy "pills" when she was in high school, specifically Oxycontin.

Freddy also told me that Chase had contacted him once, saying he needed a gun for protection. Chase wanted a gun because Tatyana had sicked her dealer on him for giving away the pot. Chase feared for his life. Freddy showed me the private messages he had received from Chase, back in March 19th, 2014, to support these claims.

Chase: "I need to move out dude."

Freddy: "Lol what why?"

Chase: "cause dude this girl is crazy."

Freddy: "You tripping bruh lol what are you doing right now, my boy has a room for rent.

Chase: "no she is crazy literally."

And on April 13th, 2014:

Chase: "eyyyyy. I needa new crib but with a chick. I got some black dude trying to kill me. Tatyana put him on me. She pulled a knife on me."

Chase: "Some random dudes tried pulling me out of my car and they seemed mad but I don't know why. They were trying to throw me in a taxi and I pulled my brass knuckles on them and next thing I remember was waking up with my car broke down on the side of the highway."

Freddy: "So wait. What's wrong with it?"

I also learned about one of Chase's and Freddy's friends who needed a ride out of state. Apparently he was in trouble and needed to avoid law enforcement. So on the spur of the moment Chase gave him a ride. There were two other riders for the trip, including Freddy. Freddy said Chase liked to drive fast. On their way back to North Carolina, Chase got pulled over. I got the "Failure to Appear" notice in the mail a couple of weeks after the funeral. Chase was going over 90 miles per hour in a 70 zone.

One of the other occupants of the vehicle was a convicted felon and Freddy had a pistol with him. The police asked Chase for permission to search his vehicle. Chase didn't have the street smarts of Freddy so he gave the police permission and they found Freddy's pistol. Somebody was going to have to go to jail. The other kid in the car decided to take the hit to protect Freddy. He became angry with Chase, however, and later made threats against him until Freddy says he got him calmed down.

While I was helping Freddy prepare to go to treatment, I drove him around. He often got bored and wanted to go hang out with his friends. I kept cautioning him to be careful about the people he hung out with. He wouldn't want to sabotage his chances at getting into Teen Challenge. One night in mid-August, when I picked him up, he asked me to drop off two of his friends.

One was Ferdinand and the other was named Corey Davis. Corey was a shy, polite kid messed up on drugs. He was a handsome, mixed-race fellow. Freddy told me that Corey was adopted and his mother raised him on her own. Ferdinand was pleasant enough, had never been violent, but he had been deported several times because he kept getting in trouble for drugs and stealing. He kept slipping back across the border into the United States. Freddy said that Ferdinand's father was a member of the Drug Cartel in Mexico. We stopped by Freddy's trailer and I sat with Ferdinand and Corey in my truck while we waited. I was quite comfortable with them sitting in my truck. They seemed to respect me. They had known Chase, and liked him. They thanked me for giving them a ride and were polite.

By now it was late August. Freddy began spending time with a young lady named Stephanie. She was petite, slender, and attractive. She looked mixed race, definitely Latina, with bronze skin, big brown eyes, and dark hair. She had high cheekbones, a very pretty smile and a lot of very good amateur modeling photos on her Facebook timeline. Stephanie was part of the rave scene. A rave is a large dance party featuring performances by disc jockeys playing electronic dance music. Apparently she got paid to dance at various clubs in the Raleigh area, scantily clad in outlandish outfits. I invited Freddy to attend a high school football game with me one night. Freddy wasn't much into football and the game was a blowout. Freddy had met me at the stadium. Stephanie and some of her friends waited for him in the parking lot. They kept texting him and he left at halftime.

I got a call the following Sunday from Freddy. Freddy was in jail in Hanover County, near the North Carolina coast. He told me that he had gone with Stephanie and her friends to the beach after he left the football game. A young man Freddy knew from the Raleigh area ran into him at the beach. Freddy went for a ride with him in his car.

This young man thought it would be a good idea to take his car out onto the beach. They got stuck and had to call a tow truck. Freddy's friend didn't have the money to pay the tow truck driver, so Freddy's friend drove away and later got pulled over by the police. Freddy had been ticketed several months back by a Park Ranger for under-aged drinking. He had failed to appear in court and never paid the fine. When the police stopped the car and ran his name, they found out that he owed this fine.

I drove to the beach to bail Freddy out of jail. On the way I called Freddy's mother. He had called her from my phone a couple of times when he was trying to track down his shot records, so I had her number in my call logs. I let her know that I was going to bail Freddy out and try to get him into a treatment program as soon as possible.

This was the only time I've ever bailed anyone out of jail. All of the staff there was friendly and helpful. After I completed the proper paperwork, the staff sent me to a room where I had to pay the bail money to the magistrate. At one end of the room was a thick piece of Plexiglass with a built-in speaker and a slot at the bottom. There was an empty chair behind the Plexiglass. Finally an officer came into the room and a woman appeared behind the Plexiglass. After she helped the officer, she waited on me. I had to have cash in the exact dollar amount. I was finally able to learn from her that there was a convenience store several miles up the road where I might be able to get change if they were open.

Since the jail was in the middle of nowhere, and I felt fortunate to find a place so close by that was open. I got the change I needed and I went back to the room to pay the magistrate. The chair behind the glass was again empty. I pressed the help button and thirty seconds later, the magistrate showed and took my money. Then Freddy and I headed back to Cary. He didn't have a shirt and I happened to have on both a T-shirt and a long sleeved shirt, so I gave Freddy my T-shirt to wear back home. We stopped for fast food and I dropped him off at Lilith's dad's trailer.

A few days after dropping Freddy off, he called and asked me to pick him up at the trailer. He said Lilith had shown up in the middle of the night. The front door apparently wasn't very substantial, and she had forced her way in. Lilith had learned that Freddy was moving on to a better life. He said that she was out of her mind from a night of drinking and drugs. She stood over him with a knife and threatened to kill him as soon as he fell asleep. When she finally left the room, he could hear her sharpening the knife with an electric knife sharpener. He didn't get much sleep that night. He told me that he had to move out of the trailer to get away from Lilith, so I let him move in with us.

It was now early September. It was bothering me that we had not been able to find Chase's medallion, so I called a local rental facility and reserved a metal detector. Justin went with me when I went to pick up the metal detector. A man was testing it out to make sure it worked properly. He showed me how it worked. It was simple to operate. He asked me what I was using the metal detector for. I explained to him that we were looking for Chase's medallion at the crash site. He told me that his son had died from lupus at age fourteen. It had been years, but it still affected him. He asked me how my wife was doing. He knew how hard the death of a child is on the mother.

Justin and I headed over to the site of the wreck. The cross Ross had put in the ground was still there. In addition there were other items on and around the tree that some of Chase's friends and acquaintances had left. We pulled out the metal detector and began to search. There is a strip of woods a hundred yards wide and several hundred yards long that separates the lanes of very busy highway. We searched in these woods first around the tree where the car had come to a rest and then we searched further into the woods. Tiny pieces of windshield glass were strewn through the woods from the point of impact at the tree for about 100 feet.

Suddenly we heard: Honk! Honk! Justin and I jumped. It was a bright yellow-orange truck that assists stranded motorists along North Carolina highways. The driver had spotted my Yukon parked on the side of the road and was stopping to see if we were okay. He hadn't seen us in the woods. I walked up to the passenger side of his truck, and he rolled down the window. I told him why we were there.

I thought he was going to cry as he told the story of a relative of his who was an alcoholic. It seemed like everyone I came in contact with had a story about a family member or friend whose life was wrecked by substance abuse. Justin and I found a nickel that was minted in the year 2000 buried six inches deep there on the side of that busy highway. We also found all sorts of car parts, some of which belonged to Chase's car, but there were parts that belonged to other vehicles, too. We stumbled upon a large stash of very old mason jars. The metal lids set off the metal detector. We examined each one. We found a lot of things, but after four solid hours of careful searching, we had not found Chase's medallion.

Obviously it wasn't there. That was okay with me. I had eliminated that one possibility, and I now could rest easy knowing I had done my best. Maybe Chase had sold it to buy drugs or to get a little more money to pay for his move to Florida. I wanted to find it so that I would know it meant something to him. Had he valued my gift enough to keep it? I couldn't believe the police hadn't found it in his car, but they told me they had searched it twice.

Finally in late September, the only thing left for Freddy to do to be accepted into Teen Challenge was to clear up his legal matters. That meant turning himself in to the police and serving about fifteen days in jail. Freddy agreed on a time for me to drive him downtown to turn himself in. The closer it got to that time, the more nervous Freddy got. He then told me he had been involved with a gang a few years back. He hadn't had the money to pay his membership dues so they wanted him to stand on the street corner and sell drugs. That's when he had disappeared. He had moved from the area where he had been staying without telling anyone, including his probation officer where he was going. Freddy claimed that there were gang members in jail who knew him and would probably be a huge threat to him. I finally realized that Freddy was not going to turn himself in. Had I done all of this for nothing?

About this time I was telling a friend I met online who lived in California, about Freddy. He told me about a program in Los Angeles where he had volunteered his time. I passed on the information to Freddy, and he went online and filled out an application. It wasn't long before they had accepted Freddy into their program.

They didn't pry into his criminal background. Freddy was going to go to treatment. They wanted him there within a few days. This program did not require any kind of fee. Freddy had a list that he printed off with everything they said he should bring. By this time, the $100 Freddy had made helping me out on Bob's farm was long gone. Kim and I went shopping. We bought Freddy new clothes, toiletries, and a brand new

Bible. I bought his airline ticket and made arrangements for ground transportation from the airport to the location of the treatment center. Then Freddy wanted to spend time with his family before leaving.

It was getting late, and he wasn't back at our house yet. We had to be at the airport early the next morning. I kept trying to call him and text him. Freddy finally got a ride back to Cary in the wee hours of the morning but I had to drive across town to pick him up. We barely made it to the airport. I went in with him. Freddy hadn't flown before, so I made sure he got checked in and got his boarding pass. There were still a few minutes to spare, so we went to a restaurant in the terminal and had coffee. I finally accompanied him to the line where he would get checked by airport security.

Finally on September 29th 2014, Freddy was airborne. Most of his friends didn't believe he would go through with it. Ferdinand sent me a message on Facebook and asked me if Freddy had left yet. "Yeah. He's airborne right now," I said. "He should be over Georgia right about now."

"What time did he leave," he wrote back.

"Wheels up about 8:23." Freddy had somehow lost the only cell phone he had the night before, so he had no way to communicate with the bus driver who would pick him up. I was able to call the bus driver and describe Freddy to him. He picked Freddy up and dropped him off at the treatment center. The next day Freddy called me from the treatment center.

"This is not what I thought it was going to be," he said. "Teen Challenge had a program you could get into once you'd gone through the initial stages. They would send you to a community college to learn a trade. They don't have that here. I've talked to a lot of people who have been here for a while. Most of them are a lot older than me and I don't see a way out of here. As you advance in levels, they keep looking for any little rule you are breaking and bust you back down to keep you here. This is a moneymaking scam! They are getting funding based on how many people they have here. You have to work menial jobs like working in the kitchen, serving people. This is not what I thought it was going to be."

"Freddy, calm down man," I said in a soothing voice. "Any treatment program is going to be difficult and uncomfortable, especially at first. You just got there. Give it more time."

"Okay, man. I'll try."

The next day he called me again. "I got in trouble for taking prescription drugs that another guy in the program offered me. I had a headache and it was the only thing available at the time. I wasn't about to turn it down. I also keep getting in trouble for looking at girls or talking to girls. I'm starting to think the guy, Chris, who is in charge of the new people is gay."

I called and talked to the leadership at the treatment center. They said they didn't know what Freddy's problem was but that he had a bad attitude and was not going along with the program. After about a week, I got a call from Chris. He told me that Freddy had been kicked out of the program and told to leave the property immediately. There had been a big argument between him and Freddy, and Freddy had slung a plate full of food at Chris. A few minutes later I had a call from a security guard at the treatment center.

"Hey. This is Tyrone. I got Freddy here with me. They kicked him out of the program. I'm gonna let him spend the night in the chapel. I could get in a lot of trouble if I get caught, but I can't just let my brotha spend the night out there on the street. He ain't got no place to go."

"Can I speak to Freddy?"

"Yeah, but just for a minute." He put Freddy on the phone with me for a couple of minutes and I worked out the details for him to come back to North Carolina. The next morning he was to get on a shuttle bus to the LAX airport. Freddy handed the phone back to the security guard.

"I don't know what Freddy's problem is. I been in this program for six years now. I work here part-time as a security guard and they helped me out a lot. I was able to get off drugs and alcohol and get another job on the outside too. I'm thirty-four."

I bought a plane ticket for Freddy to come back to North Carolina. I thought about the bus, but the cost was about the same. Freddy didn't have any place to stay, so when he arrived at the Raleigh-Durham airport, I picked him up and he moved back in with us.

A few days later Freddy told me that he needed deadlines to help him get things done. He said he had things he had to clear up first, but he gave me a date when he would like to go turn himself in. His life was going nowhere. He was on a treadmill, hanging out with the same group of friends, partying, getting wasted, and not making any money. The date came and went. Freddy had every excuse in the book for not following through with his plans.

Then one night in mid-October, he was in Stephanie's car with friends. Stephanie got pulled over for a taillight that was out. The police found drugs in Stephanie's car and arrested Freddy. The police charged him with possession with intent to distribute. They claimed it was Molly.

Freddy told me that bag the police found wasn't his and it wasn't Molly but rather Himalayan Salt. This is sometimes used to cut Molly so the dealer is giving the buyer less product for the money. This salt comes as large light-pink crystals. He explained to me that most of the Molly sold in the Raleigh area is what is known as an RC or research chemical. It's not MDMA, but rather a chemical designed to give the user a high similar to MDMA. He told me that he would plead guilty to the charges, because otherwise he was going to be sitting in jail a long time waiting on the results of the drug tests to come back.

There were two court hearings. I attended the first. Freddy was represented by the public defender. I had spoken with his attorney on the phone about Freddy and told her I would be there. When I arrived, I saw a lot of attorneys. A clerk was talking to the various attorneys. When she walked by me, I asked her if she knew which one the public defender was.

She laughed. "I have no idea, hon. They don't last very long."

I was finally able to figure it out on my own and let her know I was there to support Freddy. There were quite a few cases to be heard before they got to Freddy. I was amazed at how many people pleaded guilty to what I thought were serious drug charges and walked out with nothing more than probation. When it was Freddy's turn, the public defender told the judge I was there on Freddy's behalf and pointed me out. She also told him that Freddy was making plans to go to Teen Challenge. The judge told him that he hoped he would take advantage of that opportunity and get himself cleaned up.

Freddy had to spend a few more weeks in jail. Every so often he would make a collect call to me. I accepted the charges. He updated me on his situation and asked me to send him money for food and cigarettes.

"The food in here is terrible. I have to have snacks from the vending machine once in awhile or I'm gonna starve to death."

I wired him a few dollars every now and then to keep him going. He finally got out and once again, he came back to our house. By this time his legal matters were cleared up. I urged him to get back in touch with Teen Challenge and get on their waiting list.

He told me he had contacted them, but Freddy always found ways to stall. He would tell me that he was waiting to hear back from them about something. In the meantime, he didn't miss an opportunity to hang out with his friends. My patience with Freddy was growing thin.

Freddy had lost a cap on one of his front teeth while he was in jail. He was trying to get it replaced at a clinic, but was having trouble making an appointment. Kim was having oral surgery done at the time and mentioned this situation to her oral surgeon. He thought he might be able to find Freddy free dental care, but all of his contacts were booked solid. Freddy finally booked an appointment at the clinic he had first gone to and got his crown repaired.

He told me that he still wanted to go to Teen Challenge and that he only needed to get some of his legal paperwork from downtown to fax to them. He continued to stall by telling me he just had a few personal matters he had to get cleared up first. He claimed he owed favors to friends.

I was surprised one day to find out that Freddy was interviewing for jobs at local restaurants. This wasn't what he needed to do. It was only a short-term plan. He needed to go to Teen Challenge, then to community college and learn a trade, but at least his trying to get a job was something positive. He had found a new girlfriend who sometimes stopped in front of our house and picked him up.

After high school, Wendy had been accepted at Ole Miss. She invited Kim, Justin, and me to come out to Ole Miss for a football game on November 7th, 2014. They were going to play Presbyterian College, a small Division 1 school in Clinton, South Carolina. Ross, Chase's close friend and old teammate from Hargrave was playing defensive end for Presbyterian, so this trip gave us the opportunity not only to see Wendy, but to also see Ross, and to enjoy a college football game.

On the drive out there, I called Freddy's mother, to inform her of how he had been doing since leaving jail. "Darryl, I know you have a good heart and I know you're trying to help him, but he doesn't want to help himself. This whole time he has been telling you he wants to go to Teen Challenge, he's been telling me he doesn't *need* to go to Teen Challenge, that he's going to get straightened out on his own. His mind is so messed up from all those years of doing drugs. I love him and I want to help him, but he needs to help himself. He's a liar and a manipulator. He's just using you for a place to stay, and for food and money. You do whatever you want to, but if I were you, I'd cut him off.

I can't take it any more. I had to call the police on him once because he stole from us. I love him, but I don't know when he's going to grow up. I hope to God nothing bad happens to him, but I won't be surprised if it does. I don't know what he's told you about us, but he always wants to blame his problems on everybody else. Yes, his daddy did go to prison and yes, his daddy was a liar, but for the most part, Freddy has had a good life. When he was growing up he had everything he ever needed or wanted. He didn't lack anything."

We went on to the game and enjoyed spending the afternoon with Wendy and watching Ross play. We had a chance to visit with Ross briefly after the game and ate dinner with Wendy before driving home.

On November 10th, while Freddy was out with his new girlfriend, Sally, interviewing for jobs I was doing a load of laundry. Freddy had thrown a pair of pants in the laundry basket. It's a habit for me to check the pockets of a pair of pants before I throw them in the wash. When I checked the front pockets of Freddy's jeans, I found a plastic bag with pink crystals in it. I assumed it was Molly.

I carefully searched the other pockets and found two used syringes in one of the hip pockets. There were traces of a dark brown material still inside them. I assumed that was heroin. A few hours later, Sally dropped him off at our house and he came to the front door. When he knocked on the door I opened it and immediately went outside with his suitcase in my hand. I put it down on the front porch beside him. I had already packed it with all of his belongings. I told him what I had found and told him that he could no longer stay with us.

"What? Why not?" he asked.

"Because I found drugs in your pants pockets."

"I didn't have any drugs. What did you find?

"I found a bag of pink crystals."

"That's not Molly. It's Himalayan Sea Salt."

"What are you doing with Himalayan Sea Salt in your pants pocket?"

"It's used to cut Molly."

"That's not something you would need to carry around with you unless you're selling Molly."

"I'm not selling Molly."

"Then why do you have the Himalayan Sea Salt?"

"It's not mine. It belonged to one of my friends." Freddy was beginning to get visibly upset. He raised his voice and his eyebrows furrowed. "So that's it? You're gonna kick me out just like that because I had salt in my pants?"

"I can't have drugs in my house, Freddy. I have a fourteen year-old son."

"I didn't have drugs in your house!"

"I also found two syringes in the hip pocket of your pants. They had brown residue in them. I'm guessing that's heroin?"

"That was from a long time ago when I was hanging out with Lilith. Those syringes belonged to her. I picked those pants up from her Dad's trailer when I moved out. Those syringes have been in there the entire time. I just forgot they were in there."

"I don't care where they came from or how long they've been there. I can't have drugs in my house."

"I didn't have drugs in your house!" I noticed that Sally had driven away while he and I had argued. She had no way of knowing that I wasn't going to let Freddy in.

I looked Freddy straight in the eye. "I suggest you call your ride." I continued to argue with Freddy until his girlfriend showed up a few minutes later. He stormed away, got in her car, and they drove off.

Freddy got two part-time jobs working in restaurants. Once in awhile he would still call me and fill me in on how his life was going. A month later, we met again for lunch at the Mellow Mushroom. Freddy talked about how his life was so messed up and how he knew he needed to go to Teen Challenge, but there was some business he needed to take care of first.

Samantha, whom Chase had met in Florida, and I were friends on Facebook. She had been deeply hurt when she heard Chase had been killed in the car wreck. Occasionally some of her posts would show up in my news feed. I had messaged her several times when I was looking for Freddy to ask her if Chase had told her anything about him. One day I noticed a post on Samantha's timeline about Grayson. I messaged her and she wrote that Grayson had died of an overdose. Grayson was the kid Chase met at Peaceful Plantation and who later went to the same halfway house. He liked to use cough syrup for a cheap high. I asked Samantha what he had overdosed on. She said she didn't know for sure but that she thought it was opiates.

At Christmas we went to Greenville, South Carolina to spend time with family and friends. When we returned, we had Kylie and Shannon over to our house for dinner on December 30th. Kim was in the kitchen finishing the dinner preparations and I was sitting in the living room talking with Kylie and Shannon when I saw someone through the blinds walking to our front door. The doorbell rang. Inga was standing there with a basket in her hands. I invited her in right away. I enjoy listening to Inga speak. She shows respect by addressing Kim and me as Miss. Kim and Mr. Darryl.

"Hi, Mr. Darryl. I brought you guys a gift basket. I came by to see you right after Christmas, but you weren't home. I know how difficult the holidays must be for you and Miss. Kim." Kylie and Shannon excused themselves and went to the kitchen while I finished chatting with Inga.

"You didn't need to do this, Inga."

"Oh, it's the least I can do. I know the holidays must be a difficult time for you and Kim."

"How is Tatyana doing?"

"She's seems to be doing better. She has a steady job now. She feels terrible about what happened to Chase. That really bothers her."

"I'm sure it does. Maybe if I could talk to her..."

She shook her head, "She's not ready for that."

I nodded my head. "I understand." I didn't think I was ready for that either, but Tatyana and I had never met face to face. I thought I might be able to let go of my anger if we met.

"She's a little worried about the court date coming up in February, but other than that, she seems to be doing okay."

Kim had heard Inga and me talking and came into the living room. "Hi, Inga!"

"Hello, Miss. Kim. I brought you a gift basket. I'm so sorry you are going through this. I know the holiday's must be a difficult time for you and Mr. Darryl."

"Oh, that's sweet," Kim said. "Thank you."

"You're very welcome."

"I can see you have guests. I don't want to keep you. I'm going to head back home."

I saw Inga to the door. "Thank you so much for coming by, Inga, and for the gift basket. That was very thoughtful of you."

"You're welcome. Good night, Mr. Darryl."

Only a few days after Inga had stopped by in the late afternoon I was sitting in the recliner in our living room with my laptop on a Skype call with my friend Les. Kim was on her way home from work. I had an incoming call on my cell phone. It was from a telephone number I didn't recognize. It wasn't stored in my contacts. I answered it, out of curiosity. It was Freddy.

"Did you hear?"

"Hear what?"

"Tatyana is dead. She killed herself."

We were both silent for a brief moment. "How?"

"She set herself and her apartment on fire."

"Are you kidding me?"

"Why would I kid about something like that? Turn on the news."

"It's not that I don't believe you, Freddy. That's just so bizarre!"

"I know, right? That's what everyone I've told has said."

"When did this happen?"

"She set the fire yesterday afternoon and she died in the hospital today, just a little while ago. There were twelve families displaced as a result of the fire. Are you sorry about Tatyana?"

"No." At the moment, I was numb. I didn't feel anything. "Are you sorry, Freddy?"

"No."

There was a knock at my front door. I peeked out the blinds to see one of my neighbors standing there. I hung up and went out the door.

"I came by to tell you about the girl who was driving Chase's car."

"I heard a minute or two ago."

"Really? That's so crazy, isn't it? I guess she never got over Chase's death." Kim pulled up in the driveway and walked to the front door. The three of us stood there and talked for a few minutes. She was as shocked as everyone else to hear the news. According to the fire marshall, Tatyana had poured gasoline all over the floor of her apartment, stood in the middle of it, and ignited it. There were reports that she had jumped from her second story window onto a patio below, but an eyewitness said he saw her run out of the front door of her apartment naked and on fire. I believe that is the accurate report. Apparently her clothes had been burned right off of her.

A lot of people were under the impression that Tatyana and Chase were still romantically involved when the wreck occurred. Nothing could be farther from the truth. Chase was leaving for Florida, and Tatyana was staying behind. Wendy was on her way to see Chase before he left, and she told me that Chase told her in one of their last conversations that he knew the two of them, Wendy and Chase, would wind up getting married some day. Tatyana may have still had feelings for Chase, but if she did she never mentioned him in the suicide note that she posted on her Tumblr blog.

At first I didn't feel bad about Tatyana. I felt relieved that I no longer had to struggle with getting justice for Chase. I felt bad for her mother, though. As it began to sink in, I felt bad for Tatyana too. It was a horrible way to die. Obviously, Tatyana had been dealing with a lot of issues. Kim and I attended Tatyana's funeral. I was dreading it, but I wanted to go. I needed to go. I wanted to support her mother. Tatyana's parents didn't have a lot of money, and funerals cost a lot. Someone started a fundraiser on Facebook to help them pay for the services.

We drove to the small church a few miles away. When we pulled up in the church parking lot, Inga was standing there. It was as if she had been waiting for us even though she had no way of knowing whether we were going to come or not. When Kim got out of the car the two of them practically ran to each other. They began sobbing as soon as they made eye contact. Kim and Inga embraced for a long time and cried in each other's arms. Only a mother who has lost a child can understand the pain that another mother goes through at a time like this.

I stood there until they had calmed down, and then I embraced Inga. What could I possibly say to her? It was bad enough that she felt responsible for the part Tatyana had played in Chase's death, but now her own child was dead and it was a result of a terrible suicide. How awful! I felt sick inside.

We went into the church sanctuary and found a spot to sit about mid-way down on one of the pews. "Come closer, come closer," Inga begged us. We moved closer to the front. We were several rows behind the family.

Dylan Smith came in with his mother and aunt. Aside from us, Tatyana's family, and one or two others, most of those there were drug-addicts. Inga spoke. She is a very strong woman. I was in no shape to speak at Chase's memorial service. Several of Tatyana's friends took turns at the microphone recounting Tatyana's life. Only a few of them had any spiritual or religious foundation that I could tell. Yet here we were in a church sanctuary and their friend was dead. Tatyana had been openly critical of Christianity, yet we were remembering her life in a church building. After the funeral I spoke briefly with Tatyana's stepfather. Inga's mother was there too, visiting from the Ukraine. Kim and I made our way towards our car. We had parked near Dylan Smith's mother. She came over and talked to us as we stood by the car. "It's so sad," she said. "We lost another one."

"Yeah, it is sad," I said.

"She never got over Chase's death and she was so worried about her upcoming court appearance."

"The court appearance was not going to be that big of a deal for her," I said. "She was going to get off light."

"I know, but she had built it up in her own mind as something terrible. She thought everyone was going to be there pointing fingers at her and judging her." Tatyana was right. I would have been there along, with Kim, Justin, and every friend and family member I could round up. I would have made sure that she saw me and heard from me. I wanted Tatyana held accountable, but what she did to herself was something much worse than I could have imagined.

Tatyana was very close to her uncle, Inga's brother. He still lived in the Ukraine. The healthcare in the Ukraine is not what we're used to here in the U.S. He had a heart condition and Inga struggled with whether to tell him about Tatyana or not. She had Skype calls with her brother on a regular basis, so it was difficult to keep the news from him. Finally she told him. He died a few days later. When they found him, he had Tatyana's pictures spread out around him on the floor. Sometimes it seemed as if there would be no end to the people who would be hurt by the crash.

I had stayed in touch with the police about the car, and finally Officer Mancuso sent me an email on January 6th 2015, letting me know it had been released. I called the towing service that had it and asked if I could come out and look through it. They told me I could come and to bring my I.D. to leave with them while I was on the lot. I learned that it had been stored outside with no tarp over it. I called my friend, Bob and asked if he would mind going with me for moral support.

I met Bob at the Home Depot in Apex, and we talked as we rode together in his truck to the lot where Chase's car was stored. I wasn't sure what to expect. The rain and sunshine had probably long since removed any bloodstains. I didn't think viewing the car would bother me, but I wasn't sure. I forgot to bring gloves, but Bob had an extra pair of work gloves in his truck. We walked in and talked to the ladies behind the desk and got permission to go onto the lot and search through Chase's car.

"Be careful out there. Watch your step," one of the ladies behind the desk warned.

"Okay, we will."

We made our way through the lot and finally spotted Chase's car all the way at the back. We had to weave our way through other junked cars and wrecks. There were parts scattered on the ground in some places and jagged pieces of metal and glass protruding from vehicles. We wove our way past the other vehicles until we got there. I looked at the car in disbelief. The frame was bent so badly that the back wheels weren't even touching the ground.

"Wow! Look how badly the frame is bent, Bob."

"I know. That's crazy."

The roof was mostly gone and what was left of it was rolled up into a cylindrical shape, exposing most of the interior. The driver's side rear door was bent in so badly that it was in the shape of a U. Debris of all sorts was scattered all throughout the interior of the car. The driver's seat was jammed up next to the steering wheel. It's difficult to imagine that Tatyana had at one time been wedged between that seat and the steering wheel. It was such a tiny space. Looking at the condition of the car, it was difficult to see how *anyone* could have survived that crash, much less two people who weren't wearing seat belts. I said to Bob, "No one has searched through this car for Chase's medallion or anything else."

"I agree," Bob said. "You can tell by the way things are positioned. Most of the items scattered throughout the interior look like they've not been touched. If you were looking for something, you would have had to have picked up some of these items to search under them."

"That's exactly what I was thinking, Bob. It doesn't look like any of this stuff has been touched since the day of the wreck." I'm not sure why, but I started searching on the driver's side at the rear door. Bob had brought along some bags and I began removing items from the car, methodically and placing them in a bag. I worked my way around the back of the car and searched through the trunk. I found a dozen music

Chase's car on the lot eight months after the wreck.

CDs in a backpack. Most of them were rap and the latest popular songs. I did find two CDs with worship music on them.

"Hey, Bob! Look at this."

"What'd you find?"

"Worship music." I held up the CDs.

"Interesting."

"Look at this one. It's titled, "Reggae Worship." The cover was decorated Bob Marley-style. The musicians even wore dreads. "If you're a stoner Christian, I guess this might be what you'd listen to."

We both chuckled. In spite of the fact that it wasn't music I would have chosen, I was encouraged that at least some of the time Chase's mind was on something positive and uplifting, on the things of God. I worked my way around to the rear door on the passenger's side and then to the front where Chase had been sitting. The bottom part of the seat was still in the car, but the seat back was lying face down on the hood. There were EMS personnel gloves scattered throughout the interior. There was a good inch or more of water in the floorboard of the car. I searched all around and under Chase's seat.

Next I opened the glove compartment. When I did, water gushed out. Even though a lot of water had come out of it, the glove compartment was still full of murky water. I removed the gloves Bob had loaned me and began carefully searching through it. The temperature was slightly above freezing and my hands quickly began to ache. I stopped for a moment. I was beginning to lose hope that I would ever see Chase's medallion again.

"Why don't you take a break and warm up your fingers," Bob suggested. "Let me take over for a few minutes."

"Okay." I reluctantly stepped aside as I cupped my hands and blew into them. My fingers were throbbing.

"I'm going for the low-hanging fruit," Bob said. Bob reached over from the door where Chase had been sitting to the middle of the car. Slightly in front of the gearshift lever at the bottom of the dash was a small compartment with a little door that had a handle molded into it. I was standing to Bob's left and had a clear view of the door. He tugged on the handle and the little door, hinged at the bottom, popped open.

"There it is," I exclaimed. Bob stood there for a second and then he got a huge grin on his face.

"That's it?" he asked excitedly. "Really?"

"That's it. Don't touch it! I want to take some pictures of it right where it is."

Bob stepped aside while I took several photos of the medallion lying right where he had found it in the little cubbyhole at the bottom of the dash. It was in there among a few other things including a set of ear buds with wires. I pulled it all out. That little cubbyhole had stayed bone dry while the rest of the car was soaked. The medallion was in as good condition as it was the day I gave it to Chase.

Bob and I hugged. We headed back to the counter and told the ladies there what we had found and then we headed out. I had a bag with several other items in it, including some of Chase's clothes, the CDs I had found, and a couple of books. It was a good day. Now I knew that Chase had the medallion with him. It meant something to him. To me it was a sign. After all this time we had finally found it.

I posted on Facebook that I had found the medallion and included photos that Bob had taken of me holding it next to the car. A lot of people congratulated me on Facebook. Kylie sent me a private message that she would like to see the car. "I want to see the last place Chase was. Is that weird?"

"No. I don't think it's weird at all," I said. "Seeing the car helped me. It didn't have the negative affect on me that I thought it might. I can take you to see it if you would like to go."

We agreed on a day and time. Justin was available and wanted to go as well. I forgot there had been a lot of rain the day before. The lot where the car was parked was muddy. I was able to find car parts and place them down in a line so that Kylie could protect the new shoes she was wearing by stepping from one car part to another. We spent time at the car, and I spotted little items I had missed before. There were personal effects that had belonged to my parents in the trunk, including a small hand-written note in my mother's handwriting and one of my Dad's Bibles with notes in the margin. The Bible, however, was not salvageable.

Kylie and Justin were amazed at how badly the car was damaged. We looked around the lot. There were other vehicles close by that had been involved in fatal crashes. There was a Chevrolet Suburban that had rolled over and the roof had caved in on the family inside. There

I finally have Chase's medallion back.

was the child's seat and the toddler's shoe on the floorboard. Then there was the Volvo wagon that had apparently run up under a semi truck. The hood had peeled straight back and gone through the windshield, taking out the driver. These were startling reminders of how deadly automobiles can be.

Freddy called me out of the blue one day in mid-January. He sounded groggy, like he had just woken up. "The curse is real," he said.

"Huh?"

"The curse is real."

"What curse?" I asked.

"Lilith's curse. You know...the curse she puts on her ex-boyfriends. She told me that she puts a curse on any boy who breaks up with her. Chase and three others have died in car wrecks now. I'm in the hospital. I was in a wreck."

"What happened? Are you okay?"

"I think so. I'm very sore. I was riding with one of my friends and this girl turned right into us at an intersection. It wasn't my friend's fault."

"Was your friend impaired?"

"No. I don't know but let's say no. The wreck wasn't his fault," he insisted.

I called Freddy's mother and she already had been to see him in the hospital.

"He's fine," she said. "Just banged up a little. This makes the fifth wreck he has been involved in over the last twelve months! He wasn't driving in any of them."

"Wow. I didn't know that."

"You would think he would learn," she said.

"Since he doesn't drive, I guess he's at the mercy of his friends."

"That's true."

"He needs to find different friends, but that's not going to be easy and he's not ready to make the necessary changes."

Freddy was released from the hospital the next day. Incidentally, during the time Freddy was living with us, three of his friends were involved in two car wrecks. Drugs were part of the equation in both. Ferdinand was a passenger in one of those wrecks when the young woman behind the wheel passed out and crossed two lanes of oncoming traffic at night before running off the road. Because Ferdinand was an illegal alien and was always in legal trouble, he jumped out of the car and ran. The other wreck landed the female driver of the car in the hospital in a coma. Freddy keeps telling me that he is going to pay his own way to go to Teen Challenge soon, but it hasn't happened yet. He told me he wanted me to let him know when I was writing about him because he wanted his story to be a positive ending to the book.

When we first met Lilith's mother, she had told me that Lilith had had a baby when she was thirteen or fourteen that she put up for adoption. When I met with Freddy one day in January he confirmed that and said that Lilith hated the baby. According to Freddy, Lilith got pregnant again while he was living with us after he got back from the treatment center in Los Angeles. She claimed Freddy was the father and wanted him to pay for an abortion. I told him not to do it, that God would not approve. Freddy says that a kid named Leonard paid for the abortion. Leonard is part of the local drug scene and has had an on and off relationship with Lilith and a lot of other girls. Freddy says that Leonard has paid for all of Lilith's abortions, because somehow she has convinced him that he is the father. He said she'd had about three abortions in the last twelve months.

Freddy called me again in late January 2015 to tell me he had come into some money.

"Hey man," he said, "I need some advice. I'm getting $18,000 from the insurance company. You remember, I was in a wreck and they're giving me a check to cover my hospital bills. People are giving me all this advice about what to do with it. Sally wants me to get an apartment with her. Some people say I should buy a car with it. Everybody has some advice for me. Honestly, having this much money is making me nervous. I don't know what I should do."

"Freddy. I don't have a dog in this hunt. I don't want your money."

"Yeah. I know. That's why I called you, because you're the only person I trust to give me good advice about this."

"Freddy, are your medical bills paid?"

"Yes."

"How were they paid?"

"Medicaid."

"The right thing to do is to reimburse Medicaid with that insurance check."

"I don't know about that. The hospital got paid."

"Yeah. I didn't think you would want to hear that."

"If you're not going to reimburse Medicaid, the next best thing I can think of is to invest the money in mutual funds. I could help you pick something out. It would be a long-term investment. You would need to leave the money in there and not touch it for a very long time. You should diversify it among several funds. Then I would recommend that you go to Teen Challenge. When you graduate fifteen months from now, you will have a trade and be able to start a new life. In the meantime, your money will have grown. If I were you, the last thing I would do is use the money to buy a car. Cars depreciate fast. They're not a good investment."

"I've been thinking about Teen Challenge a lot, honestly. I'll get back in touch with you when I get the check."

"Okay."

A couple of weeks later, Freddy called to tell me that his friend had passed out at work. Corey Davis had been doing a lot of Xanax. His body had built up a tolerance to it and he was taking crazy amounts of it according to Freddy. Freddy said that Corey was also using fentanyl. I looked it up. It's bad stuff. It's a prescription drug used mostly for anesthesia. Fentanyl is approximately eighty to one hundred times more potent than morphine and roughly fifteen to twenty times more potent than heroin according to the information I found online. Corey was working at a local Burger King when he passed out. His co-workers called the authorities, and the police were on the way. Somehow Corey woke up and discovered that the police were coming. He bolted out of Burger King. Now he was in the woods in a neighborhood close by. Freddy didn't have any transportation and he wanted me to go with him to find Corey.

"Let me think about this a minute." Did I really want to get involved in this? Corey was a gentle kid, but messed up on powerful drugs, I had no idea what he might be capable of. Besides that, the police were looking for him. I didn't want to interfere with them.

"Maybe the right thing to do here, Freddy, is to call the police."

"No. We're not calling the police."

"Freddy. Life is fragile. I hope he's going to be okay, but if he's in as bad a shape as you say he is, maybe they could help us find him and prevent something bad from happening."

"It's not time for that yet. I will know when it's time to do that, if the time comes."

"Okay, man. I'd just hate to see this turn out bad."

"I have a call coming in from Corey. I need to go."

"Call me back." I waited, but after ten minutes, Freddy had not called me. I called him.

"What's going on with Corey?"

"He's still out there in the woods by himself. He kept passing out while I was talking to him and now he's not answering."

"I'll be right there." I grabbed two large, powerful flashlights and headed over to Freddy's girlfriend's house. By the time I arrived, Freddy had secured a ride with his girlfriend, Sally.

"It's okay. I'll handle it," Freddy said. "I don't need you now."

"I'm already here and I have two good flashlights. You could still use my help finding him. Besides that I was a medic in the military for six years."

"Okay. Let's go, then." We split up once we got to the neighborhood where Corey was at large. The plan was that whoever found him first would call the other. Finally I got a call from Freddy. "I found him," he said. "He's in the emergency room at Wake Med." His heart stopped twice while he was in the hospital.

Corey got out of the hospital, and the last I heard he was back to doing the same things.

I didn't hear from Freddy again until March. He sounded excited. "Hey. What's been going on?"

"Not much. What's new with you?"

"I bought a car."

"Freddy, a car is about the worst investment you could ever make."

"What? A car is a *good* investment."

"No it's not! It begins to depreciate the moment you buy it.

"I told you that before."

"Guess what kind it is?"

"What?"

"A Mercedes."

"A Mercedes? You have to maintain it and parts for a Mercedes are expensive. You have taxes and insurance you have to pay."

"I know how to work on cars. I can do the maintenance myself."

"You still have to buy parts."

"Things are crazy around here. I need to get away from everybody. I need to change. I'm doing things I shouldn't be doing to make money. I only want to double my money quickly and then get out."

"Then you shouldn't have bought a car, Freddy. Forget about doubling your money quickly. You're going to get yourself in deep trouble. Look—you know what you need to do. Whenever you decide to do it, all you have to do is call me and I'll drive you there."

"I have other people in the car with me right now. I'll call you later," he said.

On May 25th, 2015, only four days before the anniversary of the wreck that took Chase's life, I received a private message from Freddy on Facebook.

"Hey."

"Hey man. How's it going?" I asked.

"Horrible. It's been a bad year."

"So what's new? Why am I awake at 2:20 a.m.?"

"I'm asking myself the same question. Guess who called me at 4 a.m. yesterday asking to spend the night at my house?"

"Lilith?"

"No."

"Corey Davis?"

"He's in jail. And don't say something negative about that, because I'm really mad about it already."

It was too late. I had already sent him the following message. "Why am I not surprised?"

Freddy wrote, "You see. I knew it. I don't want or need to hear that."

I tried to smooth it over. "I like Corey. He's polite and easy-going, but he makes bad decisions and his life is a wreck."

It was too late. Freddy was angry, and disrespectful and I wasn't in the mood for that. I tore into him. I admit now that I was in the wrong to lose control of my temper. Angry words flew back and forth between us. I told him he was a boy who needed to grow up and stop blaming others for his problems. I had done so much for him, and had desperately tried to help him. I never expected anything in return, but couldn't he at least show me a little respect?

Freddy went on to say that I had never cared about him, but only used him for material for this book. He insinuated that I was an overbearing father who had pushed my son too far. He vowed to sabotage this book by going to the media and exposing all of my angry private messages to him.

That's the last I've heard from Freddy. I'm not a betting man, but if I were, I would bet that within a year, Freddy's Mercedes will be gone, and he will be flat broke again. If he doesn't see the light, he will likely end up in prison or dead within a few years. Otherwise he'll only live a life of bouncing from one mishap to another, always with barely enough money to survive.

What does Freddy do to relax? Mostly he smokes marijuana and drinks alcohol. If you ask him, he will tell you he's not an addict and that he rarely uses hard drugs, but I've never met any sane people who live the way he does. My sincere hope and prayer is that Freddy will prove me wrong and get the help he needs, acquire a trade, and become a successful, productive member of society. Let's hope Freddy's life will not be another "Life Half Lived."

Dylan Smith was expelled from high school last year. Judging by his Facebook posts, he is depressed over what happened to Chase and Tatyana. That's understandable. It appears he still smokes weed regularly and has a rebellious attitude, which isn't serving him well. He was arrested on May 18th of 2015 for possession of marijuana and drug paraphernalia. The last time I talked to Freddy, he told me Ferdinand had been deported and was trying to work his way back into the United States again through his father's connections with the cartel.

On May 29th, 2015, we had a nighttime balloon release to remember Chase. Initially, Kim's idea was to release Chinese lanterns. They are made of paper stretched over a frame and are made to rise by a small flame suspended underneath an opening, similar to a hot-air balloon. I thought these might pose a fire hazard. I was excited when I found balloons with multi-colored flashing LED lights. We released thirty-four of them to symbolize Chase's football jersey number, 34. They were bright, colorful, and beautiful. We had so many good friends in attendance.

On Saturday, June 27th, another tragic incident involving marijuana took place at Walnut Street Park in Cary, the very same place where we held the nighttime balloon release in Chase's memory weeks earlier. A sixteen-year old girl had arranged to meet four other young people there to sell them marijuana. When they tried to steal her marijuana, she jumped onto the step of the step-side pickup of the four as they sped away in. After the driver punched her four times in the face, she fell to the street and later died in the hospital. When will this madness end?

In the very beginning of this book, I talked about the meaning of Chase's names. Chase Morgan Rodgers: Hunter/Warrior by the sea—Prowess with a Spear. Chase was a hunter in more ways than one. He was born with a hunter's and a warrior's heart. He was a warrior and hunter on the football field. Those who played with him and against him know what I mean. He was a hunter in the field and at sea. He sought adventure at every turn. He lived in the moment. He didn't worry about tomorrow. He fought for answers to the issues that plagued him while he was in treatment in Florida—by the sea. He fought right up until the very end and was planning his trip back to Florida—by the sea, to continue his hunt, his fight to resolve those issues.

Even now after he has left this world, his warrior heart lives on in the lives of those he touched. He is fighting for you right now, through the very words in this book by sharing his story with you. That's how Chase would have wanted it. He wants you to learn from his story. It's interesting to me how we never planned his name according to the meanings, but that he seemed to live up to the meaning of his name in every way imaginable.

Chase's friend, Kylie, who had participated in the intervention and who was instrumental in getting him to go to treatment, is attending college and has decided to pursue a career in substance abuse counseling. She was inspired by her experience with Chase.

Luke, who was the punter at Cary High School and who spoke at Chase's memorial service, enlisted in the Navy. He graduated from basic training and will be in electronics school by the time this book is published. He says Chase inspired him to join the military because of his participation in NJROTC and military school.

Chase's friend Ross who played on the line at Hargrave and who made the cross for Chase's roadside memorial is playing college football at Presbyterian in Clinton, South Carolina, and excelling in the classroom. He's a junior and he tells me he thinks of Chase every day.

Chase's little brother Justin is a sophomore at Cary High School. He starts at cornerback on the Varsity team and wears Chase's number—34. He's a good student, a good kid, and a tenacious football player, like his big brother.

Wendy transferred from Ole Miss to LSU, and plans to work with special needs kids. She recently made an A on a paper she completed about Chase.

Dylan's Uncle Carter recently earned his bachelor's degree and is planning to become a medical doctor. He graduated from East Carolina University and was accepted into the Boston University School of Public Health. He's a very bright young man.

The last I heard, Samantha, the red head Chase met in Florida, had been sober for over six months. I also saw on Facebook recently that she was baptized. It appears she is still on a good path.

Chase's first real girlfriend, Shannon, is studying Speech Pathology at UNC–Greensboro, and doing well.

Katherine, the girl next door, graduated from Appalachian State with a degree in Spanish. She took a teaching job and we recently attended her wedding. It was beautiful and she was a beautiful bride. Katherine's younger brother Alex who spent many hours playing with Chase when they were little recently transferred from UNC-Greensboro to N.C. State where he is pursuing a degree in tourism.

Brice, Chase's roommate and good friend from Hargrave, is working his way through college at Florida Gulf Coast University. He's majoring in Bio Technology. There are other positive stories to tell, but there's not enough room to tell them all. How will you, my reader, write the story of your life? Will it be a story of drugs, alcohol, disappointment, and tragedy, or will it be a success story like some of the ones I shared above? The good news is that you get to choose. Choose wisely. Don't let your life be another "Life half Lived."

EPILOGUE

IN MANY WAYS, Chase crammed forty years of living into twenty years of life. He wasn't going to miss any opportunity to have fun, and he made life fun for those who were around him. He had so much potential that was never realized. I didn't see a good future for him, however, once he started using drugs, but I always hoped he would get his life together. He was my son and I loved him with all my heart. I couldn't give up.

Chase touched a lot of lives while he was here. That was evident by the people who attended his funeral and sent us cards. How many more lives might he have touched had he not been cut down in his prime? There are no words that can make you understand how much I miss Chase. I miss him every minute of every day. He is on my mind constantly. I would give up all of my worldly possessions to have him back here with me if I could. Some days it doesn't seem real that he's gone. A part of me keeps expecting him to walk in the front door with a big smile and say, "Hi, Dad!" To this day I wear Chase's medallion around my neck. It makes me feel like he is with me.

It has been my sincere desire in writing this book that you, the reader, may learn some vital lessons. I hope you have learned from the mistakes that I made as a parent throughout this book. My spying on Chase hurt our relationship. It created another barrier to open communication between us. Instead of attempting to force him to behave, I wish I had worked harder at understanding why he behaved the way he did.

I hope the teenagers who read this book will learn from some of the bad choices made by the young people I wrote about. Marijuana will probably be legalized across all fifty states over the next several years, but that doesn't mean you have to use it. A lot of people will argue that it's less dangerous than alcohol, but even if that's true, does that mean it's good for you? I don't think so. Scientific studies have shown that the frontal lobe is not fully connected to the rest of the brain in most of us until we reach the age of twenty-five. The frontal lobe is where your adult-type logical decisions are made.

Scientific studies have shown that using marijuana prior to age twenty-five can stunt the maturation process. How does that happen? It slows the growth of the membrane that covers the nerves connecting the frontal lobe with the rest of the brain. Think of this membrane as insulation on wiring. When it isn't present, something is lost in the communication between the frontal lobe and the rest of the brain. This affects not only your ability to make decisions like an adult would, but it also slows your emotional maturity.

I've seen the effects time after time, and you can see them in the characters in this book. People who are using marijuana don't want to believe that. Is marijuana responsible for Chase's death? Absolutely! It's not the only thing responsible for his death, but it is one of the leading contributors. It made his decision-making even worse than it would ordinarily have been. It caused him to hang with a crowd he wouldn't have otherwise been hanging out with. One other factor to be aware of is that marijuana is approximately three times more potent than it was in the 70's and 80's. Growers have increased the potency of marijuana through the crossbreeding of plants. I'm still not certain that Tatyana wasn't impaired that day, regardless of what the police may say. I never saw the toxicology report and the THC was never quantified.

I loved Chase with all of my being. His birth changed me, his life changed me, and his death changed me in very profound ways. I am not the same person today that I was all those years ago when Chase was born or even a few months ago when Chase died. I pray for the guidance and the will to become a better person each and every day, to become the person I was created to be, to help others when it is possible, and to do my part to leave the world a better place after I am gone. I look forward to the personal growth that will come from the struggles ahead and to the rewards this life sometimes has to offer. I also am looking forward to the day that will eventually come when God is ready for me to see Chase again. We're going to have a good time and a lot more adventures together in a place much better than this.

THE END

For more information about Chase, substance abuse, or to book me as a speaker, visit my website http://speedy34.com